WEB *of* CONSPIRACY

A GUIDE
to Conspiracy Theory
Sites on the Internet

James F. Broderick
and
Darren W. Miller

D1262496

Information Today, Inc.
Medford, New Jersey

First printing, 2008

Web of Conspiracy: A Guide to Conspiracy Theory Sites on the Internet

Copyright © 2008 by James F. Broderick and Darren W. Miller

Publisher's Note: The author and publisher have taken care in preparation of this book but make no expressed or implied warranty of any kind and assume no responsibility for errors or omissions. No liability is assumed for incidental or consequential damages in connection with or arising out of the use of the information or programs contained herein.

Many of the designations used by manufacturers and sellers to distinguish their products are claimed as trademarks. Where those designations appear in this book and Information Today, Inc. was aware of a trademark claim, the designations have been printed with initial capital letters.

Library of Congress Cataloging-in-Publication Data

Broderick, James F., 1963-
   Web of conspiracy : a guide to conspiracy theory sites on the Internet / James F. Broderick and Darren W. Miller.
     p. cm.
   Includes index.
   ISBN 978-0-910965-81-1
    1. Conspiracies. 2. Internet. I. Miller, Darren W., 1979- II. Title.

HV6275.B76 2008
025.06'0019--dc22

2008009171

Printed and bound in the United States of America

President and CEO: Thomas H. Hogan, Sr.
Editor-in-Chief and Publisher: John B. Bryans
Managing Editor: Amy M. Reeve
VP Graphics and Production: M. Heide Dengler
Cover Design: Laura Hegyi
Book Design: Kara Mia Jalkowski
Copy Editor: Pat Hadley-Miller
Proofreader: Barbara Brynko
Indexer: Beth Palmer

www.infotoday.com

A good conspiracy is unprovable. I mean, if you can prove it, it means they screwed up somewhere along the line.

—Mel Gibson as Jerry Fletcher
in the 1997 film *Conspiracy Theory*

Contents

Acknowledgments vii

About the Web Site ix

Introduction xi

Chapter 1
Roswell/Area 51 1

Chapter 2
The Death of Princess Diana 13

Chapter 3
TWA Flight 800 25

Chapter 4
AIDS 39

Chapter 5
The Shakespeare Authorship Question 53

Chapter 6
The Order of Skull and Bones 67

Chapter 7
The Jesus Controversy 81

Chapter 8
The Moon Landing 95

Chapter 9
The Death of Marilyn Monroe 107

Chapter 10
Protocols of the Elders of Zion 121

Chapter 11
Pearl Harbor 135

Chapter 12
The Trilateral Commission 149

Chapter 13
The Hindenburg 163

Chapter 14
The Philadelphia Experiment 175

Chapter 15
Freemasonry 189

Chapter 16
The JFK Assassination 203

Chapter 17
September 11, 2001 217

Chapter 18
Bodies of Evidence: The Lindbergh, Lincoln,
Hoffa, and Morrison Mysteries in Brief 231

List of Featured Web Sites 243

About the Authors 255

Index 257

Acknowledgments

Jim Broderick wishes to thank the following people: Bruce Chadwick, my colleague at New Jersey City University, for his guidance and suggestions about book-related matters. I remain indebted for all of his support, inspiration, and insight; John Sitnik, Helen Beckert, and the entire staff of the Glen Ridge (NJ) Public Library, for their assistance in locating essential resource materials; my colleagues Carlos, Ron, and John—the members of the Park Tavern Writers' group—for their fellowship, encouragement, and breadth of knowledge; and especially my writing partner, Darren, who understands what it takes to write a book but goes ahead and does it anyway (and what's worse, somehow convinces me to join him). Darren is a gifted writer whose zeal for perfection of expression keeps him up at night. I thank him for spending his sleepless hours improving my words and adding so many inimitable ones of his own. The steak—and even the asparagus—are on me next time, writing partner.

And then there is Miri, whose contribution to my work, and my life, can't be stated in words. Reporter, writer, editor, and confidante, Miri is the best of all possible partners. All of our collaborations have turned out well—most especially Olivia and Maddy. I dedicate this book to her, with affection and gratitude for our life together.

Darren Miller wishes to thank the following people: Scotty Medford Ellis, executive director of the Haywood County Tourism Development Authority, for her unconditional support of this project; Jan and Bob Roberts, whose enthusiasm for and interest in this book has re-energized me time and again; and my parents, for their constant promotion of my work. I would be remiss if I did not express my gratitude to Jim—there is no other writer I'd rather create with. I admire his prose and need his editing (which has salvaged my work countless times). Most of all, I value his friendship. I do not know if I would have survived this often-arduous process without our late night (perhaps early morning is more accurate) conversations about writing, music, movies, and, of course, wine. The laughter was always much needed and greatly appreciated.

Web of Conspiracy, or at least my participation in helping craft it, would not have been possible without my wife, Heather. Throughout the writing process, she kept me sane, even as I drove her crazy. Her encouragement kept me going. Thank you—a thousand times over— for your advice, your honesty, your friendship, and your love.

Both of us wish to thank the following people for their support and counsel: First and foremost, our editor John Bryans, whose passion and commitment to excellence are tempered by his wit, warmth, and sense of hospitality. Writing this book for him has been both a pleasure and an honor. Our managing editor, Amy Reeve, has consistently improved the pages of our work, and we remain in her debt, as do the readers of this book. Marketing coordinator Rob Colding has offered many helpful suggestions, and we are grateful to have access to his marketing acumen.

We also wish to thank the following for inspiration, which every writer needs: Francis Ford Coppola, Charles Bukowski, Larry David, William Zinsser, Seymour Hersh, Cameron Crowe, Lewis Black, and J. S. Bach. Thanks, fellas.

About the Web Site
www.TheReportersWell.com

The authors have created a Web site in support of this book and their other writing projects. The *Web of Conspiracy* page at www.The ReportersWell.com is a user-friendly portal from which readers can quickly access all the Web sites featured in this book, along with links to additional sites, books, movies, and news stories of interest.

At www.TheReportersWell.com, readers can explore extensive coverage of the world of nonfiction writing, from lists of significant books and authors to opinions about trends in journalism. To learn more about the authors of *Web of Conspiracy*, click on the site's "Who We Are" page.

Jim Broderick and Darren Miller welcome comments and questions from their readers. Email them at News@TheReporters Well.com.

Disclaimer

Neither the publisher nor the authors make any claim as to the results that may be obtained through the use of this Web page or of any of the Internet resources it references or links to. Neither publisher nor authors will be held liable for any results, or lack thereof, obtained by the use of this page or any of its links; for any third-party changes; or for any hardware, software, or other problems that may occur as the result of using it. This Web page is subject to change or discontinuation without notice at the discretion of the publisher and authors

Introduction

The list is as intriguing as it is well known: Area 51, the Grassy Knoll, the New World Order, the 9/11 Truth Activists. These phrases summon up some of history's most infamous events and the people and organizations behind them. For decades, readers have been treated to a steady stream of books that testify to the nefarious influence of public and private groups in covering up the truth. Whole libraries could be filled with books that explore various conspiracy theories. But people interested in any of the dozens of persistent theories that have congealed into a formidable body of writing have always had to seek out the information, to search for books and articles in the usual places: libraries, bookstores, archives. To be an informed conspiracy theory devotee, you needed a lot of time—and patience.

Enter the Internet.

With a couple of keystrokes, the dossier on Lee Harvey Oswald, a video of the World Trade Center collapsing, or the history of the Freemasons will appear on your computer screen in seconds.

This technological tidal flood of argument and information has allowed armchair conspiracy theorists to learn as much about their pet theories as the renowned experts who used to have a monopoly on the information. Now, anyone with an Internet connection can review pictures from the 1969 Apollo Moon landing (why are there no stars visible?), William Shakespeare's surviving signatures (sloppily written and misspelled by the supposed "bard" himself), and Marilyn Monroe's autopsy report (if she took a fatal overdose of pills, why weren't any drugs found in her stomach?).

While perhaps not a brave new world, it is at least a brazen one, with many skeptics posting their own Web sites and promoting their "evidence" in favor of some long-suspected conspiracy. There are also sites set up by amateur sleuths, aficionados of some celebrity or historical event, professional researchers, students, and the merely curious. Everyone, it seems, has an opinion about the likelihood of conspiracy.

Why so much interest in these theories—many of which run the gamut from mildly intriguing to bizarre and even ludicrous-sounding? Are people becoming more suspicious? More gullible? More cynical?

Psychologists and social scientists have proposed lots of different reasons for the interest in conspiracy theories, but a factor that is often dismissed is the actual, verifiable existence of certain conspiracies in the recent past, from the Gulf of Tonkin incident to Watergate to the Iran-Contra affair. When the world learned that the recent invasion of Iraq was based on the now-disproved charge of "weapons of mass destruction," that only fueled the fire of suspicion about what else the government has done to mislead the public.

And as historians and researchers continue to probe the causes and sequences of events from Pearl Harbor to the attacks on 9/11, every new discovery leads to new questions—and the growing suspicion in some people's minds that what we *think* we know might be suspect. Formerly fixed ideas are replaced by gnawing uncertainty. As one academic noted in a recent article about this phenomenon in the *San Francisco Chronicle*, "some people turn to conspiracy theories in a genuine attempt to understand an inexplicable tragedy, to assemble order from chaos."

In the chaos and tumult of the modern world—and with easy and instant access to all kinds of information at the press of a key—interest in conspiracy theories, ancient and recently minted, seems likely to continue to increase.

Web of Conspiracy focuses on more than 20 conspiracy theories—from those everyone has probably heard of to some that are lesser known but equally compelling. Each chapter examines an individual conspiracy theory, beginning with a comprehensive essay about the theory, tracing its origins and history to its prevalence in popular culture. After readers are thoroughly acquainted with the alleged "alternate history" or the supposed "secret society," attention turns to those places on the World Wide Web that deal with the conspiracy theory in some way—whether promoting evidence in support of the theory, highlighting the signs of a "cover-up," or attempting to debunk the claims cherished by conspiracists. Each chapter reviews those Web sites that are essential for understanding the theory in all its permutations.

Though largely neutral, the book does alert readers to some theories that have yet to gain credibility and might be, as some would term it, on the margins of credibility. Other times, the weight of evidence often seems to suggest that the "official" story might arguably be called into question. Each chapter, however, merely attempts to present the evidence. Conclusions are the function of the open-minded reader, not the authors.

All excerpts reprinted in this book are taken directly from Web sites and other sources referenced in the text. The opinions presented in these excerpts are strictly those of the cited authors, and all excerpts have been reproduced as originally written or posted—typos, misspellings, grammar errors, and all.

Part reference book, part Internet guide, *Web of Conspiracy* aims to serve as an invaluable resource—one we hope proves both informative and entertaining—for anyone captivated by the conspiratorial world and how it manifests itself on the World Wide Web.

Roswell/Area 51

Have you ever found yourself gazing skyward at night, contemplating the stars, and wondering if, among all the vastness of the cosmos, there might exist intelligent life far beyond Earth?

Have you never heard of Roswell, New Mexico?

It was there that one of the most famous encounters with alien life supposedly took place. And in the 60 years since that fateful summer night, when a mysterious "flying disk" (to quote the newspaper reports at the time) crash-landed in a farmer's field near Roswell, the legend has persisted and the question about intelligent life has been answered, some say (though the government persists in denying it). In the decades since that seminal evening, the science of UFO-ology has gained some serious traction, and everyone from backyard videographers to government agencies has joined the search. Countless sightings of mysterious lights, hovering spacecraft, and even alien abductions have been reported, scrutinized, and written about. But no single sighting has garnered the attention of the alien-interest community like Roswell, a tribute, in part, to its enduring mix of documentation, speculation, and elevation as a pop cultural myth.

Wedded to the idea of the recovery of an extraterrestrial spacecraft—and possibly some alien bodies themselves—is the equally compelling theory about a super-secret government installation, known as "Area 51," where scientists study the remnants of alien spaceships and "reverse engineer" what they find from these advance technologies for use by the military. Conspiracy theorists who allege

1

that such a staging ground exists for the collection and study of alien technology point to a very real plot of land in northwest Nevada that remains off limits to all but those with high-level security clearances (even military personnel who fly over the site are not allowed to photograph the property).

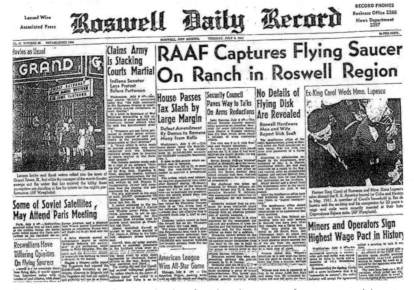

This newspaper article ran shortly after the discovery of mysterious debris in Roswell, New Mexico, in 1947. (Photo source: wikipedia.org/wiki/roswell_UFO_incident)

Flying saucers. Little green men. Secret military installations. Codes of silence. A government cover-up. Conspiracy theories do not come any more ready-made than this. The question for true believers is not "Is there intelligent life in the universe?" but "How long does the government plan to go on lying to the public about our contact with alien beings?"

Neither side seems likely to cede any ground. The government continues to maintain that the whole alien discovery scenario is more suited to pulp science-fiction novels. Proponents of the conspiracy theory say it's the government that's spinning wild stories.

Weather or Not

The two camps do agree that something happened in late June 1947 on a ranch near the Roswell Army Air Field. A farmer named William Brazel reported in early July that he discovered some metallic-type debris a few weeks earlier on the property, about 70 miles from Roswell. He contacted the local sheriff, George Wilcox, who in turn contacted Major Jesse Marcel at the airfield. Marcel and at least one unidentified assistant went to the ranch and gathered some additional metallic pieces that Brazel had not picked up and took all of the pieces back to the army base.

On July 8, the Roswell Army Air Field issued a press release, which read in part:

> [T]he intelligence office of the 509th Bomb group of the Eighth Air Force, Roswell Army Air Field, was fortunate enough to gain possession of a disc through the cooperation of one of the local ranchers and the sheriff's office of Claves County. The flying object landed on a ranch near Roswell sometime last week. Not having phone facilities, the rancher stored the disc until such time as he was able to contact the sheriff' office. ... Action was immediately taken and the disc was picked up at the rancher's home. It was inspected at the Roswell Army Air Field and subsequently loaned by Major Marcel to higher headquarters.

The "disc" was then flown to Fort Worth Army Air Field, where officials identified the debris as belonging to a type of weather balloon that carries radar deflectors. The Army issued a press release dismissing the "flying disc" idea. However, Brazel was quoted in news reports the next day challenging the Army's assertions, claiming he had seen remnants of weather balloons on the ranch before, adding "I am sure what I found was not any weather observation balloon."

From that point on, there is little agreement. In fact, some researchers even dispute those findings, arguing that the debris was taken to several military installations for inspection, ending up at the infamous base known as Area 51, a 60-square-mile tract of land that borders the Yucca Flats region of the Nevada Test Site, where the U.S. Department of Energy tests nuclear weapons. Some conspiracy theorists maintain that the bodies of the pilots of the alien vessel that crashed at Roswell are preserved in an underground lab at Area 51 and that military engineers continue to study the flying saucer's remains in an attempt to replicate the advanced engineering that makes interplanetary travel possible.

Dormant for Decades

One of the curious aspects of the whole Roswell conspiracy theory is that, for much of the past 60 years, there *was* no conspiracy theory.

Military personnel display pieces of debris they say came from a weather balloon—and not a flying saucer—that was discovered on a farm near Roswell, New Mexico. (Photo source: www.crystalinks.com/area51.html)

In fact, there was little interest at all in the largely forgotten incident of the "weather balloon" recovery of 1947. For more than 30 years, Roswell remained as unknown to the general public as it had been before the revelation of the recovery of mysterious sky debris there. But in 1980, a book titled *The Roswell Incident*, by Charles Berlitz (who had written previously about the Bermuda Triangle) and William L. Moore, ignited a wave of fervid Roswell reinvestigations. The book features interviews with several witnesses and people involved with the original investigation, including Major Marcel, who had gathered the debris at Brazel's ranch. Marcel was quoted as saying the material he collected was "nothing made on this earth." The book also argues that the U.S. military was engaged in an effort to discredit belief in UFOs and that the debris the Army showed to the press in an effort to bolster its weather balloon theory was actually switched from the debris collected near Roswell.

After *The Roswell Incident*, several other researchers rushed into the vortex. Throughout the 1990s, a number of important books on the subject were published, many of which included testimony from additional witnesses, generally supporting the claims made in the 1980 book but extending the reach of the conspiracy. Some of these books suggested that there were actually two separate crashes near Roswell, and many of these authors built further on the original implication of Berlitz and Moore that those closely involved in the recovery of the debris had been intimidated and coerced into silence.

By the time the Air Force published its own report in the mid-1990s, which not surprisingly found no credibility in the spaceship crash/cover-up theory, the conspiracy advocates had gained sufficient ground to plant the seeds of doubt in the public's mind. Opinion polls conducted in the past few years have found continued widespread belief that *something* happened in Roswell. Occasionally, a major news network or cable television channel will produce a documentary about the Roswell crash, though such enterprises are often beset by the failing memory of those who claim firsthand knowledge of the event, as well as the regularly changing stories of the principals, such as Brazel and Marcel. Additionally, there is a split in the UFO-believing community, with many researchers arguing that Roswell is a dubious event—one that eclipses the thousands of other, more credible "sightings" that should be getting more attention.

But it is Roswell that is, for good or ill, the focal point of UFO-ologists of all stripes, from amateur sky watchers to serious researchers. The town itself has taken advantage of its reputation to become a magnet for conspiracy theorists, sponsoring a four-day "UFO Festival" every year, which features a mix of academic symposia and carnival silliness.

Area Codes

While the town of Roswell has rolled out the welcome mat for the perpetually suspicious, Area 51 has taken the opposite approach, remaining absolutely shrouded in secrecy. The installation—also known as "Groom Lake" (because of the body of water to the southwest)—is surrounded by checkpoints and signs warning trespassers not only that "photography is prohibited" but also that "the use of

This photograph, taken in Green Bay, Wisconsin, in 2007, captures what thousands of people each year claim are genuine visitations by UFOs. (Photo source: www.ufoevidence.org)

deadly force is authorized." Some satellite photos of the parcel of property have become public, but these reveal little more than a couple of hangars and some airstrips. (The base's history includes use as a bombing practice facility in World War II and a test site for the famed U-2 spy plane.) Yet conspiracy theorists argue that all the real action happens underground, where facilities are said to include everything from advanced aerospace research labs to morgues containing alien bodies. There's even a contingent of conspiracy-minded individuals who argue that Area 51 was the staging ground for the Moon landing of 1969 (see Chapter 8), which they say was filmed in an underground TV studio made to resemble the lunar surface.

The very words "Area 51" have become shorthand in popular culture for some super-secret location, off-limits to all but those in the corridors of power. Internet sites that seek to acquaint users with the scope of Area 51's activities inevitably rely on speculation and recirculated rumor. No one is allowed to visit the property, which is reportedly patrolled by ground vehicles, helicopters, and radar. Whatever is going on at Area 51 is likely to remain secret—catnip to conspiracy theorists.

The Internet, in fact, seems like the perfect place for fans of a government-sponsored cosmic cover-up to gather: the distances of outer space conflated to the virtual proximity of cyberspace, with no military or government censor redacting the free flow of evidence and speculation. There are many sites that are thorough and credible—but given the admittedly far-fetched "little green men" component of the conspiracy, surfers are urged to remember that there are some Web sites that are as far out as their subject matter.

Computer Crashes

Before moving directly into the Roswell controversy, readers might want to get their bearings with the universe of UFO research. A great site is the UFO Evidence Web site (www.ufoevidence.org/topics/government.htm). This site offers a helpful and thorough overview of UFOs and the evidence for their existence. A number of articles deal with government secrecy and the military's role in studying and concealing UFO information. Other topics addressed include "U.S. Presidents & UFOs," "Public Opinion Polls on UFOs," and "UFO Crashes & Retrievals." The site offers extensive links to government documents, other UFO-related Web sites, and a catalog of books and articles about the UFO phenomenon. There are also message boards related to each of the topics discussed on the site.

An updated and extensive archive of Roswell crash information can be found at The Roswell Incident page (www.subversive element.com/roswell1_home.html), maintained by Subversive Element. Users are greeted by a pages-long list of links to Roswell-related documents, from newspaper and magazine articles to excerpts from books, video, and print transcripts of interviews with government officials, as well as author interviews, photo archives, and statements from witnesses to some aspect of the Roswell incident. The site is not the most visually arresting—it seems to have been designed with the same care that goes into listing the specials on a menu at an all-night truck stop—but there's no denying the wide utility of its selections.

Less extensive but engagingly presented is the Roswell page of the Skeptic's Dictionary (skepdic.com/roswell.html). The site combines a sober and thorough retelling of the sequence of events in July 1947 with an insider's perspective:

> The actual crash site was on the Foster ranch 75 miles north of Roswell, a small town doing big business feeding the insatiable appetite of UFO enthusiasts. Roswell now houses two UFO museums and hosts an annual alien festival. Shops cater to this curious tourist trade, much as Inverness caters to Loch Ness crowd. This seems a bit unfair to Corona, New Mexico, which is actually the closest town to the alleged crash site. Roswell is the nearest military base, however ....

In addition to the helpful general overview, the site includes a section for further reading and a message board for reader comments.

There are also lots of links to related sites connected to the Skeptic's Dictionary, such as "Area 51" and "Alien Abduction."

The fairly objective tone of the Skeptic's Dictionary is somewhat at odds with many of the other Roswell sites, most of which tend to espouse a belief in the alien crash landing and subsequent cover-up. One of the more distinguished voices on a variety of conspiracy theories is CoverUps.com, which, of course, has a Roswell section (www.coverups.com/roswell). If you've had some difficulty convincing your friends or family of the validity of the crash and cover-up, you might want to spend a few minutes online with this site—ferocious in its belief and equally adamant in its assertion of a cover-up:

> It would seem logical to conclude that an intelligence matter classified two secrecy levels higher than the Hydrogen bomb is unlikely to be revealed except to those with the very highest security clearances. Even at that level, the degree of information shared would be kept severely compartmentalized. In other words, those who learned the "truth" about UFOs did not necessarily know the WHOLE TRUTH, nor all of those who had the same level of saucer/alien knowledge as they did. The old fable of the blind men describing an elephant comes to mind.

Much of the discussion on the site (not surprisingly) tends to deal with the cover-up rather than the actual event. The motives of the government to keep secret the whole "aliens have landed on Earth" scenario are analyzed and critiqued, with the site's authors rather dryly concluding that: "It is unlikely that the fabric of society would be destroyed if selected facts were released."

But why such secrecy surrounding Area 51, a military base that everyone seems to agree exists, though no one talks about what actually happens there? Well, some people are talking about it, including a PhD in metaphysics named Ellie Crystal, whose Web site Crystalinks contains an extensive section on Area 51 (www.crystalinks.com/area51.html). The site offers extensive geographical information providing Area 51's specific location and an overview of the various military projects undertaken there. In an acknowledgment of the rather "Alice in Wonderland" status of the property, Crystal notes that: "The U.S. Government does not explicitly acknowledge the existence of the Groom Lake [Area 51] facility, nor does it deny it." Crystalinks provides an immense amount of information about the facility (including the protocol followed by base personnel when they arrest a trespasser: "Modest fines, of around $600, seem to be the norm, although some visitors and journalists report receiving follow-up visits from FBI agents."). The site offers a measured tone that never descends into breathless indignation or encyclopedic detachment. It's a very entertaining read.

Less dramatic but quite useful are the extensive articles in Wikipedia under "Roswell UFO Incident" (en.wikipedia.org/wiki/Roswell_UFO_incident) and "Area 51" (en.wikipedia.org/wiki/Area_51). These entries offer the usual Wiki mix of fun facts, serious scholarship, and unproved allegations. But there's a wealth of

The U.S. government denies, officially, the existence of Area 51 despite clear indications that something is going on within this highly protected parcel of land. (Photo source: wikipedia.org/wiki/area_51)

information (so much so that first-timers to the world of Roswell or Area 51 might want to start with a smaller Internet bite, such as the provocative, brief entry at www.armageddononline.org). The Wikipedia articles are particularly strong on the post-1980 world of conspiracy theorizing that has swirled around Roswell/Area 51 since the first wave of alien cover-up books began appearing in 1980. The overall tone of the Wikipedia entries is one of healthy skepticism: "While new reports into the 1990s seemed to suggest there was much more to the Roswell incident than the mere recovery of a weather balloon, skeptics instead saw the increasingly elaborate accounts as evidence of a myth being constructed."

As has become clear to regular users of the Internet, the prime benefit of Wikipedia articles might be their often impressive bibliography of sources, pointing the Web surfer to a variety of documents available both online and in libraries and research collections. The comprehensive list of approximately 50 or so sources at the end these two entries testifies to the breadth and depth of research on the subject.

But there's nothing like firsthand research. Those who are truly interested in the Roswell controversy might want to visit the town itself. The chamber of commerce has set up a terrific Web site for potential tourists at www.roswellnm.org, featuring all the usual information one would expect from a municipal site (accommodations, directions, cultural events), as well as extended coverage of the town's marquee event: the UFO Festival, "a family-oriented festival with plenty for the serious UFO/Alien buff." The festival features speakers, conferences, book signings, contests, a carnival, hot air balloons (some in the shape of large, alien heads), and "fifty other events and attractions taking place" during the four-day celebration.

Connections

If the UFO-seeing-crowd is as large as some Internet stargazers suggest, there are thousands and thousands of documented, inexplicable cases of UFO sightings. In the pre-Internet age, these witnesses might have felt inclined to keep their rather astounding accounts to themselves. But the Internet has changed all of that, of course, opening a portal into worlds we've never encountered—at least officially. Was the incident at Roswell one such encounter? Many people think it was, and many others remain open-minded, perhaps because of what they've seen with their own eyes. It's been 60 years since the alleged crash on that ranch just north of the military base at Roswell, and it would appear that an increasing number of people—brought together on the Web to consider otherworldly contact—have firmly concluded that we are not alone.

Roswell, New Mexico, has made the most of its reputation as a home for UFOs— and UFO enthusiasts. (Photo source: www.roswellnm.org)

The Death of Princess Diana

Revered and admired in life, and iconic in death, the late and deeply lamented Princess Diana seemed to touch something in her admirers, who ranged from working-class tradesmen to dewy-eyed teenagers from all parts of the globe. It would be hard to think of anyone whose life—and death—triggered such an outpouring of affection and admiration among all strata of society. The adulation she engendered approached a religious frenzy, as if she were the matriarch of the Church of the British Royalty, though it found expression among all segments of the population, Anglophile and otherwise. Diana, or Lady Di, represented the dream of many a callow schoolgirl, and, to more worldly and mature admirers, she stood for the good that can happen to one in this life and the good one can do for others. Her death was, for a country of her peers and a world of her acolytes, a loss incalculable.

And for many reasons, her tragic death in an automobile accident in Paris in 1997 remains troubling—not only to her legion of fans but to those who find the official explanation of the accident sorely insufficient.

A Fairy-Tale Life

Diana wasn't a modern-day Cinderella, scrubbing floors and laundering hand-me-downs while dreaming of the good life. Her upbringing was replete with the privilege of the aristocracy—but she symbolized for many people the modern day fairy-tale princess:

young, beautiful, and swept off her feet by a real-life prince. She was born of wealthy and socially significant parents, educated at the top private schools in England and Switzerland, and circulated among the sons and daughters of the Continent's well-heeled. Her alliance with Prince Charles, while certainly not predictable, wasn't inconceivable. Diana was, to borrow a phrase describing her maternal grandmother's actual job, very much a "Lady in Waiting."

Diana had a suitable upbringing for her future role as princess—including education at the best private schools and interaction with the most well-heeled strata of British society. (Photo source: www.coverups.com/diana)

And if ever there was a storybook wedding, it was surely Diana's. Setting the standard for pomp in the modern era, the wedding of Diana and Charles in 1981 was viewed by an estimated 750 million people around the world. Tens of thousands of Britons lined Diana's carriage route to Westminster Cathedral, waving signs, throwing flowers, and blowing kisses to the soon-to-be "Her Royal Highness."

Diana's grip on the popular imagination only seemed to tighten as her marriage unraveled, fueling a cottage industry of tabloids trumpeting the royal dissolution and exchanging front-page salvos about who was cheating on whom (both were, it has been alleged). Throughout her marriage, its unraveling, and her subsequent life as the world's best-known divorcee (the marriage formally ended in 1992), Diana involved herself with a couple of high-profile charitable campaigns for which she became even more admired. She helped spearhead an international effort to ban landmines (going so far as having herself photographed in a flak jacket walking through a minefield), and she campaigned for more humane treatment and widespread acceptance of AIDS victims.

Shortly before her death, Diana became involved in a relationship with Dodi Al-Fayed, a multimillionaire and heir to the Harrod's department store empire. Diana and Al-Fayed were returning to his apartment in Paris after dining at the Ritz Hotel when the car in which they were riding crashed, killing Al-Fayed and the car's driver, Henri Paul, immediately. Diana was taken to a hospital, where doctors were unable to save her from severe internal injuries. A fourth passenger, Al-Fayed's bodyguard Trevor Rees-Jones, survived the crash.

Curves and Swerves

From the very first media reports of the accident, through the police report and subsequent high-profile investigations, a number of inconsistencies and questions have emerged that continue to fuel speculation that the crash was no "accident."

The official version of events goes like this: Henri Paul, the driver, was inebriated—three times over the legal limit. As he drove the couple from the Ritz Hotel to Al-Fayed's Paris apartment shortly after midnight, Paul was being chased by the paparazzi, which had been stalking the couple throughout their stay in Paris. Paul drove the black Mercedes with tinted windows through an underpass tunnel that had been the site of several previous crashes along its sharp curves and narrow lanes. In an effort to outrun the pursuing shutterbugs, Paul lost control of the car and hit a pylon. Given the excessive speed of the vehicle (which remains in some doubt, with estimates ranging from 60 mph to more than 100 mph), the crash demolished the driver's side of the car (killing Paul and Al-Fayed instantly) and severely damaged the passenger side (with Rees-Jones, in the front seat, surviving, and Diana, behind him, sustaining internal injuries). Paramedics responded to the crash, removed Diana from the semi-crumpled vehicle, and transported her to a local hospital, where she was pronounced dead shortly after arriving.

Yet conspiracy theorists contend that each one of those facts misrepresents what actually happened, as well as leaving out whole swaths of facts that can't simply be explained away. And lurking behind the facts, they argue, is the undeniable presence of motive: The royal family simply couldn't accept the romantic coupling of the

This security camera video captured Diana exiting the Ritz Hotel moments before her fatal crash. (Photo source: www.time.com)

Princess of Wales and a Muslim with ties to the Saudi ruling family. The prospect of Muslim half-brothers to the future Kings of England must have riled the Queen, theorists suppose. Add to that Diana's out-spoken criticisms of Prince Charles and the Royals in general. In short, she had become a problem for the crown.

Conspiracy-minded Diana fans see the hand of the British Secret Intelligence Service, the MI6, behind the crash. So, too, does Dodi Al-Fayed's father, Mohammed Al-Fayed, who has been outspoken in his criticisms of the "cover-up" of the accident. The elder Al-Fayed has continued to maintain that his son was intending to marry Princess Diana, and that once the Royals got wind of that fact, they put a stop to the relationship by creating the "accident." (Many pro-ponents of the conspiracy also contend that Diana was pregnant at the time of the crash—a supposition that the coroner's inquest refuted.)

Mystery Vehicles

Those who allege that the Princess was done in by foul play point to a couple of factors that have remained largely unexplained. A handful of witnesses who were also traveling though the Place de l'Alma tunnel in Paris at the same time as Diana and her entourage claim to have seen a black sedan and a smaller white car, alleged to be a Fiat Uno, following Diana's limousine quite closely. These vehicles were said to be far ahead of the paparazzi, and trailing her dangerously closely, according to witnesses. One thing investigators have never been able to explain away is the mysterious streak of white paint along the side of Diana's vehicle after the crash. There was no white car found at the crash scene. Even the findings of the high profile "Operation Paget" investigation into Diana's death, which were released in December 2006 and concluded that there was no conspiracy, noted that: "We believe there was glancing contact between the Mercedes, driven by Henri Paul, and a white Fiat Uno just before the Alma underpass. … Who was driving the [car] and why they did not come forward are questions we have considered. The French investigation carried out a major search for the Fiat Uno but could not locate the car."

Witnesses traveling in the opposite direction have also said they saw a motorcycle come out of the tunnel, then make a U-turn, and race back into the tunnel in the direction of Diana's limousine just before the crash. One witness told the Associated Press that he saw a motorcycle cut right in front of Diana's vehicle, followed by a bright flash. Another witness told French police he saw a motorcycle swerve in front of the car just before it crashed.

Conspiracy theorists have noted that the very fact the car was in the tunnel is suspicious. The underpass tunnel is well out of the way for the destination the couple was headed to (Al-Fayed's apartment). Investigators have acknowledged that there were far quicker routes for the couple to take than the out-of-the-way Place de l'Alma tunnel. This has raised doubts about whether or not the driver, Henri Paul, was acting under orders from the MI6 to drive the couple through the tunnel. (Paul was head of security for Al-Fayed, not his chauffeur. The man who was his chauffeur, Phillipe Journot, had driven them all around the evening of the crash but had been sent ahead of Diana and Al-Fayed as a decoy to fool the waiting press.)

Doubters also point to the inconsistencies in the accounts of Diana's condition just after the crash. She was determined by the first

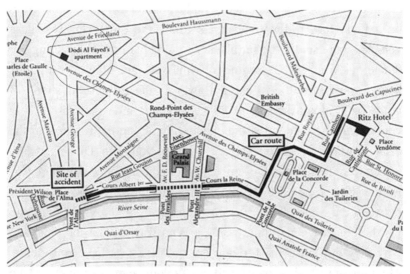

This map shows the extreme out-of-the-way route taken by Diana's driver on the night of her death. (Photo source: www.coverups.com/diana)

doctor on the scene to be "not catastrophic." Paparazzi photographs reportedly confiscated by French police show Diana with her eyes open, appearing unhurt. The first news account of the accident said that Diana sustained only minor injuries. She wasn't even put into an ambulance for more than 50 minutes after the crash. Perhaps most suspiciously, the ambulance ride to the hospital—which was less than four miles away—took 45 minutes, with a mysterious 10-minute stop along the way. If Diana was suffering from life-threatening injuries, why wasn't she rushed to the hospital? The dark answers to those questions, conspiracy theorists allege, suggest that something was done to Diana *en route* to the hospital—something that the crash itself wasn't able to accomplish.

The last piece of damning evidence offered by conspiracy theorists is the decision on the part of the British Royal Family to have Diana's body embalmed on the day of her death—*before* the British post-mortem could be conducted. Such a decision has created the impression among doubters that the Royals were trying to cover up evidence that would have suggested Diana did not die as a result of the crash—or even that she was pregnant. As one Web site dedicated to the conspiracy notes, "We have still not been given any plausible reason why Diana's body was embalmed in France and not sent back to the U.K. for the proper procedures to take place."

And for those who think the British Crown could never have engineered anything quite so nefarious, there's an alternative line of thinking that might provide some comfort: Princess Diana never died—she faked her own death. This theory takes its root in Diana's increasing dissatisfaction with being followed everywhere she went, even though she was no longer an ambassador of the royal court. She wanted her life back, some argue, and this "accident" was a way of killing off the old Diana and starting life anew (with a little help from a plastic surgeon, of course).

Royal Site Seeing

Although the Princess Diana conspiracy is a relatively recent entry in the pantheon of great conspiracy theories, its advocates have made impressive strides in raising questions and getting the word out. There are lots of sites that offer intriguing angles on the untimely death of the world's most beloved woman. A good place to start is the Diana, Princess of Wales Web page (www.londonnet.co.uk/ln/talk/news/ diana_conspiracy_theories.html). The site offers a brief overview of what it calls the "Big Three" conspiracy theories: that British Intelligence officials killed Diana, that Dodi Al-Fayed was the target of an assassination, or that Diana faked her own death. Regarding the latter, the site explains: "Fed up with the constant intrusions into her private life by the media, Diana arranges a spectacular 'death' from which she can retreat into blissful isolation. One version of the theory claims that the crash was an attempt at a faked death that went terribly wrong." Good, general overviews of the theories can also be found at CoverUps.com (www.coverups.com/diana), which tersely announces that "the 'Paparazzi killed Diana' theory turns out to be bull," and the Princess Diana section of ConspiracyPlanet.com (www.conspiracyplanet.com), which offers links to an archive of articles about the "accident" in the British tabloid press.

Once you have a handle on the general outlines of the major theories, you're ready to immerse yourself in one of the more comprehensive Web sites dedicated to this conspiracy: The Murder of Princess Diana (www.dianamurder.com). This site is impressive in its breadth of resources and its fair-minded scrutiny of the events before, during, and after the crash. The site claims its aim is "to ask a few questions, to make people ponder on a few facts and to help share information that may help lead to the REAL TRUTH." The first page of the site greets readers with a list of "Latest News" about Diana or the investigation into her death. There's an impressive array of links to other Diana-related Web sites and to recent interviews in the press with British officials or people involved in Diana's death. There are also updates about books and films involving the Princess of Wales and links to excerpts of previously published books and articles on the subject. The site deals with each of the major areas of the conspiracy, from the alleged appearance of the mysterious white Fiat entering the tunnel at the same time as Diana's vehicle (claiming to have been "the FIRST website to reveal the involvement of a white

Fiat Uno merely hours after the crash—yet the media refused to acknowledge it for several months") to the rumors of her pregnancy. The site's clearheaded nonalarmist tone provides some genuine cause for reconsideration, as in its discussion of how quickly, and uncritically, the motorcycle-riding paparazzi were blamed for causing the crash:

> Diana and Dodi were used to photographers chasing them. The driver was also aware that photographers would be following. ... Why should the driver risk life and limb from photographers that were a continual nuisance anyway?
>
> In any case, it's virtually impossible to take photos from a moving bike at high speed, especially when playing cat and mouse with a sturdy Mercedes. You can't take photos through a glass car window using a flash at night without getting a nice photo of your own flash as a reflection.

The site offers no firm conclusions but echoes the sentiments of many other conspiracy theorists that the princess might have been getting under the skin of the British government with her frequent political criticisms and activism. As they put it, "Diana was increasingly becoming involved in politics, and rattling a few cages on the way ... She had, in the words of some insiders, 'become a loose cannon.'" The site also notes that if Diana were, in fact, pregnant with Dodi's child, "it could have given the secret services a motive to eliminate her."

The architects of the WeThePeople Web site share that opinion. The site's "Diana Forum" (www.wethepeople.la/diforum2.htm) states bluntly that: "Queen Elizabeth ordered the murders of Diana and Dodi because she could not stomach the idea of William and Harry having a Muslim step-father." The site's main contribution to the conspiracy is an annotated set of photo stills taken by the paparazzi after the crash that show Diana's ambulance after it had pulled off the road for a 10-minute stop and an unidentified man standing outside the ambulance having a conversation on his cell phone. As the site puts it:

Here you have a French official talking on his cell phone, while not more than ten feet away the mother of the future King of England's life drains away, when this official and every other official present should have been YELLING AND SCREAMING AT THE TOP OF THEIR LUNGS FOR THE AMBULANCE TO DISPATCH WITH ALL HASTE TO THE HOSPITAL WHERE A MEDICAL TEAM OF 25 OF PARIS' MOST EXPERIENCED MEDICAL PROFESSIONALS HAD BEEN ASSEMBLED AND COULD VERY WELL HAVE SAVED THE POOR WOMAN, IF ONLY THEY WOULD GET THE AMBULANCE TO THE HOSPITAL!

The answer to that, and hundreds of other questions, can ostensibly be found in the official British inquiry from 2006 called "The Operation Paget inquiry report into the allegation of conspiracy to murder" (www.direct.gov.uk/en/Nl1/Newsroom/DG_065122). The

This photo purports to show an unidentified French official talking on his cell phone while Diana languishes in an ambulance parked 600 yards from the hospital. (Photo source: www.wethepeople.la/diforum2.htm)

report was Scotland Yard's response to the growing chorus of public doubt about Diana's accidental death. The 800-plus-page document affirms the earlier, official version of events: an inebriated driver racing to get away from the paparazzi and losing control of his vehicle while speeding through an underpass. (And regarding the ambulance stopping just a few miles from the hospital, the report says that Diana's blood pressure was dropping and the medical staff asked the driver to stop so they could work on the Princess's condition.) The report is thorough, sober, and detailed—and a total whitewash, according to some conspiracy theorists. After the report's public release, Al-Fayed's father, Mohammed, said, "It's completely outrageous that the leading Scotland Yard officer can come up with such unbelievable judgment."

Lord Stevens, the lead investigator of the report and a retired Scotland Yard official, concluded, "I have seen nothing that would justify further enquiries with any member of the Royal Family." Another major inquiry, launched in October 2007 and completed in April 2008, supported the earlier findings and put the full blame for the crash on driver Henri Paul and the pack of photographers that persued the Mercedes through the tunnel. "The verdict is unlawful killing, grossly negligent driving of the following vehicles and of the Mercedes" carrying the couple, the jury foreman announced.

But there is certainly more to Diana's enduring appeal than the questions surrounding her death. There are a number of Web sites that offer tributes, retrospectives, photographs, and essays dedicated to the life of the "People's Princess." Best of the lot is *Time* magazine's Diana archive (www.time.com/time/daily/special/diana). This site offers dozens of articles, an extensive photo essay, and a reprint of the magazine's "Special Report" on Diana's life in 1997. Also worth a look is The Work Continues (www.thework continues.org), a site maintained by the Diana, Princess of Wales Memorial Fund. Visitors to the site will learn about the many charities the princess was involved with and can also read Diana's own words about her firsthand experiences dealing with victims of illness and poverty.

Image and Reality

Princess Diana's life, star-studded and star-crossed, touched so many people that it's no surprise she remains, even in death, transfixing. Much of the theorizing about her death is due, no doubt, to genuine curiosity and a fervent belief that the whole truth has not been revealed. But to some admirers, the lingering questions simply offer a valid reason to remain obsessed with Diana, the "People's Princess." In the years since her death, Diana has become larger than life, and the number of sites aimed at exploring the shadowy circumstances of her death continues to multiply. And while the British government has concluded that Diana and Al-Fayed died as a result of reckless behavior on the part of their driver and pursuing paparazzi, there will always be those for whom motive, influence, and evidence lead straight to the gates of Buckingham Palace.

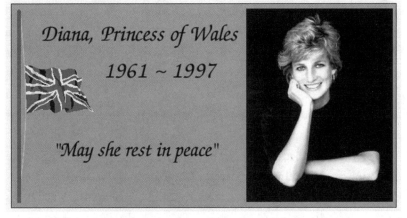

Diana's death has inspired dozens of Web sites, most of which feature a mix of loving tribute and questions about her death. (Photo source: www.dianamurder.com)

TWA Flight 800

In the annals of commercial aviation, the night of July 17, 1996, is one of devastating proportions. But it all began so routinely. On a clear, warm summer evening in New York, John F. Kennedy International Airport hummed with its usual high volume of traffic. Consistently ranked as the top "gateway" into the U.S. for international air travelers, JFK handled nearly 50,000 passengers per day in 1996.

One of the planes that touched down on the JFK tarmac that July afternoon was a Boeing 747 from Athens, Greece. The plane, Trans World Airlines (TWA) Flight 881, arrived at its assigned gate just after 4:30 PM without incident. Despite an hour-long delay (due to "a disabled piece of ground equipment and a passenger/baggage mismatch," according to the National Transportation Safety Board [NTSB]), the Boeing 747, now tagged TWA Flight 800, departed from JFK at about 8:19 PM, bound for Charles de Gaulle International Airport in Paris with two pilots, two flight engineers, 14 flight attendants, and 212 passengers aboard. The plane ascended to an altitude of about 13,000 feet over the Atlantic Ocean several miles off the southern shore of Long Island without incident.

Twelve minutes after takeoff, the inexplicable happened. The plane, as it followed instructions from air traffic control to climb another 2,000 feet, horrifically and mysteriously exploded, raining fiery debris seaward.

The plane was lost. All 230 people aboard were dead.

With the flames still illuminating the darkened ocean that night, experts and laypersons alike, publicly and privately, had already begun asking the perplexing question that surfaces after these type of terrifying tragedies: "Why?"

Despite the longest and most expensive investigation in American aviation history, many are still wondering what really happened.

A Spark of Doubt

Immediately, the search for survivors commenced. But the rescue would morph into a recovery sooner rather than later. Boats with divers and high-tech equipment, led by the Navy and Coast Guard, trawled the waters, pulling out bodies and wreckage.

With three possible culprits—mechanical failure, a bomb, or perhaps even a missile—in play during this early post-crash stage, the Federal Bureau of Investigation (FBI) and the NTSB each launched investigations, which created a sometimes-tenuous relationship and disagreements with respect to the cause of the crash. The FBI bowed out in November 1997, saying no physical evidence had been found to substantiate criminal or terrorist involvement. More than four years after the demise of TWA Flight 800, the case was, officially, closed. And the plane itself—not a foreign object or person—was to blame.

This mechanical failure, as proposed by the official report issued in August 2000, begins with the 25-year-old 747 as it sat on the tarmac at JFK. While attempting to find a passenger who had checked baggage but had not boarded the plane, the crew ran the aircraft's air-conditioning units—located inches below the center wing tank in the belly of the fuselage between the wings—to keep passengers comfortable during the hour-and-a-half delay. (The missing passenger, they realized, had been on the plane the entire time.) The heat created from these units, according to the NTSB version of things, created a vapor from the minute amount of jet fuel contained in the center wing tank, producing a highly ignitable gas/air mixture. Then, as the flight approached an altitude of 13,700 feet, something ignited it: "A short circuit involving electrical wiring outside the center wing tank somehow transferred excess voltage to the fuel quantity indication system,"

Many agree with the idea presented in this NTSB slide—that the air-conditioning packs (right) heated fuel in the center wing tank (left). But what caused the volatile vapor to ignite remains a point of contention. (Photo source: www.ntsb.gov/events/twa800/default.htm)

stated Bernard Loeb, NTSB director of aviation safety, during the public presentation of the final report. Though this fuel quantity indication wiring inside the tank is designed to limit voltage to "a very low level," he added, a short circuit could allow excessive voltage to enter these wires and create a powerful enough spark to ignite the catastrophic cocktail, causing an explosion that ripped the plane in two.

Though Loeb was guarded in his rhetoric (the findings of aircraft crash investigations are typically labeled with a "probable cause" tag), several factors bolster this conclusion, according to the NTSB. For starters, investigators discovered two microsecond dead spots toward the end of the Cockpit Voice Recorder tape—what they assert represented the device's momentary loss of power and corroborating evidence of a short circuit. "We cannot be certain that this, in fact, occurred," he said, regarding the NTSB's explanation of events, "but of all the ignition scenarios we considered, this scenario is likely."

Or was it?

Commander William Donaldson, a retired naval officer who conducted an independent investigation and pursued other possible explanations until his death in 2001, said such a scenario is, in fact, unlikely. "They have demonstrated that the fuel could explode if there's a large enough spark, but they haven't demonstrated how that large spark could have gotten into the center wing tank," he said, adding that government tests at Cal Tech used a spark 63,000 times greater than what officials claimed could cause the gas/air mixture to explode. Donaldson called the spark that supposedly caused the devastation and the spark actually needed to ignite it during tests "two completely different beasts."

He is not alone in this line of thought. While there seems to be agreement that the center wing tank did indeed explode, the reason why and when that happened remains a point of contention. Did a spark cause the explosion that, in turn, caused the breakup? No, argued the International Association of Machinists and Aerospace Workers (IAMAW). Instead, the group—privy to the investigation, along with Boeing, TWA, and the Air Line Pilots Association (ALPA)—proposed that the explosion was a result, not the cause, of TWA Flight 800's in-flight breakup. "A high-pressure event breached the fuselage and the fuselage unzipped due to the event," the IAMAW asserted. "The explosion was a result of this event."

If indeed this explanation of the breakup/explosion sequence is true, the actual cause of TWA Flight 800's demise—this "high-pressure event"—remains a mystery. To some, it's no mystery at all.

It's a Bird, It's a Plane ... and a Missile?

On that summer evening in 1996, hundreds of people—more than 700, in fact—saw something strange in the sky over the Long Island shore. One man explained that it seemed like a cheap firework rising from the beach. More than 250 reported seeing a streak of light. Several dozen witnesses described it as ascending; others said it originated from the horizon or the Earth's surface; many also recounted seeing a trail of smoke, or a contrail. Then, the mysterious streak of

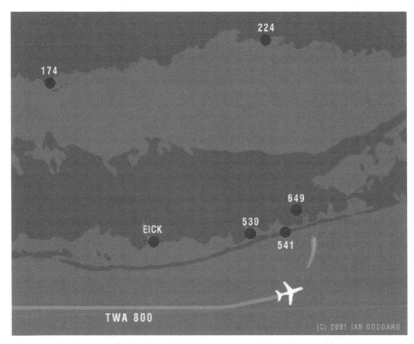

Researcher Ian Goddard's animation pinpoints the location of six witnesses who saw a "streak of light" (more than 700 saw "something") moving left to right across the sky on a collision course with Flight 800. (Photo source: users.erols.com/ igoddard/TWA800)

light disappeared for a few seconds, only to result in a series of explosions and fireballs, according to a bevy of eyewitnesses.

While a majority of witnesses were well within the range of visibility, perhaps no one had a better view than Major Fred Meyer, a New York Air National Guardsman and search-and-rescue pilot who served in Vietnam. Co-piloting a Black Hawk helicopter along the coast to perform a mid-air refueling training exercise and only 10 miles from TWA Flight 800, Meyer, too, saw something: a streak of light resembling a shooting star. "That's exactly what it looked like except it was red-orange in color and I saw it in broad daylight," he said. Then, as other witnesses described as well, the streak disappeared. What Meyer observed next—a sudden "high velocity explosion" followed by two to three more explosions and finally a "slowly forming, low velocity" fireball—was unmistakable to this experienced flyer with a military background:

> When you fly a helicopter at 120 knots over North
> Vietnam ... you see a lot of missiles, you see a lot of flak.
> I know what it looks like ... what I saw explode in the sky
> on July 17, 1996 was military ordnance ... *Somebody shot*
> *this aircraft down.*

Meyer and the scores of other witnesses talked to the FBI, which rather than recording their full accounts with a detailed transcription instead penned summaries of what it heard during the usually brief interviews.

Nonetheless, the witnesses still saw what they saw, and what they saw overwhelmingly resembled a missile. The NTSB, however, attributed the so-called streak of light to a result of the mechanical failure. After the center wing tank exploded and the fuselage cracked in two, the nose of the plane plummeted to the sea while the fiery aft section tilted back and climbed more than 3,000 feet for 30 seconds before its descent. The zoom climb, as it has been called, met harsh criticism when mainstream broadcast media aired a CIA-produced animation portraying the theory. This is what hundreds of eyewitnesses mistook for a missile, officials claimed. (At other times, they identified burning fuel and descending debris as "the missile.") Physicists, aviation experts, investigative journalists, and many witnesses counted themselves among its critics, arguing that the laws of physics and aeronautics, the plane's speed, and eyewitness accounts rendered the theory ridiculous and the animation a "CIA cartoon."

Ray Lahr—a retired Navy pilot, a former United Airlines captain, and a former safety representative with ALPA—has said that the zoom climb could not have happened. Instead, he argues, the plane—minus the forward third—pitched up and subsequently stalled in less than two seconds, causing it to free fall.

"The most the aircraft could have climbed would be about 200 feet," said Lahr, who assisted in seven NTSB airplane crash investigations prior to TWA Flight 800. "If the zoom climb never happened, then they've got to find out what the eyewitnesses saw, and the only logical conclusion is that they saw a missile."

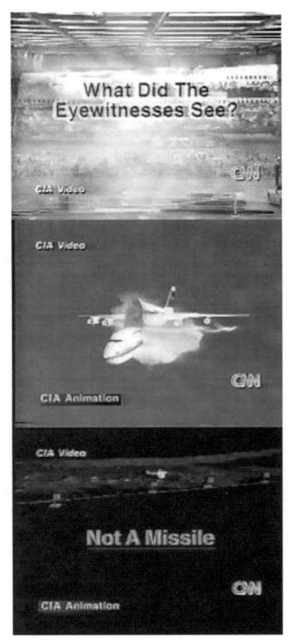

In this video aired on CNN, the government asserted that witnesses did not see a missile but rather the burning aft section of the plane climbing 3,000 feet after the nose was blown off. (Photo source: www.flight 800.org)

Investigating the Investigation

The official government line regarding the crash of TWA Flight 800 has been difficult to accept for many who have studied, or simply followed, the case. Many of the alternate theories not only allege that the official investigation simply got it wrong but also that the final conclusion was a result of a massive cover-up. Along with the various technical and eyewitness details, the timing of the event has fueled such suspicions. The crash of TWA Flight 800 occurred two days before the opening ceremonies of the Olympic Games in Atlanta; during the trial in New York of alleged terrorist Ramzi Yousef for his plans to attack airliners; during the midst of President Bill Clinton's re-election efforts; and only weeks after Clinton, based on intelligence reports, raised the country's state of alert to its highest level since the 1962 Cuban Missile Crisis.

In order to understand why belief in an alternative theory is so prevalent, knowledge of the official version is paramount. Spending some time on the TWA Flight 800 section of the NTSB's Web site (www.ntsb.gov/events/twa800/default.htm) will provide just that, from a summary of the investigative process to details of the investigation's findings to explanations of the final conclusion. A public hearing in December 1997 and a public board meeting in August 2000 serve as the main sources of information presented on the site. Full transcripts are provided, along with an abundance of what the NTSB calls "factual reports"—studies and analyses of all aspects of the case—that support its conclusion. Images, animation, and video provide information about everything from the aircraft's post-explosion trajectory (zoom climb) and fuel explosion tests to details of the center wing fuel tank and the debris field. The transcript of the two-day public hearing is useful in that readers are presented with the NTSB case from the NTSB officials themselves—at times convincing, at others lacking definitive explanations. Reports submitted by those groups privy to the investigation—Boeing, TWA, ALPA, and IAMAW—are available for download as well, parts of which criticize the investigation process and contradict the NTSB's assessments.

With a high level of technical expertise involved in this case, many of the NTSB documents are lengthy and the details complex. For a simpler and quicker introduction to the official theory of what happened to TWA 800, check out the National Geographic Channel's "Seconds from Disaster" reconstruction of that fateful flight, which is available at YouTube in three segments titled "Flight TWA-800 (mid-air explosion)" (www.youtube.com/watch?v=w581BiSBzQA). The site also offers an opposite but equally compelling view. Check out "TWA Flight 800 Shot Down by Surface-to-Air Missile" (www.youtube.com/watch?v=L6BUXu0AEpg) to watch Jack Cashill's *Silenced*, a six-part hour-long documentary proposing a scenario in which two missiles blew the plane from the sky. A writer and producer, Cashill explores this possibility, as well as that of a government cover-up, on the TWA Flight 800 page of his Web site (www.cashill.com/twa800/index.htm). Dozens of articles deal mostly with issues of a cover-up and not with the terrorist- vs. friendly-fire debate.

"Whether the missile strike is a tragic misfire by Navy or NATO forces or an act of terrorism is no longer relevant," he writes in the last installment of a 10-part series published on the disaster's 10th anniversary. "What is relevant is that some individuals know what happened and decide to conceal the truth."

Coupled with his claims of a cover-up, and even some circumstantial evidence, a summary of his main allegations and assertions makes a provocative argument—and a reason to visit his site: A high-speed projectile "merged" with the doomed plane, according to FAA radar data, which prompted a White House meeting the night of the crash; the Navy's presence in the "immediate vicinity" of the crash, though initially denied, included a warship and three submarines; a fast-moving "surface vessel" that fled from the area of the crash site, though initially denied, remains unidentified; supposed photo evidence of a missile was seized by the FBI, and that of a contrail was described as a "speck of dirt"; explosive residue discovered on pieces of wreckage was dismissed as the remnants of a dog-training exercise; red residue found on three rows of seats was dismissed as glue used in those seats, though independent tests revealed strong similarities to residue left by a warhead; officials tampered with the black boxes, along with the floor of the center wing tank, which was supposedly "sweeping upward" in early photographs of the wreckage—evidence of an external force—but later hammered down; officials discredited eyewitness reports, creating the zoom climb theory to explain away what people "really" observed.

The lynchpin of the official investigation, the zoom climb remains a fiercely disputed scenario. Lahr, who has fought for NTSB and CIA documents, calculations, and records pertaining to the theory using the Freedom of Information Act (FOIA), argues that "the investigation was shaped to fit the zoom climb hypothesis," steadfastly maintaining such an increase in altitude was aerodynamically unachievable under the circumstances. His Web site, The Impossible Zoom Climb (ray lahr.entryhost.com), highlights the reasons for such a belief. Though the NTSB diminished the importance of its own theory toward the end of the case, the entire investigation hinges on the question of whether Flight 800 climbed 3,200 feet after the explosion and loss of its cockpit. Lahr's site—which includes the CIA animation, eyewitness animations, and videos of expert testimony, along with news articles, court documents, and affidavits detailing his FOIA legal battle—is persuasive in its effort to debunk the zoom climb and, in turn, the basis for dismissing hundreds of eyewitness accounts.

If it wasn't the flaming plane increasing in altitude or falling debris, what did witnesses observe? The TWA 800 section of Ian Williams Goddard's Web site (users.erols.com/igoddard/TWA800) attempts to answer the question, using FBI witness reports and providing analysis and animated versions of its sketches. Referring to an affidavit filed by Colonel Lawrence Pence, whose job it was to interview military personnel who witnessed missile attacks in Vietnam, Goddard insists: "It is manifestly inaccurate to assert that eyewitness accounts are not consistent with a surface-to-air missile strike." But for Goddard, witnesses offered not only circumstantial evidence of a missile strike but also of heavy military activity—on the water and in the air—near the crash site, just to the north of an active military warning zone known as W-105. "Based on the established precedent in aviation accident investigation, the eyewitness evidence in the

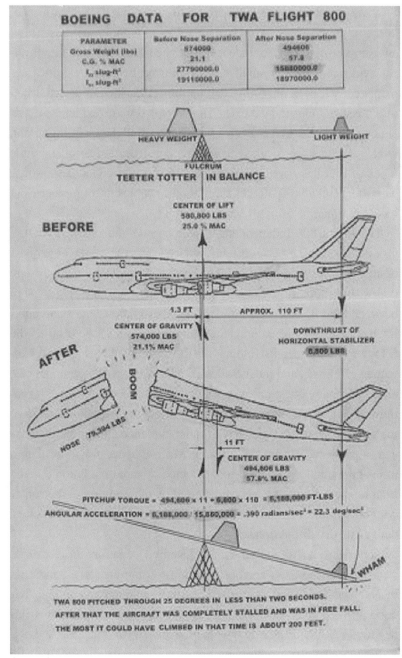

Ray Lahr, a former Navy and commercial pilot, proposed on his Web site that the so-called zoom climb is aerodynamically impossible, bringing witness statements back into play. (Photo source: raylahr.entryhost.com)

Flight 800 case is *more than sufficient* to determine 'felled by missile' as the probable cause," Goddard writes, even without the presence of any supporting physical evidence. But, according to Goddard, physical evidence—namely small holes produced by high-velocity fragments caused by a proximity detonation (rather than a direct strike) of a missile—does indeed exist. That, coupled with "evidence of evidence tampering," makes eyewitness accounts all the more important, which should have resulted in serious consideration of all possible types of missiles—including the classified variety. Goddard, whose site offers linkable footnotes throughout, enables users to check out more information from his various sources.

The Flight 800 Independent Researchers Organization (FIRO), a group formed in 1999, has established itself as a major player in questioning the investigation and lays out its stance on its Web site (www.flight800.org)—that because of "an unusual relationship between the FBI and NTSB during the investigation," the final report is "inconclusive and incomplete." As outlined in its petition of the NTSB to reconsider its findings, FIRO's claims center around eyewitness, forensic, and radar evidence. Investigators, the group argues, either left many questions unanswered or produced dubious explanations, trying to make the evidence jibe with a predetermined cause of the crash. The group's analysis of radar evidence alone—that wreckage moving away from the plane at Mach 2 speed for more than a mile at the time of the explosion, detected by radar but ignored in the final report, could not have been caused by the eruption of the center wing fuel tank—makes its site an important component of the "alternative" theory discussion.

The Web site of the Associated Retired Aviation Professionals (www.twa800.com) is arguably the most comprehensive source on the subject. The group, comprised of former military and civilian aviation professionals, proposes that one or more shoulder-fired missiles destroyed TWA Flight 800, likely a result of terrorist activity. Extremely detailed in its support of the missile theory, the site explores, in expansive sections, eyewitness accounts (with some using Google Earth to pinpoint their locations in relation to the plane), radar data, explosive residue, the FBI's search for missile parts among the wreckage, facts about shoulder-fired missiles, official investigation documents, news accounts, and more. With the amount of information here, acquiring at least a bit of background knowledge before reviewing the site would help users from becoming totally overwhelmed.

Flying the Friendly (Fire) Skies

Despite all of the questions, doubt, and suspicion surrounding the official investigation, from charges of withholding and tampering with evidence to allegations that certain explanations are simply impossible scenarios, the NTSB has not wavered from its "probable cause" determination. In fact, the reconstructed wreckage is now used to train accident investigators, and the findings spurred aviation officials to install equipment in passenger airplanes to reduce the flammability of gases and vapors within the center wing fuel tank. "It is unfortunate that a small number of people, assuming their own agendas, have persisted in making unfounded charges of a government cover-up in this investigation," said NTSB Chairman Jim Hall.

But one of the remarkable aspects of the TWA Flight 800 case is the involvement of so many credible, expert professionals who have challenged, and continue to question, the official version of events. While the most popular theory among these dissenters focuses on missiles, disagreement as to what type and in what manner they destroyed the plane has led to splintered groups—and, at times, contradictory arguments. And though the theory that terrorism brought down TWA Flight 800 continues to circulate, friendly fire from the U.S. Navy—the result of a test missile missing its target drone and instead locking on the commercial aircraft—has dominated the "who-pulled-the-trigger" debate. The destruction of a commercial airliner by a Navy missile, some say, would force the government to engage in a massive cover-up. As a federal judge said in his 2006 decision regarding Lahr's FOIA suit, "Taken together, this evidence is sufficient to permit the plaintiff to proceed based on his claim that the government acted improperly in its investigation of Flight 800, or at least performed in a grossly negligent fashion."

A group of witnesses took out a large ad in the *Washington Times* on August 15, 2000, alleging that government agencies had "silenced" them during the investigation. (Photo source: www.twa800.com)

AIDS

In the early 1980s, the mainstream press sought to get a handle on a new, mysterious disease that seemed to be ravaging certain sectors of society (primarily homosexual men and members of the African-American community). But long before the growing corps of puzzled journalists—or even the medical community—began to discern the contours of this unnamed malady, some of those from the groups being afflicted began putting out their theory about where the disease had come from. By the time the illness had a name—AIDS: Acquired Immune Deficiency Syndrome—many of its victims had named the culprit they claimed was responsible for introducing this virus into society. Perhaps shockingly to some—though not, perhaps, to die-hard conspiracy theorists—the guilty party was identified as the U.S. government.

In the decades since, AIDS has become an all-too-familiar plight for countless people around the world, and conspiracy theorists have put forward lots of arguments and evidence that they say proves their thesis: namely, that the U.S. government funded a secret military program to develop a biological weapon that would destroy the immune system of any subject who was injected with the virus.

The arguments and refutations have raged for decades as the disease has continued to spread. And it's precisely *who* has suffered from this disease that adds fuel to the conspiracy fires. From the homosexual community, which was the focal point of the first wave of the illness, to African-Americans, and, now, the whole of the

African continent (which is, in the estimation of some world health experts, approaching epidemic status), conspiracy theorists argue that these communities have been targeted for elimination by the government.

But within the conspiracy community, there are sharp divisions over such basic questions as whether AIDS is even fatal, or rather if it's the *treatment* for AIDS that kills instead. A bruising disagreement continues between those who argue about whether the human immunodeficiency virus (HIV) causes AIDS, with some medical experts arguing that HIV is as harmless as the common cold virus. And, just to make things interesting, there's a small but vocal camp that argues that AIDS is not a man-made illness at all but rather the result of extraterrestrial tampering. These adherents argue that the spread of AIDS coincided with the rash of alien abductions that came to light through some best-selling accounts of humans being transported aboard UFOs. Since AIDS was a completely unknown condition, never having appeared in human history, it must have come from an otherworldly source, these theorists argue.

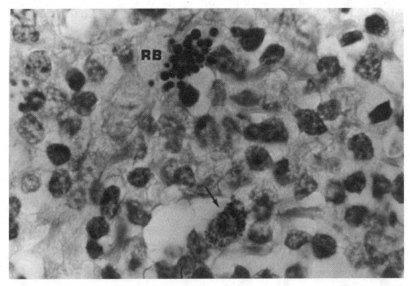

A close-up look at the AIDS virus in one of the earliest known cases. (Photo source: www.conspiracyplanet.com/channel.cfm?ChannelID=34)

Is there a basis for such speculation? After decades of scientific research, hasn't the origin of the AIDS virus been established scientifically? Could this just be another case of knee-jerk alarmists blaming the usual suspects?

Whatever agreement exists among the mainstream scientific community, there's little but fragmentation, accusation, and indignation among conspiracy theorists. And as the disease continues to spread, the theories continue to multiply.

Here a Theory, There a Theory

In most conspiracy theories, there is a split between the "official version" (usually supported by government and scientific officials) and the "untold story" (promoted by those who suspect a conspiracy). The AIDS conspiracy is different in that not even those in the "official" camp can agree on its origins. Many scientists and medical researchers disagree—at conferences, in medical journals, and in books—about the sources and treatments for AIDS. A large cohort of doctors and immunologists seems to agree with the findings that AIDS is caused by HIV. Many researchers see a clear link between HIV and AIDS, with HIV destroying various cells of the immune system, which leads then to AIDS (basically, an inability of the body to fend off infection). However, there is a persistent and vocal group of researchers who suggest that HIV has nothing to do with AIDS; in fact, they argue, many people who have the HIV virus will live happy, healthy lives—unless they begin treatment for HIV, which often involves highly toxic drugs. The cure, they argue, is what often leads to AIDS, not HIV. Some researchers have even speculated that AIDS is not caused by a virus but rather by certain social factors, such as malnutrition or pollution.

Another difference between the AIDS conspiracy theory and other, popular conspiracy theories is that it is almost impossible for a non-specialist to wade through the scientific research and come to an independent conclusion. The material published by medical journals on AIDS is, well, as eye-glazing and indecipherable as most other medical writings. Even Web sites aimed at general readers often lapse into medical jargon baffling to the nonspecialist (for example: "HIV is a retrovirus, necessarily employing the enzyme RNA transcriptase in its replication. RNA transcriptase is notoriously prone to transcription errors, resulting in numerous viral mutations [sudden marked genetic changes]. Viral mutations can be expected to select for properties favouring survival, such as drug resistance and increased infectivity.").

And there's one other important distinction between those suspicious of the origins and causes of AIDS and proponents of other conspiracy theories. Supporters of the mainstream argument—that HIV causes AIDS and is *not* the result of a Western government plot to eliminate "undesirables"—say that the life-saving fight against AIDS is being dangerously set back by the persistence of conspiracy theories. Many researchers and public health officials have argued that it's the conspiracy theories that are often keeping people from seeking treatment—especially in Third World countries, where AIDS remains a widespread lethal presence. (South African President Thabo Mbeki expressed skepticism about mainstream AIDS theories, suggesting that the many deaths from AIDS in Africa might be attributable to the disease's "treatments"—the toxic drugs manufactured by profit-seeking pharmaceutical companies with the active support of Western governments.)

Spreading Like a Virus

Within the conspiracy community, most adherents believe that there is, in fact, an HIV virus, and that it will turn into full-blown AIDS and kill you if left untreated. Further, they are fairly strongly united in their belief that the HIV virus was deliberately concocted in a U.S. government laboratory. There's some disagreement, however, about whether the U.S. government ever intended to release HIV into select populations. One of the first examinations of the AIDS conspiracy came from Jakob and Lilli Segal, a pair of East German scientists who authored a startling report in 1986 titled *AIDS: USA Home-Made Evil*. In this document, the scientists detailed what has become widely accepted among conspiracy theorists: the "spliced theory" of HIV. In this theory, HIV is widely accepted to be the result of splicing a nonhuman virus (in their report, it's a sheep virus) with a human virus. They claimed that the splicing was part of a biological warfare research experiment at Fort Detrick, Maryland, and they went on to suggest that the virus was introduced into the U.S. prison population, and those inmates then spread the disease to New York's gay community.

The AIDS conspiracy theory, then, only makes sense if one believes that the government would authorize germ warfare and then unleash the product of that experiment on unsuspecting members of the public. Theorists are quick to point to a number of such apparent instances of lab-based virus creation. As one Web site dedicated to the subject notes:

> The US Government has an established history of performing atrocious experiments on its own citizens without their knowledge or consent. Between 1932 and 1972, the United States Public Health Service conducted a covert experiment called the Tuskegee Study of Untreated Syphilis in the Negro male. In this experiment, the Public Health Service deliberately deprived black, syphilis-infected residents of Tuskegee, Alabama of treatment in order to see what would happen to them. Between 1953 and 1972, the CIA conducted secret experiments on unwitting human subjects under the umbrella of projects MK Ultra. The full nature and scope of these experiments may never be known, since most of the records on MK Ultra were deliberately destroyed by the CIA in 1972. What is known, however, is that some of these experiments involved: electro-shock treatment, sensory deprivation, sleep deprivation, administration of psychoactive drugs, psychosurgery, the effects of radiation, the testing of chemical and biological weapons on American city streets, "brainwashing" and "mind control," interrogation and torture techniques. The US Army has admitted to conducting similar experiments.

A federal official takes a blood sample as part of the "Tuskegee Study of Untreated Syphilis in the Negro Male." (Photo source: wikipedia.org/wiki/Tuskegee_Study_of_Untreated_Syphilis_in_the_Negro_Male)

So there it is, the foundation that undergirds the conspiracy theory. If the government deliberately infected a select group of its citizens in the past, theorists argue, why not believe they would do it again? And from there, it's a short leap—in some people's minds—to the supposition that certain "undesirables" (such as sexually active gay men) might be targeted by the government in a modern use of germ warfare.

It all makes for some grimly diverting reading on the Web, with contributors ranging from established medical researchers to politically active (and angry) private citizens, all of whom seem eager to add their piece of the AIDS picture to the overall puzzle.

Framing the Issue

There are so many avenues to pursue in the AIDS conspiracy theory that first-timers to this topic need a good, general introduction before exploring any of the dozen disparate paths laid out on the

Internet. It's easy to get swamped by confusing, complex, and contradictory information. A good place to get started is the "AIDS Conspiracy" page of SourceWatch: A Project of the Center for Media and Democracy (www.sourcewatch.org/index.php?title=AIDS_ conspiracy). The site lists most of the major theories and players in the conspiracy and also annotates each theory, explaining not only what is believed, but *why*. For example, one finds such notations as:

> Some conspiracy theories on the origins of AIDS carry anti-Semitic overtones. … Some African-Americans in the US believe that HIV was invented by Jews as a way to destroy the black race. … Some believe the claim that AIDS was created by scientists to be false and to have originated from a communist Cold War plot to destabilize the Western World … [with] KGB agents seeking to undermine the faith of citizens in their own government.

The site helpfully categorizes each of the arguments and makes for a relatively easy at-a-glance score-carding of the major arguments.

Most of the larger sites dedicated to this topic tend, not surprisingly, to endorse the idea of a conspiracy. A spirited presentation of the various theories can be found on the AIDS pages of the popular Conspiracy Planet Web site (www.conspiracyplanet.com/channel.cfm? ChannelID=34). Much of the information on this site carries the bylines of various medical researchers, though the articles are clearly intended for an audience of nonspecialists—a fact easily deduced from the roster of somewhat nonserious titles, like "Monkey Biz: Cancer-Causing Vaccines, Polio, and AIDS" and "WHO Murdered Africa (The Man-Made Origin of AIDS)." The tone of most of the articles is, well, pretty angry. And the scope of suspects is comprehensive, from the World Health Organization (the "WHO" in "WHO Murdered Africa") to the KGB. As one article, written by William Campbell Douglass, MD, states, "You will understand why the other suspects, the homosexuals, the green monkey and the Haitians, were only pawns in this virocidal attack on the non-Communist world." The site doesn't lack conviction.

An author and researcher named Boyd Graves has established himself as one of the more active proponents of the AIDS conspiracy theory, and his Web site (www.boydgraves.com) is a good example of the kind of private passion this subject has worked up in some people. This site features an AIDS timeline (dating back to 1878, "when the United States passed a federal Quarantine Act ... and began a significant effort to investigate 'causes' of epidemic diseases"), a message board, and an online "People's petition calling for immediate review of the U.S. Special Virus Program and the evidence of the laboratory birth of AIDS."

Similarly, a physician named Alan Cantwell has written extensively about the development and spread of AIDS; much of his work can be found in the archives of the AIDS Conspiracy site at Sonic.net, including his provocative article titled "AIDS Biowarfare" (sonic.net/~doretk/ArchiveARCHIVE/Aids/Aids.html). Cantwell theorizes that the government developed the virus, and then injected it into "New York, San Francisco and Los Angeles gays who volunteered for a hepatitus vaccine experiment." He also speculates that

"The World War with the AIDS weapon continues to rage."

Dr. Boyd Graves, an outspoken critic of the U.S. AIDS policy, holds what he claims is a flow chart detailing research into the development of the AIDS virus in U.S. government laboratories. (Photo source: www.boydgraves.com)

large-scale inoculations administered by the WHO in Africa could have been responsible for transmitting the AIDS virus. As he notes, "The 'official' African Monkey story does not adequately explain how a black African heterosexual epidemic could have transferred itself into a white homosexual epidemic in Manhattan, or how AIDS could have started *in Africa and in New York City* at the same time."

Well, one way to explain it would be to blame it on extraterrestrials, which is exactly what a researcher argues in an article at Flying Saucer Review (www.fsr.org.uk/fsrart37.htm). Building on the argument that AIDS appeared at widely distant places at roughly the same time, Phillip S. Duke, PhD, notes that "The origination of these two different viral strains, in two different locations, at the same time, in two differently susceptible human populations, is entirely contrary to how natural infectious disease works." And why would aliens want to infect the human race with AIDS? That's a question Duke deals with after presenting his case, complete with a discussion of cattle mutilations and reported human abductions:

> I suggest there is only one real form of cosmic wealth, and that is cosmic real estate in the form of a world rich in life, like ours. When enough people are sick, dying, and dead from AIDS, human civilization will collapse, eliminating any opportunity of organized, meaningful resistance, including the possibility of atomic retaliation.

Duke is far more suspicious of alien life forms than he is of the fellow members of his own species, as he questions in his article: "What human being or human organisation would purposefully develop and unleash the infectious lethal virus HIV, which threatens to destroy human civilization and possibly even our species?" He concludes by dismissing the prevailing notion of the disease's origin: "The concepts of HIV's origination in simians, or by human science, are invalidated and must therefore be discarded." Well, it's a position.

Not everyone in the world of AIDS conspiracies sees an evil motive behind the spread of the disease. One particularly compelling argument suggests that the disease might be natural but the government's

Some conspiracy theorists believe that the AIDS virus resulted from an alien plan to infect and weaken the human species. (Photo source: www.ufoevidence.org)

response to the disease was badly bungled. In the "AIDS Conspiracy" section of Totse.com ("Raw data for raw nerves"), one can read an article accusing the government and pharmaceutical companies of "unconscionable neglect and mismanagement" (www.totse. com/en/conspiracy/the_aids_conspiracy/aids.html). The article's author, John S. James, lays out a convincing-sounding case, laden with facts and historical background about the development of prospective treatments of AIDS—many of which were ignored, underfunded, or refused. James's article suggests there are indeed "life-saving treatments" available but that researchers and government officials need to work together: "The consistent, severe mismanagement of this research will stop when doctors, scientists, journalists, and organizers stop passing the buck to other experts, and begin to inform one another and the public." So, in a bit of a departure from others who have written on the subject, James sees a conspiracy—but of a different, less nefarious type: "With thousands dead, millions of people affected, and thousands of doctors, scientists, and journalists involved, there has been a conspiracy of silence around the central issues of AIDS treatment research."

Silence always makes people suspicious, and in the case of AIDS, one of the most consistently suspicious groups of people regarding the cause and spread of AIDS has been African-Americans. To gauge the depth of that suspicion, check out PubMed (www.ncbi.nlm.nih. gov/pubmed) and search for the article "Do Blacks believe that HIV/AIDS is a government conspiracy against them?" Readers will find a summary of a lengthier article on the topic (as well as links to other articles on that subject) that suggests "Twenty-seven percent of blacks held AIDS-conspiracy views and an additional 23 percent were undecided," according to a recent survey. The article concludes that "such beliefs must be addressed" as part of any larger public health policy aimed at controlling the spread of AIDS.

And controlling the spread of AIDS is the primary focus of an impressively extensive site maintained by a worldwide AIDS charity AVERT. The group's site addresses the spread of the disease in a detailed but user-friendly essay titled "The Origins of HIV" (www.avert.org/origins.htm). There's none of the alarmist rhetoric of the majority of conspiracy-minded sites but rather a clearheaded, scientific-sounding discussion of how HIV likely crossed over from monkeys to humans, and how the disease has continued to spread. The authors of the article don't feign certainty, but they do endorse the arguments put forward by mainstream researchers—that AIDS leaped from African monkeys to mankind: "Given the evidence we have already looked at, it seems highly likely that Africa was indeed the continent where the transfer of HIV to humans first occurred (monkeys from Asia and South America have never been found to have SIVs that could cause HIV in humans)." And, in a departure from those conspiracy sites that look backward to establish the cause,

This poster, which aims to raise awareness of AIDS in Ho Chi Minh City, Vietnam, demonstrates the global reach of what many experts now classify as a pandemic. (Photo source: wikipedia.org/wiki/AIDS)

AVERT urges a scientific focus "not on how the AIDS epidemic originated but how those it affects can be treated, how the further spread of HIV can be prevented and how the world can be changed to ensure a similar pandemic never occurs again."

Next Move?

In the many ways that conspiracy theories about AIDS differ from those about other historical events, one stands out: AIDS is continuing to kill. The phenomenon of this epidemic can't be studied from the safe remove of decades or centuries, with the historical distance necessary to sort out truth from fiction. There's a chilling immediacy to the subject, a dire gravity that keeps all the theorizing from being merely a diverting intellectual exercise. And yet, it might turn out that the very questions being raised by the conspiracy theorists are the ones that need to be answered by the medical community—or a skeptical public. There's no doubt that questions about the origin and treatment of this lethal disease will continue to fester, as surely as its roster of worldwide victims continues to swell.

The Shakespeare Authorship Question

Who wrote the works of Shakespeare? The question seems preposterous, with an answer so obvious. It's a no-brainer, right? William Shakespeare, the most famous literary figure in history, wrote the works of Shakespeare. The commoner with humble beginnings in Stratford-upon-Avon—a town of 1,500 people and a four-day journey from London, the heart of Elizabethan England—wrought the 37 plays, two narrative poems, and 154 sonnets that have come to form the heart of the canon of Western literature.

Maybe.

In the late 18th century, more than 150 years after the death of William Shakspere (as his name was spelled in his baptism record), a clergyman and scholar named James Wilmot came to a startling conclusion as he wrapped up his investigation, in and around Stratford, into the biography of the supposed author: Noting an overwhelming lack of evidence connecting the man to the works, he decided Sir Francis Bacon, not Will Shakspere, was the true author. Wilmot never published his findings, notes of which he demanded be burned when he died, but he did confide in a friend who later passed the secret on to a literary society. Wilmot's research and conclusion, however, was not discovered until 1932, long after the authorship debate had commenced.

Since the time Wilmot settled on Bacon as author of the Shakespeare canon, some five-dozen additional candidates have been proposed, from Queen Elizabeth I to Christopher Marlowe, from Sir

Henry Neville to Edward de Vere, 17th Earl of Oxford. And even the idea that the works were penned by a collaborating group of writers has been suggested. Through the years, just as the number of candidates proposed has increased, so has the prevalence of the authorship question: in PBS documentaries, hundreds of books, scholarly papers, newspaper articles (in such popular periodicals as the *New York Times*, the *Atlantic*, and *Harper's*), and even a moot court debate presided over by several Supreme Court justices.

The Shakespearean authorship question, however, is still relatively obscure. Academia is not exactly embracing the debate (good luck trying to find it in the course catalogs of university English departments), and Stratfordians—those who steadfastly subscribe to the long-held notion of Will Shakspere, the Bard of Avon, as the author Shakespeare—often dismiss the question altogether, as kooky, as conspiratorial and extreme, as irrelevant. For the uninitiated, the doubt regarding the byline of the greatest literature ever composed might indeed seem surprising, even shocking. So, one might wonder, what, if anything, lends the supposed literary mystery, the "historic whodunit," any credence?

A Shake-y Bio, an Unliterary Will

The problem that arises from ascribing the works of Shakespeare to the man from Stratford is, as Wilmot discovered in 1785, the sheer lack of concrete, or even circumstantial, evidence. Despite being one of the most researched figures in all of history and the subject of an inestimable number of biographies, the record regarding the life of Will Shakspere is sparse (although some say more is known about him than other commoners and most dramatists of the time).

In a 2005 essay, Rachel Donadio, a writer and editor for the *New York Times Book Review*, mused whether Stephen Greenblatt's best-selling biography, *Will in the World: How Shakespeare Became Shakespeare*, more appropriately belonged on the fiction list:

> Outside of his astonishing body of work, the playwright
> didn't leave the materials of the kind biographers have

traditionally relied on. So in order to unite the Shakespeare who left a will and one surviving letter with the Shakespeare who wrote *Hamlet* and *King Lear*, Greenblatt took imaginative leaps. The result is a book shot through with "might haves," "could haves" and "may well haves," ... In valuing imagination over evidence Greenblatt is essentially using fiction techniques in nonfiction writing.

But, as Donadio points out, Greenblatt was not the first, and likely not the last, Shakespeare biographer to use imagination, inference, conjecture, assumptions, and pure speculation in his or her efforts to paint a picture of Will Shakspere of Stratford as the greatest poet and playwright in history. Without doing so, the authors of such biographies would find it difficult to fill a chapter, never mind an entire book. Mark Twain—one of many literary and intellectual giants who has, at minimum, expressed skepticism about the Stratford man's claim to authorship—compared Shakespeare's biography (in *Is*

Many Stratfordians believe the Shakespeare monument in Holy Trinity Church (left) helps proves that Will Shakspere was indeed the author. But others point to the statue's depiction in William Dugdale's *The Antiquities of Warwickshire* in 1656 (right), which shows Shakespeare holding a sack of grain instead of a pen and paper. That's the real Shakspere from Stratford-upon-Avon, they say. (Photo source: www.shakespeareauthorship.com)

Shakespeare Dead? From My Autobiography) to a museum dinosaur: a few bones and lots and lots of plaster.

So what do we know about Will Shakspere of Stratford-upon-Avon? Born in April 1564, he was the son of a leather worker and glove maker, John Shakspere. At the age of 18, he married Anne Hathaway, who was pregnant and eight years his elder. A daughter was baptized six months later, and twins were born two years after that (a boy, who died at age 11, and a girl). Legal documents, which provide nearly all we know about Will Shakspere, show him to be a successful businessman: a moneylender, a grain dealer, and an investor in real estate and theaters (he may have been a bit-part actor as well). But there is no evidence that he obtained any formal education, nor is there any record of him traveling outside of Stratford or London—both seemingly essential prerequisites for this "worldly" author to possess.

Nothing from his day reveals a literary life of any kind, and in many cases, the records and documents seem to indicate quite the opposite. His father, wife, and two daughters are believed to have been illiterate, based on their signatures (simple marks on the page). While the inability to read or write was not uncommon, the thought that the greatest literary mind in history failed to teach his daughters either is certainly striking. Shakspere's own signatures—three from his will, three from other legal documents—do not instill much confidence: "They look like a child's attempt to copy a signature," one scholar noted. "The smooth flourish of a signature, whether legible or illegible, that would be expected of a writer who had penned nearly a million words, is missing." And his will itself disappoints. Despite its length and detail regarding who should receive varying possessions—sword, clothes, silver bowl, silver plate, his second-best bed—Shakspere makes no mention of any books (although it was common to do so in wills), and no other evidence has ever surfaced to suggest he maintained a library of any kind. He also fails to note in his will the 18 plays yet to be published when he died—a curious omission. And when the Stratford man did die in 1616, the event, a major one if indeed he was the great author, went totally unnoticed and unrecognized—a curious silence.

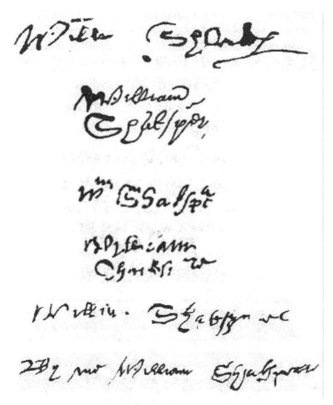

For someone who penned thousands of famous lines, Shakspere's six known shaky signatures are not what would be expected from the prolific author. (Photo source: wikipedia.org/wiki/Shakespeare_authorship_question)

The Genius Defense

Stratfordians are quick to dismiss the absence of evidence from Shakspere's life, arguing that none of it amounts to definitive proof that he was not the author, while anti-Stratfordians believe the cumulative weight is quite persuasive. Stratfordians also tend to point to the prefatory material of the *First Folio*, which was printed seven years after Will Shakspere's death and contained 36 plays (half of which had never been published before), claiming it makes clear that Shakspere of Stratford was indeed Shakespeare the playwright. Supporters of another authorship candidate, however, dispute that interpretation, arguing it is merely another piece of circumstantial evidence that can, in fact, be read in a way that casts even more doubt over the Stratford claim while propping up their own nominee.

This is essentially the problem with the authorship debate: It revolves around circumstantial evidence, interpretation vs. interpretation. There is no smoking gun; so the controversial question—Who

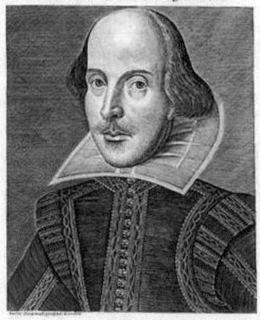

Many skeptics look at this illustration from the *First Folio*—a key piece of evidence for Stratfordians—with a suspicious eye, claiming that Shakspere's face (note the prominent jaw line) masks the true author. (Photo source: shakespeare.palomar.edu)

wrote Shakespeare?—remains a question with no definitive answer, leaving only theories, some much stronger than others.

Skeptics wonder how this apparently uneducated man with no access to books or experience of significant travel, this grain dealer and moneylender, son of a glove maker, from the hinterland of Stratford, could have written the works of Shakespeare, which are drenched with sophisticated thoughts and ideas; immersed in an understanding of the ways of nobility, aristocracy, and courtly life; steeped in the classics (often using sources not yet translated into English); and bursting with a keen knowledge of law (among many other disciplines), foreign languages, and distant lands (especially Italy).

Genius. Unparalleled genius. Superhuman genius.

That's the response the orthodoxy offers—quite predictably—when confronted with this dichotomy of inexperience displayed in the life vs. erudition exhibited in the works.

But is genius, and genius alone, a reasonable enough defense?

As Richard Whalen, author of *Shakespeare: Who Was He?*, wrote in his clear dissection of the Shakespearean authorship debate:

> In the nineteenth century they called it "Divine Inspiration." Literary genius, however, must have the raw material to draw upon. The richer and more diverse the content of the writing, the greater the need to draw on diversity and intensity of experience. Unlike music or mathematics, great and sustained writing is the result of genius working on life experience and acquired knowledge, neither of which can be part of the innate gift of genius. Even if endowed retrospectively with a genius that is almost superhuman, Will Shakspere still, according to the records, had precious little time to gain the life experience demonstrated so dramatically in the early plays.

All the great writers throughout history, Whalen asserts, "draw directly on what they have seen, heard, and learned, transmuting their experience into their most effective art"—an assessment difficult to dispute when looking at his examples: Tolstoy, Proust, Twain, Melville, Kafka, Mann, Moliére, Joyce, Dickens, Hemingway, Faulkner, O'Neill, and Updike.

As Ralph Waldo Emerson aptly pointed out in 1850, referring to the supposed Stratford author, "Other admirable men have led lives in some sort of keeping with their thought; but this man, in wide contrast."

If this argument is to be believed—that the works of Shakespeare could not have flowed from the quill of Will Shakspere of Stratford because his experience and education (or lack thereof) ill-prepared and ill-equipped him to be able to create such masterful dramas— then the true author is missing, waiting for recognition that is long overdue.

Searching for "Shakespeare"

Shake-speare (a hyphenated version frequently appeared on the title page of the works; hyphenated bylines often indicated the use of a pseudonym) is, in fact, a perfect nom de plume for a playwright: Athena, Greek goddess of wisdom and the arts, was born to Zeus, shaking a spear at birth. But among doubters of the Stratfordian theory, there is some debate as to whether the similarity between the supposed pseudonym and Will Shakspere's name was merely a coincidence or if the Stratford man was paid to serve as a "front man" for the *real* author—whoever that might be. Since the Shakespearean authorship question first took root centuries ago, some 60 candidates have been proposed as the right man—and in some cases, the right woman—for the byline.

The first choice for the Shakespeare throne was Sir Francis Bacon. Although he has fallen out of favor as a leading contender, Bacon is still regarded in some circles as the man who was Shakespeare. Although not the most aesthetically appealing site on the Internet, a Web site called Sir Francis Bacon's New Advancement of Learning (www.sirbacon.org) highlights the Baconian theory; clicking the "Summary of Baconian Evidence" link on the site's homepage directs users to a page full of quotes, essays, book excerpts, and other analysis that present the case for Bacon's authorship.

Poet and playwright Christopher Marlowe, another popular candidate, was supposedly murdered in 1593—the same year Shakespeare's works began to appear. Marlovians, however, argue that he faked his death—either to avoid an imminent execution for heresy or to cover up his work as a spy for the crown—and went on to write the works of Shakespeare. For an introduction to the Marlovian theory, check out the Marlowe Lives! Association's Web site (www.marlovian.com), which also lacks visual sophistication and does not nearly come close to providing the amount of information presented by the aforementioned Baconian site. It does, however, serve as an adequate introduction and provides a limited but useful list of links for further investigation into the Marlowe-was-Shakespeare theory; be sure to check out "The Marliad," a somewhat bizarre but equally fascinating Marlovian treatise described on the site as "a rap epic-in-progress about Christopher Marlowe and the age of Shakespeare."

In 2005, a fairly surprising development occurred: A new candidate was proposed to the list, which previously consisted of mostly long-standing challengers, like Bacon and Marlowe. Brenda James, co-author of *The Truth Will Out: Unmasking the Real Shakespeare,* claims Sir Henry Neville to be the true author. James's Web site (www.henryneville.com) complements the book and the theory that Neville—an Elizabethan English diplomat—used a distant relative named Will Shakspere to hide his identity as author. The site, set up much like a blog, is limited in explaining the Neville case that is presented in the book and instead "contains extra background material." There are, however, dozens of articles, all written by James, that highlight aspects of Neville's life and touch on his connection to the works of Shakespeare.

But, without doubt, one candidate—mainly because of the captivating persuasiveness of the theory behind his candidacy—has risen above all else, gaining increasing popularity as the leading contender during the last three decades. That man is Edward de Vere, the 17th Earl of Oxford, who was known at court as a "spear shaker" and whose family crest contains a lion shaking a spear. In 1989, PBS's *Frontline* aired a program investigating "The Shakespeare Mystery," which aided in bringing de Vere's credentials, as well as the authorship debate in general, to the forefront. Several years after broadcasting the program again in 1992, PBS dedicated space on its Web site for the Stratford vs. Oxford case (www.pbs.org/wgbh/pages/front line/shakespeare). The site remains one of the best designed, most easily navigated, and clearly written on the topic. Because it never really gets bogged down with too much microscopic detail, the site is the perfect introductory course to de Vere's challenge of the Bard. (At the top of the homepage, users can link to a similarly engaging site for PBS's *Frontline* exploration of the Marlowe theory [www.pbs.org/wgbh/pages/frontline/shows/muchado].) The site contains transcripts of "Three Debates/Mock Trials": a Boston Bar Association–sponsored mock trial in 1993; a national satellite conference debate, moderated by William F. Buckley Jr., in 1992 (audio excerpts are provided as well); and a 1987 moot court in Washington D.C. before three Supreme Court justices. Users can also read from several selected articles, including a 1974 *Harvard Magazine* piece by Charlton Ogburn, who a decade later would publish what amounts to an Oxfordian bible, *The Mysterious William Shakespeare: The Myth and the Reality*. Richard Whalen, author of a similarly engaging Oxfordian work, provides an annotated reading list, an extensive bibliography with a range of books that runs the gamut of Shakespearean authorship beliefs. The "Synopsis" link on the homepage, which provides a summary of the program, is a good place to start exploring this site (a full transcript of the entire *Frontline* show is available for download). And since the Web site debuted long after the program's 1989 premiere, the site includes two "Updates"—an essay from the Stratfordian side and another from the Oxfordian side, the latter of which deals mostly with the discovery and study of de Vere's annotated Bible, known as the Geneva Bible, which frequently corresponds to biblical references made in Shakespeare. Although the links listed under the "Shakespeare on the Web" heading are disappointingly few, those who have been intrigued by this initiation into

THE SHAKESPEARE MYSTERY
Who, in fact, was he?

The man from Stratford?   or   Edward de Vere, 17th Earl of Oxford?

While the list of candidates is long, the bout between Shakspere and Edward de Vere has gained a certain prominence. (Photo source: www.pbs.org/wgbh/pages/frontline/shakespeare)

the Oxford theory will find a must-visit site: the Shakespeare Fellowship.

Oxfordians, as the adherents of the de Vere theory are called, can trace their lineage back to 1920, when British educator J. Thomas Looney (pronounced Low-ney, though Stratfordians didn't miss the chance to point out his "funny" name) first proposed Oxford as a candidate. Starting with the premise that the author of the works was unknown, he listed all the characteristics—both general and specific—the author should possess. One and only one Elizabethan fit the criteria: Edward de Vere. At the Shakespeare Fellowship Web site (www.shakespearefellowship.org), the entire text of *"Shakespeare" Identified*, Looney's landmark book, is available. While that alone makes the site worth logging on to, there are many more reasons to bookmark this site. In the "Virtual Classroom," users will find a wealth of information pertaining to the Shakespeare authorship question and the Oxford case: a succinct and understandable "Beginner's Guide"; a brief FAQ explaining the authorship debate; an engaging slideshow highlighting 25 reasons why Oxford was Shakespeare; a flash presentation of the "Shakespeare Skeptics Hall of Fame" (many great minds, as users will note here, have questioned the Stratford claim); a timeline exploring the history of the authorship debate; a section containing articles and essays about "Shakespeare and the Law"; access to selected chapters (and the entire table of contents) from a 2001 doctoral dissertation detailing a 10-year study of de Vere's Geneva Bible; essays dealing with the dating of the plays (often a Stratfordian knock on the Oxford theory because some of the plays appeared after de Vere's death); and a selection of book reviews. The site also maintains a "News" section, and users can contribute to the debate in the interactive "Forum." Perhaps most impressive of all, however, is the Shakespeare Fellowship's "Links" page—an annotated listing of several dozen sites, divided into various categories (e.g., Oxfordian, Shakespeare, Stratfordian, Baconian, Marlowe, and Renaissance Literature).

Included on that list is a site by Mark Anderson, a journalist and staunch Oxfordian, who published a well-received de Vere biography in 2005 titled *"Shakespeare" By Another Name: The Life of Edward de Vere, Earl of Oxford, the Man Who Was Shakespeare.* While the site (www.shakespearebyanothername.com) functions largely as a promotional vehicle for the author and book, two of its features are wholly unique: a series of nine downloadable audio files (each free

Ralph Waldo Emerson, Mark Twain, Walt Whitman, Sigmund Freud, Malcolm X, Mark Rylance, John Paul Stevens, and Orson Wells (clockwise from left) are among a host of luminaries who have questioned the authorship of the works. (Photo source: www.shakespearefellowship.org)

"episode" is about 20 minutes) that reveal some of the mind-blowing ways in which Oxford's life parallels the works of Shakespeare, and a Google Earth interactive atlas of de Vere's life (another convincing, and entertaining, argument that he was indeed the Bard). Is *Hamlet* really Oxford's autobiographical drama?

But some scholars remain unconvinced, reluctant to accept Oxford's strong case. The Stratfordian stance—other than dismissing the authorship question altogether as absurd—is best represented and best argued by the Web site of David Kathman and Terry Ross: www.shakespeareauthorship.com. Billed as being "dedicated to the proposition that Shakespeare wrote Shakespeare," the site is part Stratfordian, arguing on behalf of the traditional byline, and part anti-Oxfordian, attempting to debunk the evidence behind the de Vere claim. Mostly a compilation of essays—many written by the hosts themselves, some from other sources—the site is easily navigated: The homepage lists all of the site's contents, with embedded links to read full articles. Here, as with aforementioned sites, the links section to other Web resources is expansive. (Note: The Shakespeare Fellowship replies to several of the Shakespeare Authorship site's positions in the "State of the Debate" section of its "Virtual Classroom.")

While the prevalence of Web sites related to the authorship debate is obviously plenty, the number of general resource sites pertaining to Shakespeare is even greater—the best of which is called Mr. William Shakespeare and the Internet (shakespeare.palomar.edu). This site functions mainly as a portal, but it also posts original material regarding Shakespeare "unavailable elsewhere on the Internet." The site contains hundreds, if not thousands, of links, categorized on several pages: "Works," "Life & Times," "Theatre," "Criticism," "Renaissance," "Sources," and "Educational." It then collects recommended sites from each section (denoted as such by the use of five diamonds) and lists them on the "Best Sites" page for quick and easy access. There is also an "'Other' Sites" page, which lists some quirky, entertaining, and certainly non-scholarly sites. While the site implicitly adopts the traditional authorship stance, it does provide a section ("The Authorship 'Problem'") of links regarding the debate on the "Life &

Times" page. Overall, if it has to do with Shakespeare and it's on the Web, this site links to it, from pages detailing life in Elizabethan England to architectural detail of the Globe Theatre to the works themselves.

Speaking of the works, the best site on which to read the words of Shakespeare, whoever he or she might be, is the Internet Public Library's Shakespeare Bookshelf (www.ipl.org/div/shakespeare). Usefully arranged onto four shelves—Comedies, Histories, Poetry, and Tragedies—clicking on the spine of a book links the user to the text of the work at the Bartleby Web site, where the 1914 Oxford University Press edition is presented in a very readable manner.

Recognition Overdue?

Those who have never heard of the authorship debate before and those who want to avoid the possibility that someone other than the Stratford man was the author often pose this question: Why does it matter who wrote the works of Shakespeare? We have the works, they say, and that's what counts. The play's the thing! But exploring the very real prospect that someone other than Will Shakspere wrote the greatest and most influential literature in all of history is of the utmost importance. If indeed the byline rightfully belongs to Oxford, or any of the other realistic candidates, the works will take on whole new meanings and provide previously undiscovered insights. And if the true author used Shakespeare merely as a front man or a pseudonym, as Whalen wrote, "simple justice requires that he receive the recognition that is his due."

The research into and the debate about the very real Shakespearean authorship question must continue, and, through the means of the Web, it undoubtedly will.

The Order of Skull and Bones

When Senator John Kerry of Massachusetts won the Democratic nomination in 2004, it appeared as if the election pitted two very different kinds of people against each other in the bid for the American presidency.

President George W. Bush, still a "Texan" in the eyes of many voters despite four years in Washington, and Kerry, a card-carrying member of the liberal Northeast elite, couldn't seem more different—in biographical background, in political affiliation, and in policy positions.

The "regular-guy" Republican incumbent and the war-protesting Democrat did, however, share a few similar experiences. Thirty-nine years earlier, on a Thursday night at the end of his junior year at Yale University in New Haven, Connecticut, Kerry was one of 15 classmates "tapped" for initiation into the Ivy League's most hallowed secret society.

"Skull and Bones: Do you accept?" a senior member, wearing a black hood and a gold skull-and-crossbones pin, would have asked as his hand rested on Kerry's shoulder on "tap" night. Kerry accepted (some do refuse, surprisingly). In return, he received instructions that—once he untied the black ribbon and broke the black skull-and-crossbones wax seal—would tell him what time to arrive at the Tomb next Tuesday night, initiation night.

The same scenario unfolded the following year when a member of the society's class of 1967 asked Bush, "Skull and Bones: Do you accept?"

Four decades later, these candidates faced a whole new set of questions—about war and peace, about the country's economy and welfare, about education and healthcare—and responded with strongly contrasting answers. Rarely, however, did the mainstream media seriously probe their connections to Skull and Bones or consider deeply the implications of those ties; when confronted on rare occasion with questions about their membership, the candidates provided much the same response.

"You both were members of Skull and Bones, a secret society at Yale. What does that tell us?" NBC's Tim Russert asked Kerry during an interview for *Meet the Press* in 2004.

"Uh, not much because it's a secret," Kerry chuckled awkwardly.

"Is there a secret handshake, is there a secret code?" Russert followed, more innocuously than exploratory.

The menacing logo of Skull and Bones, used on the secret society's stationery, includes the mysterious number 322, which some say represents the year Skull and Bones was founded (32 for 1832) as the second chapter of the Bavarian Illuminati. (Photo source: wikipedia.org/wiki/Skull_and_bones)

Kerry didn't budge: "I wish there were something secret I could manifest."

"322. Secret number?" Russert tried one last time.

Although he did not physically leave the room as Skull and Bones members are told to do when the topic arises, Kerry managed to maneuver himself to safer ground with little resistance: "There are all kinds of secrets, Tim. But one thing is not a secret; I disagree with this president's direction …"

Russert failed to get much from the president, either. "You were both in Skull and Bones, the secret society," Russert said. Bush offered nothing: "It's so secret we can't talk about it."

"What does that mean for America?" Russert asked. Seemingly expecting not to get an answer, he continued with no real pause for one. "The conspiracy theorists are gonna go wild."

"I'm sure they are," Bush said through his laughter. "I don't know, I haven't seen the Web sites yet."

It is here, at the intersection of ultimate secrecy and unparalleled power, where this particular secret society transcends the world of silly rituals and spooky symbols for a realm of profound influence and conspiratorial intrigue.

Uncovering the Bonesmen

For a group determined "to get as many members as possible into positions of power," as one critic noted, 2004 proved to be a good year, to say the least. Skull and Bones was guaranteed to have, again (for the *fourth* time), an alumnus in the biggest chair in the biggest office in the biggest house. But this kind of power is an expectation for members of Skull and Bones, not a surprise.

Since its founding in 1832 by William H. Russell and Alphonso Taft, in reaction to Phi Betta Kappa's elimination of its secrecy oath, Skull and Bones alum have filled the halls of power: U.S. presidents (three to be exact); senators and congressmen; Supreme Court justices (including chief justices); a secretary of war and national security advisor; attorneys general and secretary of commerce; directors of the Central Intelligence Agency (along with many other CIA operatives and "spooks"); the head of the Council on Foreign Relations; and a few secretaries of state. Their reach extends beyond the political sphere, with names like Dean Witter, Harold Stanley, and Henry Luce as evidence. Prominent authors, journalists, bankers, CEOs, scholars, and lawyers fill the ranks as well. Bonesmen, as members are called, served as the first presidents of the University of California, Cornell University, and Johns Hopkins University; they played important parts in the creation of major organizations, from the Carnegie Institution to the American Psychological Association.

Their clout is clear, but their secrecy—what Bonesmen obsessively protect ("guarded ... with the zeal of Howard Hughes and the nuttiness of J. D. Salinger," as one writer put it)—seems somewhat questionable. After all, it is known that the two major party presidential candidates in 2004 were Bonesmen, that George W. Bush's father and grandfather preceded him, and that William Howard Taft, the 27th president of the U.S. and the only one to go on to serve as

Each class of Skull and Bones, consisting of 15 well-heeled members, poses for a photo nearly identical to this early one (always with human bones and a grandfather clock). (Photo source: www.ctrl.org/boodleboys)

chief justice of the Supreme Court, was Skull and Bones. And the list of known Bonesmen certainly doesn't end there.

Membership in the organization, however, has never been heavily guarded. At various times, tap day has attracted crowds of undergraduates to assemble together on campus, and the group itself has published lists of new classes in, of all places, the *New York Times.*

Unlocking the Tomb

There are other secret societies on the Yale campus: Scroll and Key, Book and Snake, and Wolf's Head, among others. But none are older, more secretive, or more powerful than Skull and Bones—a mixture that propels it to nearly mythological stature, and thus the desire of outsiders (or barbarians, as Bonesmen call them) to crack its code of secrecy. That desire has typically been met with very real threats from Bonesmen, who have in some cases even taken action.

Twenty years after the society was officially incorporated as the Russell Trust Association in 1856 and took residence in a new, imposing structure, a group of students, calling themselves the Order of File and Claw (for the tools it used to gain access through a window), broke into the Skull and Bones on-campus building known as the Tomb (for its resemblance to a crypt) and then published a pamphlet with what they discovered inside. A century later, an all-women team followed File and Claw's lead, breaking into the Tomb and snapping photographs of its interior. As one might expect from a secret society named Skull and Bones with a headquarters called the Tomb, the decor—described as "funny spooky ... sort of like the Addams family, it's campy in an old British men's-smoking-club way"—is dominated by human and animal skeletons and skulls. Some even allege the collection includes the stolen skulls of Apache chief Geronimo (thanks to the efforts of a band of members that included Prescott Bush), Mexican revolutionary Pancho Villa, Cuban revolutionary Ernesto "Che" Guevara, and former U.S. President Martin van Buren, along with the gravestone of Elihu Yale, the university's namesake. As the editor of the California-based publication *La Voz de Aztlan*

Members meet at the "Tomb"—the society's forbidding structure on the Yale campus—every Thursday and Sunday evening during their senior year. (Photo source: wikipedia.org/wiki/Skull_and_bones)

mused in a *Yale Herald* article, "Do not be surprised if the skull of Saddam Hussein ends up as a trophy inside Skull and Bones as well."

There are also "pictures of the founders of Bones at Yale, and of the members of the society in Germany, when the chapter was established here in 1832," according to the "report" by File and Claw. The number 322 is one of major significance to Bonesmen, even adorning its emblem and stationery, yet its true meaning is one of debate. Members of File and Claw, and later Anthony Sutton, author of *America's Secret Establishment: An Introduction to the Order of Skull & Bones* (which Alexandra Robbins referred to, in her May 2000 article about Bush and Bones in the *Atlantic*, as a "feverish 1983 tract" that is "the most useful *omnium gatherum*" for the conspiracy-minded), claim 322 is derived from the fact that Russell founded Skull and Bones—after a trip to Germany during which he befriended a leader of a secret society at a university there—in 1832 as the second chapter of the German society called the Bavarian Illuminati.

Before entering the "sanctum sanctorium" of the Tomb, its "Inner Temple" known, of course, as Room 322, an engraving of four human skulls and Masonic symbols greets those about to enter with these words: "Who was the fool, who the wise man, beggar or king? Whether poor or rich, all's the same in death." This supposed gift from the German chapter is strikingly similar to what many believe constituted the Bavarian Illuminati initiation ritual, when the presiding member asks an initiate whether a particular skeleton is that of a king, nobleman, or beggar. Unable to decide, the initiate is told, "The character of being a man is the only one that is important."

Summarizing the initiation ritual for CBS's *60 Minutes*, journalist Alexandra Robbins, who wrote the book *Secrets of the Tomb: Skull and Bones, the Ivy League, and the Hidden Paths of Power*, said:

> There is a devil, a Don Quixote and a Pope who has one foot sheathed in a white monogrammed slipper resting on a stone skull. The initiates are led into the room one at a time. And once the initiates are inside, the Bonesmen shriek at him. Finally, the Bonesman is shoved to his knees in front of Don Quixote as the shrieking crowd falls silent. And Don Quixote lifts his sword and taps the Bonesman on his left shoulder and says, "By order of our order, I dub thee knight of Euloga."

Once initiated, Bonesmen, who are each assigned a new name, meet in the Tomb every Thursday and Sunday evening during their senior year. They are required to share the narrative of their life with the other 14 Bonesmen, as well as divulge their entire sexual history (rumors abound that this takes place while lying naked in a coffin and masturbating, which has yet been confirmed to any degree of certainty). Upon graduation, Bonesmen supposedly receive a no-strings-attached $15,000 gift.

While Skull and Bones, to be sure, isn't exactly what first comes to mind when thinking of your typical college fraternity and couldn't be further away from the world of Delta House, toga parties, and heavy drinking, it is an alumni network, on steroids—"a lifelong, multi-generational fellowship far more influential than any fellowship," Skull and Bones expert and journalist Ron Rosenbaum wrote. "It was—and still remains—the heart of the heart of the American establishment." And although outsiders most likely view, with good reason, the initiation and ensuing ceremonies as bizarre and silly, "the rituals are less important than the relationships—the bonds of power and influence that develop between Skull and Bones initiates after they graduate," he added. Initiation into this secret society is, indeed, as Rosenbaum put it, "a defining rite of passage of the American ruling class."

A World Wide Web of Power

The Order of Skull and Bones, through its alumni, unquestionably wields tremendous power and exercises incredible influence—not only in America but also throughout the world. The question is not whether Bonesmen conspire to grab as much power as possible, but whether they conspire once they have that power to dominate the course of human events across the globe.

"One doesn't need to scratch deeply to uncover accusations of sinister ties with the CIA, the Trilateral Commission, the Illuminati, the Council on Foreign Relations, even the Nazis," wrote Robbins.

All one needs to do, in fact, is log on to the Web.

A good place to start is the Conspiracy Theory Research List, where "The Boodle Boys" (old slang, as the site points out, for members of Skull and Bones) link in the "Top Features" section leads to a portal of all things Bones (www.ctrl.org/boodleboys). Kris Millegan, editor of *Fleshing Out Skull & Bones: Investigations Into America's Most Powerful Secret Society*, runs the site, which addresses everything from the society's connection to the Illuminati to George H. W. Bush's significant role in the 1963 assassination of JFK to the direct involvement of Bonesmen in the creation of the CIA. Millegan offers a wealth of other useful information on his site for those looking to dig deeper into the Tomb of Skull and Bones, including a list of Bonesmen that George W. Bush has appointed to positions within his administration. One of the enduring beliefs regarding Skull and Bones is its connection to the

American intelligence community—from the spies of the Revolutionary War to the Office of Strategic Services (OSS) during World War II to the creation and subsequent operation of the CIA. Indeed, an astounding number of Yalies, including numerous Bonesmen, have filled the ranks of the OSS and the CIA.

Perhaps the most notable Bonesman involved with the CIA was George H. W. Bush, who served as chief of the organization—a secret society, of sorts, in its own right—from 1976 to 1977 during President Gerald Ford's administration. But about 30 years earlier, another Bonesman led the charge to *create* the CIA: Robert A. Lovett chaired the Lovett Committee, which would essentially push for reinstituting the OSS and lead to the establishment of the CIA in 1947. This notion, that this secret society and this newly formed intelligence apparatus were and are kin, reached popular attention in 2006 with the release of Robert DeNiro's *The Good Shepherd*, starring Matt Damon and Angelina Jolie. The movie's Web site (www.thegoodshepherd movie.com) essentially serves, not surprisingly, as a promotional vehicle for the DVD. But it is worth a look, as is the movie itself. Stylishly designed, those who enter the site can view brief movie clips from links at the bottom of the page including "Skull and Bones," "Cold War," "C.I.A. Is Born," and "Bay of Pigs." The "C.I.A. Declassified" link is somewhat more useful, acting as a primer to the CIA. Some, however, have argued that a movie like *The Good Shepherd* only stokes the fire for the conspiracy-minded, echoing sentiments once used to characterize Oliver Stone's *JFK* years earlier.

For a different view of history, check out the official site of the CIA (www.cia.gov). There's more here than one might initially suspect: from virtual tours of its headquarters (mainly of the exterior) and FAQs to a "Library" that includes a "Freedom of Information Act Electronic Reading Room." There's not much talk of Skull and Bones. But entering those three words into the search box will produce this page: https://www.cia.gov/library/center-for-the-study-of-intelligence/csi-publications/csi-studies/studies/vol51no1/the-good-shepherd.html. This roundtable review of *The Good Shepherd* by four CIA historians attacks the movie for, what they say, are factual and historical distortions galore. "Another historical falsehood is that

Many believe Bonesmen played prominent roles in creating the CIA. Numerous members have staffed and led the CIA, including George H. W. Bush, who some conspiracists claim had been involved with the agency long before heading it from 1976 to 1977. (Photo source: www.freemasonrywatch.org)

becoming a leader at CIA hinges on membership in Skull and Bones, the secret society at Yale," wrote Nicholas Dujmovic. "No senior figure of the time at CIA ever had anything to do with that organization." The piece is even accompanied by a chart comparing the differences between the "Character" and the supposed "Real-life Model." Perhaps the fact that the term "spook"—originally used when talking about a Yale secret society member—now applies to those in the field of espionage is merely coincidence.

Despite the existence of Skull and Bones for more than a century and a half, popular interest in the secret society didn't become widespread until recently, starting in 2000 with the release of the thriller *The Skulls* coupled with George W. Bush's arrival on the national political stage, followed by the 2004 battle of Bonesmen for the

White House. Propaganda Matrix, in fact, arranges its Skull and Bones archive (www.propagandamatrix.com/archive_skull_and_bones.html) with the "Skull and Bones Election 2004" atop the page, followed by "Background" and "Bush Family Connections." The site is a treasure trove of links—to news articles and videos from mainstream and alternative media—for those wanting to dig a little deeper. Access to articles by Robbins and Rosenbaum, along with videos of MSNBC's Keith Olberman and CBS's Morley Safer paying heed to the society, is provided. There are also lesser-known but more provocative items, including a two-part documentary featuring interviews with the likes of Anthony Sutton and night-vision footage of parts of an initiation. Some of these videos are available on YouTube (www.youtube.com) in complete versions and with a larger screen size. Simply type "Skull and Bones" in the search box.

While many of the sites that deal with Skull and Bones post some form of a membership list, the one posted on www.freedom domain.com/Secretsocietes/Skullbones/skullbones.html is arguably the most useful. For the many who would struggle to recognize names alone, here the list is annotated and organized by the various professions the members pursued following graduation. The site also links to a worthwhile interview with Sutton and an informative "white paper" on the topic.

At first glance, the Skull and Bones section of the Bilderberg Web page (www.bilderberg.org/skullbone.htm) can seem a bit wild and unwieldy. But while it might not have the gravitas of polished, mainstream sites, there's no shortage of information, whether it is directly or tangentially related to Skull and Bones. Users will find, stacked vertically on the lengthy page, book excerpts on Bones, essays about occult symbolism, and source lists and links, as well as tracts asserting that Skull and Bones is tightly connected to the oil industry, helped create the "modern health establishment," "played key roles on both sides of the anti-smoking movement," and even dabbled in "population control."

In 2004, Skull and Bones received more media attention than ever when John Kerry and George W. Bush—both Bonesmen—vied for the American presidency. (Photo source: www.youtube.com)

Dangerous Secrets

Skull and Bones is a secret society that turns out some of the most powerful people in the world. One could argue, however, that these children of the elite didn't necessarily need an initiation night in the Tomb to get that kind of power; it would be theirs eventually anyway. Are their secretive ways an effort to hide sinister deeds? Or are conspiracy theories a consequence of that secrecy? Perhaps it is, as Robbins has suggested, "a society whose biggest secret may be that its secrets are essentially trivial." Even with that *there's-no-real-conspiracy-here* view, she doesn't dismiss Bones altogether as trivial:

> I don't think that the elected officials who represent our
> country, especially the president, should be allowed to have
> an allegiance to any secret group. Secrecy overshadows

democracy ... I don't think it's coincidence that what I would call the most secretive government in America since the Nixon era is run by the world's most infamous secret society.

Probing into Skull and Bones is not reserved for only the habitually conspiracy-minded. As Rosenbaum puts it, "I think there is a deep and legitimate distrust in America for power and privilege that are cloaked in secrecy ... [and] any society or institution that hints that there is something hidden is, I think, a legitimate subject for investigation." But be warned: "The alumni still care," a Bonesman once threatened Rosenbaum. And the alumni wield absolute power.

The Jesus Controversy

> And as they thus spake, Jesus himself stood in the midst of them, and saith unto them, Peace be unto you. But they were terrified and affrighted, and supposed that they had seen a spirit. And he said unto them, Why are ye troubled? and why do thoughts arise in your hearts? Behold my hands and feet, that it is I myself: handle me, and see; for spirit hath not flesh and bones, as ye see me have.

So saith the New Testament, in the Gospel according to St. Luke. But from the time of Jesus's life, death, and reported resurrection, the Word has not been the last word. In fact, one could argue that doubts about Jesus's resurrection—and even the basic details of his life, such as whether he was married and what the message of his teaching really was—have never been so public or so prevalent. Popularized by a recent high-profile work of fiction, a blockbuster film, and a cottage industry of nonfiction works, the notion that there's a secret society aimed at preserving the real story of Jesus's life, teachings, and—here's the shocker—*heirs* is as bizarre as it is compelling.

Conspiracy theorists, bolstered by decades of research and revisionism, have put forward the claim that Jesus was married to Mary Magdalene (a figure mentioned prominently in many of the gospels that didn't make the cut for the "authorized" version of the Bible). In addition, conspiracy theorists claim that Jesus might have survived the crucifixion (which could have merely been staged—a convenient way for the Romans to eliminate a growing political problem), fled with Mary Magdalene to France, and had a daughter named Sarah, the first of a family tree whose descendants are among us today. Skeptics find this inconceivable, wondering how all this could have remained a secret for centuries. It boggles the mind, skeptics argue, to think that such a conspiracy could have ever existed, much less endured for two millennia.

Certainly, the stakes couldn't be higher: the destination of the human soul and the power to serve as gatekeeper. Once upon a time, priests guarded the mysteries of the Divine word in a sort of code, the dead language of Latin. But lately, it's another code that's been getting most of the attention.

Da Vinci's Secrets

While there have always been rumblings in quasi-scholarly and theological circles about Jesus's divinity or whether he in fact ever married and had children, the idea of a conspiracy covering up his true nature had never gained much public traction. But that all changed with the 2003 publication of novelist Dan Brown's global best-seller *The Da Vinci Code*. The book obviously touched a nerve with readers with its mix of historical revisionism, mystery, and theological speculation.

The book puts forward the theory that the Catholic Church, for 2,000 years, has been living a lie. Jesus was not divine, just a mortal with a message. And, as a mortal, he did what most mortal men in Judea did 2,000 years ago: He got married. To Mary Magdalene. The New Testament suggests Mary Magdalene, a minor figure in the authorized Jesus story, was a prostitute, but *The Da Vinci Code* suggests that this was a smear campaign by early church fathers to discredit her and minimize her role in Jesus's life. And when Jesus was crucified, a pregnant Mary Magdalene fled to France, where she had a daughter Sarah—the start of the bloodline that became the Merovingian dynasty of France.

The lineage of this bloodline has been protected, the book claims, by a secret society called the Priory of Sion since the crusaders conquered Jerusalem in 1099. The leaders of this secret society have included some of the most powerful men in European history, including Leonardo da Vinci—who encoded many of his master-works (such as the *Mona Lisa* and *The Last Supper*) with cryptic visual clues revealing Mary Magdalene's place as the real "Holy Grail." (The Holy Grail is often said to be the chalice that caught Jesus's blood while he was on the cross, but in Brown's formula-tion—à la da Vinci—Mary Magdalene is the Holy Grail, the pre-server of the bloodline of Christ.)

Since *The Da Vinci Code* is a work of fiction (though Brown has peppered his pages with an immense amount of archaeological and historical fact), there are all the usual mystery-thriller components: an early chapter murder, a love interest, the double-cross, and, purely for effect, a masochistic albino monk. Brown's book became pub-lishing's perfect storm, with fans showering him with accolades—and lots of money—and theologians (mostly Catholic) seeking to undue the damage they felt Brown had done to their faith tradition. The attacks on Brown's work have been vehement and persistent, but the residual impact of this campaign to discredit *The Da Vinci Code* has only seemed to further ignite reader interest. The novel has sold more than 60 million copies and has been translated into more than 40 languages.

Before the first chapter, Brown assures readers in a note that "all descriptions of artwork, architecture, documents … and secret rituals in this novel are accurate." Many critics have challenged that asser-tion, but Brown counters on his Web site (www.danbrown.com) with the cautionary note: "The FACT page makes no statement whatsoever about any of the ancient theories discussed by fictional characters. Interpreting those ideas is left to the reader."

The "ancient theories" Brown alludes to are enumerated more fully in a 1982 book titled *Holy Blood, Holy Grail,* which served as a source for *The Da Vinci Code* and helped the Jesus controversy gain a foothold in the pantheon of conspiracy theories. That book, a work of historical investigative journalism written by a team of British researchers, argued that Jesus survived the crucifixion and fled to France with his wife, Mary Magdalene. *Holy Blood, Holy Grail*

The Holy Grail has fascinated researchers, archaeologists, and religious scholars for centuries. Some believe it is the chalice that Jesus drank from at the Last Supper, while others claim it was used to catch his blood during the crucifixion. Its mystical powers are legendary. (Photo source: www.scottbruno.com/Holy-Grail.htm)

details a two-millennium-long campaign to protect the secret of Jesus's bloodline. From a shadowy medieval group called the "Knights Templar" to the modern day Priory of Sion, the book charts the history of the secret sects that have preserved Jesus and Mary Magdalene's family tree.

Proponents of the various Jesus theories all tend to build on the established body of literature relating to the quest for the Holy Grail. All an author has to do is acquaint the reader with the wide swath of literature—fiction and nonfiction—regarding the historical quest for the Holy Grail, and then it's a short leap to argue that the Grail is not just a cup, but something more significant and earthshaking (such as a person, Mary Magdalene, or an idea, like "the feminine sacred"). In addition, many authors who have waded into the controversy have noted the patriarchal history of Christianity, putting forth their theories as a long-overdue corrective to the male-dominated church hierarchy. If one believes that the people who assembled the *New Testament* were interested in preserving and promoting the male power structure (resulting in the unwillingness to acknowledge Mary Magdalene as an equal partner in Christ's life, as opposed to his *male* disciples), then these revisionist campaigns not only seem plausible but long overdue. Brown's book is really about the devaluation of the feminine principle by a group of power-hungry men.

In all these rewritings of the traditional Jesus story, there lurks the idea that Christianity could have been much more potent as a social force if it had frankly acknowledged the necessity of the feminine as a part of an integrated whole. Christianity's failure to embrace the biological imperative driving men and women toward each other, and its decision to stigmatize sexual longing, set it on a course that has asked generations of believers to deny an aspect of their fundamental humanity. A religion built upon an abstemious Christ is far different from one that seeks to celebrate conjugal love. That's why the stakes in the Jesus debate are so incalculably high. The priesthood, the College of Cardinals, the Vatican, and the creeds of the Catholic Church itself would be revealed as erroneous. The heart of the Jesus controversy doesn't involve the traditional theological debate about the split between body and soul as much as the union between bodies, male and female.

Canvassing for Clues

The question that even the most open-minded readers surely must ask themselves when confronting the rather spectacular re-imaginings of Catholic Church history is does evidence really exist to back up these claims? Well, it depends on how you define "evidence." Everything the conspiracy theorists cite when pointing to a secret marriage—and a secret society—is the product of interpretation and speculation. There *were* early church councils in which certain "authorized" documents were approved for the New Testament, while others—sometimes called "The Gnostic Gospels," some of which discuss Mary Magdalene more prominently—were excluded. There *is* the history of the Knights Templar, a band of warrior monks from the Middle Ages whose purpose is still not completely clear. The Knights were engaged to protect someone—or something. There might or might not have been a modern secret society called the Priory of Sion, but it appears increasingly likely that the organization, and its roster of purported leaders, was an elaborate hoax. The Holy Grail—whatever it is (a chalice from the Last Supper, the cup that caught Jesus's blood during the crucifixion, a box containing the bones of Christ, the French tomb of Mary Magdalene, the family tree of Sarah)—has yet to be located, if it even exists.

And then there's the work of Leonardo da Vinci, and specifically his painting *The Last Supper*, which some theorists claim reveals the Jesus–Mary Magdalene relationship (the rather feminine figure to Jesus's right, which is often taken to be John the Baptist, is really Mary Magdalene, Jesus's right-hand partner, some say). Under the scrutiny of some conspiracy theorists, *The Last Supper* can be seen as revealing several clues about the Jesus–Mary Magdalene secret marriage. (*The Da Vinci Code* even suggests that Mary Magdalene was directed by Jesus to take over his ministry, but the Church fathers later revised history to have Jesus handing things off to St. Peter, while erasing Mary Magdalene from the picture entirely.)

The Net Impact

Medieval mystery cults and early Christian theology delivered to a 21st-century computer screen—even Biblical prophecy couldn't have foreseen the impact the Internet would have on the questions surrounding the founder of Christianity. The best single overview of the

Leonardo da Vinci's famous painting of the Last Supper is thought by some to contain clues to a secret relationship between Jesus and Mary Magdalene. (Photo source: wikipedia.org/wiki/The_Last_Supper_(Leonardo))

controversy can be found at "The Jesus Conspiracy" page on the Seize the Night site (www.carpenoctem.tv/cons/jesus.html). The site provides a quick and informed gloss on the many questions surrounding the issue, and a thorough exploration of the main points of contention in *Holy Blood, Holy Grail.* The site takes the claims of a secret bloodline seriously without explicitly endorsing them—and reminds readers of the stakes:

> Suddenly, the meandering history of Europe develops a dramatic, cohesive plot line: the persecution of the cathars by the church, the collusion of Rome in the assassination of King Dagobert, the successful conspiracy of Pope Clement V and Phillipe IV of France to suppress the powerful Templars—all were efforts to "eradicate it, Jesus' bloodline." For "it" constituted nothing less than a rival church with a more direct link to J.C.'s legacy than the Vatican could ever claim.

The site's open-minded posture and its incorporation of lots of historical details without bogging down in minutiae make this a good first stop. Readers interested in a much lengthier but nonetheless compelling discussion of Mary Magdalene and her place as the living Holy Grail should visit the Bloodline of the Holy Grail (graal.co.uk/bloodlinelecture.html). The site's author, Laurence Gardner, takes readers through the history of the Grail legend, from the first century to modern times. Gardner does a good job of establishing Mary Magdalene's place among early followers of Christ:

> The Gospels relate that Jesus said: Wheresoever this Gospel shall be preached throughout the whole world, this also that she hath done shall be spoken of for a memorial of her [Mary Magdalene]. But did the Church authorities honor Mary Magdalene and speak of this act as a memorial? No they did not; they completely ignored Jesus' own directive and denounced Mary as a whore ... To the Nazarenes, however, Mary Magdalene was always regarded as a saint.

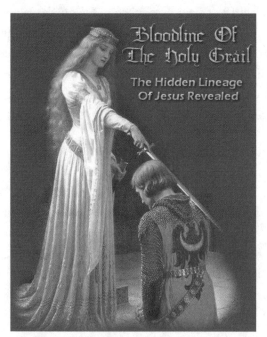

Whether Jesus's modern-day heirs really exist is a subject of great debate and historical interest among conspiracy theorists. (Photo source: graal.co.uk/bloodlinelecture.html)

Gardner's longish essay also deals with the theological components of the controversy in clear and sensible-sounding prose, even when suggesting that Christ's death was metaphoric and part of a widely understood Jewish ritual: "As for Jesus' death on the cross, it is perfectly clear this was a spiritual death, not physical death, as determined by a three-day excommunication rule that everybody in the 1st Century would have understood." He goes on to explain that "In civil and legal terms, Jesus was denounced, scourged, and prepared for death by decree. For three days Jesus would have been nominally 'sick' with absolute 'death' coming on the fourth day." The site offers lots of information about religious tradition at the time of Christ, and how misinterpretation by modern scholars—or mistakes in translation—have led to lots of inconsistent and illogical interpretations.

For those who find *The Da Vinci Code* inconsistent and illogical—and who resist the notion of a revisionist Jesus—the site to check out is TheTruthAboutDaVinci.com (www.thetruthaboutdavinci.com). The site is maintained by the Westminster Theological Seminary and was established as a sort of public service to the community of believers who find their faith threatened by the Jesus conspiracy. As the site's authors explain, "The mix of fact and fiction in *The Da Vinci Code* is reason for great concern. The film, based on the best-selling novel, is causing audiences to question the Bible's message and its impact on history." The site contains essays and articles about many of the arguments put forward in Brown's book, organized helpfully by the major points. The site maintains a measured tone throughout, though it completely embraces the party line, so to speak, of the Catholic Church. For instance, speaking of the alleged marriage of Mary Magdalene and Jesus, the site informs readers that:

> Jesus, the Second Person of the Trinity, though fully human, would not have married a mere human creature. Nor was it his mission to do so. And there is not a whiff of evidence for this anywhere in recorded history. He came to "marry" the church, which is metaphorically his bride.

Regarding the possibility of a secret society, the Priory of Sion, whose mission it is to maintain the secret of Jesus's bloodline, the site claims that "the Priory was a club created in 1956 by Pierre Plantard" and that it exists "only in the novel and in the mind of the late Pierre Plantard."

But taking seriously the idea of secret societies is the business of the Web site maintained by Scott Bruno, whose Priory De Scion & Secret Societies site (www.scottbruno.com/priory-de-scion.htm) is a fascinating consideration of the role and value of secret societies in our culture. The site endorses the idea that such societies exist and thrive in the modern world, though not all readers will willingly follow Bruno as he links the Priory of Sion with other high-profile mystery cults like the Illuminati and the Freemasons. But it's in its more sober considerations of secrecy that the site excels:

> Today we understand a secret society to be a society with secrets, having a ritual demanding an oath of allegiance and secrecy, prescribing ceremonies of a religious character, by the use of prayers, signs and symbols, etc. … however there is a more elaborate description: Secret societies are those organizations which completely conceal their rules, corporate activity, the name of their members, their signs, passwords and usages from outsiders or the "profane."

There's a lot of talk about how secret societies operate, and some amusing speculation about the significance of the number 13 in the Priory of Sion, and subsequently, in American history ("If you take a One Dollar bill out and examine it you will notice thirteens in abundance."). It's a quirky site with lots of fun facts, not all of them related to the Jesus conspiracy.

No site provides more interesting facts—and more useful information—than the "Leonardo" pages of the Museum of Science–Boston (www.mos.org/Leonardo). The site is kid-friendly—but not just for kids—in its presentation of the world of Leonardo da Vinci and his many inventions (there's not really much about *The Da Vinci Code*, though there are lots of striking images and informed discussion

The dollar bill contains lots of objects in clusters of 13—a significant number to the members of the shadowy group Priory of Sion. (Photo source: wikipedia.org/ wiki/United_States_one_dollar_bill)

about da Vinci's paintings and his love of complex puzzles and hidden ciphers). Anyone with an interest in science, Renaissance art, or the creative process would benefit from visiting the museum's site.

There are lots of close-ups of da Vinci's *The Last Supper* on *"The Da Vinci Code"* page at the Voice of Reason site (www.thevoiceof reason.com/Conspiracy/DaVinciCode.htm). In fact, this is one of the very best sites on the Web to get an explanation of the Jesus conspiracy because so many of the points made in *The Da Vinci Code* are not only thoroughly discussed but clearly illustrated as well, with lots of examples of Renaissance art. There's also a crystal clear discussion of the main points made by Dan Brown in his book, without resorting to breathless exhortations of support or insulting denigrations of the book. Though the site generally maintains a skeptical viewpoint toward many of *The Da Vinci Code* claims, it offers enough visual evidence to allow readers to make up their own minds.

Those who end up convinced of the truth or falsity of the assumptions that underlie the controversy have a great place to argue it out: www.abovetopsecret.com. The site maintains extensive message boards and forums for devout skeptics and religious adherents to battle it out in cyberspace. For those who prefer moving pictures over words, check out the Discovery Channel's Web site, which features several pages dedicated to a recent documentary that alleges that

Jesus's family tomb might have been discovered (dsc.discovery.com/convergence/tomb/tomb.html). The site also offers some useful and interesting historical background on Jesus's life, the geography of the Middle East, the practice of first-century burial, and a theological debate about the impact of Jesus's possible marriage.

Savior Self

The narrative of Jesus's life—no matter who's telling it—has long been considered "the greatest story ever told." Arguably, no one who's ever lived has had as much of an impact on the human race as Jesus, so it's easy to see why so much interest, passion, and anger attend every revision of the known life of Christ. The story of the New Testament is gospel truth, literally, to millions of devout followers. The notion that the Jesus of the Bible is incomplete—or even fraudulent—is something the vast majority of believers simply refuse to grant.

This stained glass window portrays Jesus and Mary Magdalene as a married couple. Such a shocking revelation lies at the heart of the Jesus controversy. (Photo source: www.rejesus.co.uk)

Most people have a fairly settled notion of Jesus—when he was born, what happened to him on his way to the cross (and salvation), what happened on the third day after the crucifixion, and what his legacy means to the world. Presenting the world with a vision of Jesus that includes marriage, children, and a secret society opposed throughout history to the established church is, to some, either heresy or lunacy. But still, conspiracy theorists argue, shouldn't the quest to know Jesus be guided by the truth, no matter where it leads?

"Heaven and Earth shall pass away: but my words shall not pass away," Jesus said. Neither, apparently, shall the mystery of His life.

The Moon Landing

The images are iconic: sleek, 12-story rockets blasting off into the clear blue sky, hordes of white-shirted technicians cheering in the control rooms of Houston and Cape Canaveral, images of Planet Earth transmitted from orbit. And, of course, most memorably, puffy, space-suited astronauts bouncing merrily on the shadowy lunar surface. The American space program has provided a wealth of images that have been used to inspire the national consciousness and stir our adventurer's soul. When Neil Armstrong laid his first boot on the dusty terrain of the Moon—a seminal moment in human history—he stepped across the threshold of possibility and changed the way achievement would be calibrated in the future.

Mankind's conquest of the Moon marked a new chapter in the development of our species. No single event had proclaimed the potential of humanity in such a clear and impressive manner. A new era had dawned.

"And … Cut! Print! That was great, Neil! Now, let's do a take from the other side. Come down the ladder a little more slowly, OK? Places, everybody … lights, camera … ACTION!"

What if none of it ever happened? No lunar module landing spectacularly on the crater-covered surface, no "giant leap for mankind," no triumph of technology in the face of remarkably daunting odds. What if it was all the product of cinematic illusion, a made-for-TV spectacle engineered to fool the public (and our political rivals) into thinking we had made it to the Moon before the JFK-imposed end-of-the-decade

The launch of *Apollo 11* in July 1969 made history when it took its crew to the Moon for the first time—an event some conspiracy theorists claim is more fiction than fact. (Photo source: wikipedia.org/wiki/Apollo_11)

deadline? Could the greatest moment in modern history turn out to be a fraud?

Absolutely, argue some conspiracy theorists. And they have photographic proof.

Shoot the Moon

In many cases of alleged conspiracy, there is little physical evidence to back up the claimants on either side. The Moon landing (or the *alleged* Moon landing), however, has provided a wealth of scientific data, from infrared photos to Moon rocks. One might think that would help clarify the questions at the heart of the conspiracy. But that is not the case here, with the two sides looking at the same photos and saying "See! This proves it!" What's happened in this debate has become analogous to a trial where each side presents scientific "experts" who testify that the defendant is sane or insane—both with equal passion and apparent expertise. And, as with any jury trial, who to believe depends on who appears more credible. Though the conspiracy theorists do tell a pretty incredible tale, they have nonetheless managed to persuade millions of people (according to a recent Gallup poll) that the whole Moon landing in 1969 was a hoax.

What the conspiracy crowd believes would make a pretty wild movie—in fact, it did: *Capricorn One*, an uneven but thoroughly entertaining suspense-drama. The premise of the movie is identical to the conspiracy theory: The U.S. never went to the Moon. The *Apollo* Moon landings were staged on a special set that was built to portray the lunar surface, and all of the images that have become engraved in the consciousness of spectators of the 1960s space race were faked. Mankind never put a foot down on the lunar surface—that foot was put down in an underground television studio, possibly in the famed "Area 51" super-secret military installation in Nevada (see Chapter 1). Most Moon landing conspiracy theorists argue that none of the six "successful" *Apollo* missions, between 1969 and 1972, actually took place.

What motive would the U.S. have for forging such a seminal moment as mankind's conquering of the Moon? Conspiracy theorists argue that the U.S. was technologically still several years away from being able to engineer flights to the Moon, but that President John F. Kennedy's pledge to get there by the end of the decade put the U.S. in a bind. To admit failure would be to subject American power to global second-guessing and to lose a valuable chip in the Cold War poker game. As one popular Moon hoax Web site puts it:

> [T]he main reason why the U.S. Government and NASA
> faked the "official record" is because they could not be

seen to be the weak link, especially when you consider that during the 1960's, the USA was at the height of the Cold War with Russia … it would be better to try and fool the public and hoax the footage, rather than let their biggest rival in the world strike a huge moral victory by beating them to the Moon.

One Giant Leap—or Many

The evidence put forward by proponents of the hoax theory consists of a number of "discrepancies" they have discovered, mostly in studying the photos of the astronauts that were taken during the *Apollo 11* mission—the first one to actually put a man on the Moon—in July 1969. These include:

- There are no stars visible in any of the pictures. Conspiracy theorists say the frames should be filled with stars.

- The American flag planted by the astronauts appears to be waving in the breeze. Since the Moon has no atmosphere, there's no possibility of a breeze. How could a flag blow in the wind—with no wind?

- The "feet" of the lunar landing module are visible on the surface of the Moon. Skeptics suggest that the first few inches, at least, should be buried under the dust of the lunar surface. (If Neil Armstrong's boot left a vivid imprint, why not a several-ton spacecraft?)

- In some photos, the images appear to be illuminated by multiple light sources. For example, in some cases, the astronauts have their backs to the sun yet the front of their space suits are lit clearly enough to read the lettering across the chest (doubters point to this standard technique of theatrical lighting to argue for a staged event).

- During the television broadcast, Mission Control in Houston and the astronauts spoke to each other with almost no delay. Some skeptics argue that there would certainly be at least a few second delay between question and answer. (They point to the delay that occurs even today between journalists sending a story via satellite and the anchorperson asking them questions.)

Those who doubt that the U.S. actually landed a man on the Moon in 1969 wonder why there are no stars visible in the official photographs of the mission. (Photo source: www.apfn.org/apfn/moon.htm)

If the sun is the only source of light (seen here in the background), some skeptics wonder how the front of this astronaut's spacesuit could have been so brightly illuminated. (Photo source: www.ufos-aliens.co.uk/cosmicapollo.html)

There are dozens and dozens of other questions, some technical, some philosophical, that skeptics like to pose. Many point to the fact that after the early 1970s, no other missions were ever sent back to the Moon, suggesting that NASA was abandoning the effort before its failure to actually ever reach the Moon would be discovered. Some Web sites even maintain a list of NASA employees who have died "mysteriously"—with the suggestion that these people knew of the cover-up and had to be silenced before they went public with their evidence.

One skeptical Web site notes:

> For a start, the TV footage was hopeless. The world tuned in to watch what looked like two blurred white ghosts throw rocks and dust. Part of the reason for the low quality was that, strangely, NASA provided no direct link up. So networks actually had to film man's greatest achievement from a TV screen in Houston—a deliberate ploy ... so that nobody could properly examine it. By contrast, the still photos were stunning. Yet that's just the problem. The astronauts took thousands of pictures, each one perfectly exposed and sharply focused. Not one was badly composed or even blurred.

In 2001, the Fox television network broadcast an hour-long special on the Moon landing hoax that raised most of the same questions as the Web sites dedicated to the conspiracy. The show angered some scientists and Moon landing advocates because of its largely uncritical acceptance of the hoax theory. Shortly after the broadcast, NASA itself announced it would be rebutting the conspiracy theories in an authorized book on the subject—but then just as quickly changed its mind. As the BBC reported the news,

> The US space agency (NASA) has canceled the book intended to challenge the conspiracy theorists who claim the Moon landings were a hoax. NASA declined to comment specifically on the reasons for dropping the publication, but

it is understood the decision resulted from the bad publicity that followed the announcement of the project.

NASA might have decided not to combat the hoax theory with a book-length rebuttal, but that hasn't kept other interested parties from weighing in. The Internet has become a launching pad for theories pro and con about the Moon landings. Some of the Web sites that have been developed to argue about the hoax feature some stunning photography and a pretty impressive use of technology. Almost all of them feature galleries of still photographs and even streaming video from the NASA archives. What differs is the commentary. Two sites might feature the same photo on the homepage, with one reminding viewers of the importance of the historical moment when mankind conquered the Moon, and another advising viewers to "click here for a list of suspicious points about this photograph." Just as no two people see the same thing when gazing into the sky on a dark, star-filled evening, it seems that no two Webmasters can look at the steps of one man, Neil Armstrong, without conjuring up two entirely different visions of his "mission."

Booting Up

Many of the best and most informative Web sites that deal with the Moon landing hoax also tend to be the longest (which is another way of saying that the people putting them together have a *lot* to say about the subject). One of the most useful sites, maintained by the American Patriot Friends Network, is Was the Apollo Moon Landing Fake? (www.apfn.org/apfn/moon.htm). First-time investigators of the subject might feel a bit overwhelmed by the amount of information available on this site, but the pages definitely deliver the goods. There is a lengthy, detailed overview of the questions that continue to nag the doubters, links to dozens of other Web sites (both pro and con), audio links to radio programs that feature astronauts and others talking about the hoax, excerpts from books about the controversy, and postings from readers on all sides of the issue. The site provides the usual array of photographs and commentary, but also lots of intriguing arguments not found elsewhere (for instance, under the extensive discussion of "motive" for faking, it includes: "Money—NASA raised approximately $30 billion dollars pretending to go to the Moon"). There's a lengthy list of the "Deaths of Key People Involved with the Apollo Program," with links to other Web sites for more information about each person or "mysterious cause of death," in-depth discussion of the potential effects of radiation on the Moon (from unfiltered solar exposure), and, of course, lots of links to individual investigators' Web sites. It's a useful portal site for those with time and interest, and a one-stop shop for the merely curious.

Another massive Web site that offers perhaps the most extensive photo-by-photo analysis is the Faked Apollo Landings site (www.ufos-aliens.co.uk/cosmicapollo.html). This site promises "to prove, once and for all, that we are not being told the truth about the NASA film footage of the Apollo missions" and that "the whole Apollo Moon project of the late 1960s and early 1970s were a complete hoax." Relying on close scrutiny of many official photos of the missions and links to "official NASA footage," the site allows viewers to play investigator and assess the credibility of the official documents. Among the site's worthwhile exhibits is a close-up photo of one of the more popular components in Moon landing hoax circles: the mysterious "letter C" rock. This Moon rock, captured in some NASA photos but not others, appears to have a large capital "C" carved into it, and it sits just behind a clump of dirt that, upon closer inspection, also seems to bear the letter "C." As the site explains, "The use of the letter C on film props is well known by the people in Hollywood and is used to show where the center of the scene should be." There's an intriguing discussion as to how NASA created the effect of weightlessness in a studio and at least an attempt to answer the question of how so many people could be involved in the U.S. space program but not be aware of the hoax:

> Thousands of people were employed to work on the Apollo mission, but very few people had access to the complete picture. By giving several people a small role in the missions meant that they would not see the whole project.

This close-up of a Moon rock seems to reveal a letter "C" (on both the rock itself and the ground below). Skeptics claim that "C" stands for "center"—designating its location on a soundstage. (Photo source: www.ufos-aliens.co.uk/cosmic apollo.html)

The archives at news site CNN.com provide some useful background material about the Moon landing hoax, most especially the article "NASA Debunks Moon Landing Hoax Conspiracy" (archives. cnn.com/2001/TECH/space/02/19/nasa.moon), in which researchers and conspiracy theorists exchange charges and countercharges in the wake of the airing of Fox's 2001 documentary. "The theorists point to supposed oddities in the NASA Moon shots," the article notes, advising that "reputable scientists dismiss the claim outright." The Moon landing hoax articles from the archive feature links to a not-unexpectedly robust message board called "Moon Landing: Myth or Fact?"

For those who feel the hoax is so much lunar lunacy, a site that bolsters the "fact" over the "myth" can be found on the Moon hoax pages of Goddard's Journal (www.iangoddard.net/moon01.htm). Viewers will see many of the same photos that decorate the pages of the conspiracy theorists but with rebuttals and explanations of the anomalies that bother the doubters. The site, which focuses on those discrepancies featured on the Fox broadcast, concludes: "None of the alleged photographic anomalies presented by Fox TV are true anomalies and thus they evidence neither manipulation nor a hoax." For those who are unconvinced, the site offers a generous sampling of links to sites both pro and con on the subject.

The site Bad Astronomy (www.badastronomy.com/bad/tv/fox apollo.html) offers an even more extensive refutation of the main Moon landing conspiracy theories. Viewers will find links to explanations under dozens of the so-called anomalies, such as "No stars in pictures," "Nonparallel shadows," and "Why was every picture perfect?" The site's author, Phil Plait, has established himself as the prime explainer-away of the conspiracy theorists' objections. Here's his take on why no stars are visible:

> So why aren't they in the Apollo pictures? Pretend for a moment you are an astronaut on the surface of the Moon. You want to take a picture of your fellow space traveler. The Sun is low off the horizon, since all lunar landings were done at local morning. How do you set your camera? The lunar landscape is brightly lit by the Sun, of course, and your friend is wearing a white space suit also brilliantly lit by the Sun. To take a picture of a bright object with a bright background, you need to set the exposure time to be fast, and close down the aperture setting too; that's like the pupil in your eye constricting to let less light in when you walk outside on a sunny day. So the picture you take is set for bright objects. Stars are faint objects! In the fast exposure, they simply do not have time to register on the film.

The Bad Astronomy site offers lots of clear, reader-friendly discussion of some technical topics. Plait's style is impassioned but not overheated. (Of course, it should be noted that many of the other Moon hoax Web sites disagree with Plait's analysis and have set up message boards rebutting his findings.) The Bad Astronomy site aims to set the record straight—but some conspiracy theorists read the record in a different light.

One of the most intriguing arguments against the Moon landing is put forward by a DVD director named Bart Sibrel, whose Web site (www.moonmovie.com) offers glimpses of his work, an interview that explains his skepticism, and a comprehensive "clues" link that covers the basic questions in a fun, cloak-and-dagger tone. Sibrel's Web page sets up the whole Moon landing question with an undeniably engaging—and chilling—overture:

> The Space Shuttle, so far, has killed fourteen people, merely trying to attain an orbit about two hundred fifty miles above the Earth. How is it then, that a third of a century ago, with less computing power in the entire rocket than in a present-day twenty dollar Wal-Mart watch, NASA claims to have gone 100,000% farther, six different times between 1969 and 1972, landing on another celestial body and then returning, without ever killing anyone?

To see where such theorizing leads, you can purchase a number of Moon landing-related DVDs on the site.

So did NASA go to the Moon or didn't they? "Of course we did!" states the official NASA Web site (liftoff.msfc.nasa.gov/News/2001/News-MoonLanding.asp), offering this disarmingly direct rebuttal to doubters: "Actually, it would have been harder to fake the whole thing than to do it!" The site, not unexpectedly, also offers a wealth of information about space, satellites, shuttle launches, Mars, astronaut training, and a proposed timeline for future missions—including a planned return to the Moon.

Or a maiden voyage, depending on what you believe.

Bella Luna

From time immemorial, the human species has been fascinated with the Moon. It has inspired some of the greatest paintings, poetry, and music ever conceived. And each lunar cycle only revives the

Celebrated astronaut Neil Armstrong is shown here speaking to a group of test pilots in front of a projection of the training vehicle used by NASA to train astronauts on lunar landing procedure. (Photo source: www.nasa.gov)

magic and the mystery. There is something undeniably stirring about the site of a luminous, lighted Moon, rising in the night sky, its distance daunting, its beauty coldly arresting. To think that humans have walked upon its craggy, cratered surface is a truly awesome notion. For most, the whole concept still remains remarkable.

For some, even unbelievable.

The Death of Marilyn Monroe

She was perhaps the most well-known woman in the world, a movie star in the classic mold—with a figure that broke the mold. Behind the breathy voice and the slightly coy manner, beneath the billowing white cocktail dress and the faux blonde tresses, there existed a complex woman with a past as sad as her present was bountiful. Touched by tragedy early in life, the woman the world came to know as Marilyn Monroe was beloved for her beauty and the savvy way she made it work for her—and her audience. And that audience was everybody—men and women, the powerful and the unknown, the lonely and the revered. She dined (and more) with presidents and the politically well connected, rubbed shoulders (and more) with the "A list" of Hollywood celebrities, and provided a hopeful example (and more) for anyone who started with nothing and came from nowhere. Her life seemed manufactured for movie magazines and gossip columnists, but there was more substance there than many people suspected. The excavation of the real Marilyn Monroe—born Norma Jeane Mortenson—has continued uninterrupted since her death on August 5, 1962, at the age of 36. A corps of biographers, Hollywood insiders, and longtime confidants has gradually replaced the image of the "dumb blonde" with the more accurate picture of a highly intelligent businesswoman and a focused, committed artist, but the world still remembers, mostly, the beaming, siren-like smile, the camera-ready diva, the unapologetic sex symbol.

And, of course, the world remembers her death.

In fact, there are many who can't seem to get past it, haunted as much by the vacuum her death created as they are bothered by the roster of serious, unexplained inconsistencies in the official account of her demise. The nude, lifeless body of the world-famous actress that investigators found in the middle of the night in her Brentwood home has unsettled the sleep of some police officers, private investigators, family friends, and fans around the world for almost five decades.

What was once limited to library shelves, sympathetic fan magazines, and inner-circle cocktail party chatter has now gone global. The Internet has fueled the controversy of her death and re-ignited interest in her life. For those too young to have experienced firsthand the phenomenon of Marilyn Monroe (existing as she does for many younger people merely as a relic of Hollywood's golden age), there are lots of places to re-experience the magic of her movies and her life. Yet, it's her death that eclipses much of that interest, a death many people say simply makes no sense—unless you think about who might have had something to gain from the loss of such a cultural sensation.

Charity Case

There was little to suggest that Norma Jeane would make any kind of an impact on the world when she was born in the charity ward of Los Angeles County Hospital on June 1, 1926. Her mother, the unmarried Gladys Pearl Monroe, suffered from periodic bouts of severe depression and economic hardship. Gladys placed her daughter in foster care, and Norma Jeane spent the first seven years of her life in the home of a Hawthorne, California couple named Albert and Ira Bolender.

In 1933, Gladys bought a house and briefly reclaimed her daughter, but almost immediately after moving in, she suffered a mental breakdown, and Norma Jeane was declared a ward of the state. Gladys's best friend, a woman named Grace McKee, took over the care of Norma Jeane, but she married in 1935, and her ward was sent first to the Los Angeles Orphans Home and then a succession of foster

The young Norma Jeane, born in a charity ward, spent the first seven years of her life in a foster home. (Photo source: www.crimelibrary.com/notorious_murders/ celebrity/marilyn_monroe/)

homes. Grace later reclaimed her, but she and her husband decided to move to the East Coast and concluded they could not take Norma Jeane with them, and so to keep Norma Jean from being sent, yet again, to a foster home, they encouraged her marriage, at 16, to a young man named James Dougherty, who was soon to join the Merchant Marines and head overseas.

While he was away, Norma Jeane moved in with her mother-in-law and took a job with the Radiophone Company factory, where she inspected parachutes. A photographer for *Yank* magazine named David Conover, doing a feature about women assisting the war effort, discovered Norma Jeane and was captivated by her. (He later claimed in his autobiography, *Finding Marilyn*, that the two had an affair that lasted for years.) After photographing her, he encouraged her to pursue a career in modeling, and she signed with the Blue Book modeling agency. Within a year, her picture had appeared in dozens of magazines (though with her new look: shorter, straightened hair and golden locks). In 1946, after being noticed by a talent scout for 20th Century Fox and a successful screen test, Norma Jeane signed a contract, and at the urging of studio executives, changed her name from the prosaic Norma Jeane Mortenson to the more memorable Marilyn Monroe.

That same year, she divorced her husband and spent the next four years taking bit parts in mostly forgettable films until her performance in 1950's *The Asphalt Jungle* brought her to the attention of critics. In 1952, she had her first starring role in the film *Don't Bother to Knock,*

Marilyn Monroe was featured on the cover (as well as in a considerably more revealing full-color spread on the inside) of the very first issue of *Playboy* magazine in 1953. (Photo source: en.wikipedia.org/wiki/Marilyn_Monroe)

and from there on, her popularity grew. Hugh Hefner featured nude photos of her in the very first issue of *Playboy*, and in 1954, she married Yankee slugger Joe DiMaggio. The high-profile marriage collapsed, and in 1956, Marilyn married playwright Arthur Miller, only to divorce five years later. All the while, Marilyn kept working, turning out such now-classic films as *Gentlemen Prefer Blondes* and *Some Like It Hot.*

At the time of her death in 1962, Marilyn was said to be involved in several film projects. She was commanding top-tier salaries (in excess of $250,000 per film) and was, according to some biographers, planning to remarry Joe DiMaggio.

Throughout her career, her celebrity placed her in contact with lots of powerful figures in the world of movies and politics. Although it has never been proved, many biographers and countless conspiracy theorists claim Marilyn had an affair with President John F. Kennedy and perhaps with his brother Bobby as well.

Some Like It Not

From the first press reports of Marilyn's death—officially listed as a suicide—a number of nagging questions have been raised. Why would a woman who was at the top of her career—and was planning new projects and possibly remarrying—take her own life? Many friends and co-workers who were around Marilyn in the days before her death claimed that she was upbeat and energized about the future (she had recently bought a new house in the posh Brentwood neighborhood). She left no suicide note, and no one has come forward to reveal what might have been troubling her enough to cause her to consider suicide.

The biggest impediment to believing the conclusion of suicide is based on medical evidence. Although she was said to have overdosed on barbiturates, the coroner's official report indicates that her stomach was empty. High levels of barbiturates were indeed found in her bloodstream and her liver, but not in her stomach. Medical officials and subsequent investigators have confirmed the coroner's findings, leading to the conclusion that the drugs were either injected into her (though there were no needle marks noted in the coroner's report—a finding some investigators question) or administered rectally through suppositories or an enema. (Neither method seems likely as a means of taking one's own life.)

There are several other pieces of puzzling evidence. When investigators discovered Marilyn's nude, lifeless body, she appeared to be lying peacefully on top of her bed. Most medical experts say that ingesting such a fatal dose of drugs would have brought about a series of convulsions and contortions causing the body to writhe about rather violently, not lie peacefully, as if one were napping. There are inconsistencies in statements made at the scene by her housekeeper (who, according to reports, was not available for further questioning as she moved away the next day, leaving no forwarding address), and in those of her personal physician, her psychiatrist, and people who had spoken with her the evening of her death. Witnesses, including a police officer, reportedly placed Robert Kennedy at Marilyn's home that night, and critical phone records have mysteriously disappeared.

Suspicion has often centered on the Kennedys, with many theorists suggesting JFK wanted to silence Marilyn because of the potentially damaging impact that the revelation of their relationship would create. Some think JFK orchestrated her death and used the power of his office to cover his tracks. The case is summarized in *The People's Almanac*, by David Wallechinsky and Irving Wallace:

> It is believed that Marilyn's phone had been tapped both by Robert Kennedy through the Justice Dept. and by his enemy, teamster boss Jimmy Hoffa. (Telephone toll tickets, which might have shed light on the case, have disappeared.) That a cover-up was enacted by the Los Angeles police and coroner is suspected. Sgt. Jack Clemmons, who was the first police officer to arrive at Marilyn's house the night of her death, later stated, "She was murdered by needle injection by someone she knew and trusted. I have no doubt of it. This was the cover up crime of the century."

In addition to President Kennedy, conspiracy theorists tend to cluster around a couple of other candidates: Bobby Kennedy, who some also see as having been romantically involved with Marilyn; the mafia, who saw murdering JFK's high-profile mistress as payback for his administration's attack on organized crime; and even Fidel Castro, acting in retaliation for Kennedy's failed assassination attempts.

Less sinister is a theory that centers on the possibility of an unintended fatal reaction to two drugs that should not have been in her system at the same time. As this theory goes, drugs Marilyn had taken during the day, prescribed by her physician, interacted fatally with a sleep-inducing enema prescribed by her psychiatrist and allegedly administered by a third party. Some investigators, such as Donald Spoto, who wrote a book-length biography of Marilyn Monroe, asks, "Who, at last, gave the enema? The only person who could have done it was [Marilyn's live-in housekeeper] Eunice Murray," though until the end of her life, Murray never wavered from her story that she went to bed early that night and only later discovered Marilyn's lifeless body in the early hours of August 5. But Spoto suggests that "giving an enema is not within the range of a psychiatrist's duties," and that "Eunice Murray could not point the finger at anyone else because she had done the actual deed. All she and [psychiatrist] Greenson could do was weakly state that they did not believe that Marilyn took her own life deliberately."

A number of high-profile, attention-getting books have been published in the last couple of decades, pointing to all sorts of evidence and all manner of conspiracy. But it's the Internet that has been home to the most compelling and up-to-date theorizing surrounding Marilyn's death.

Powerful Connections

"Everyone loves a conspiracy," notes the Marilyn Monroe section of truTV's Crime Library (www.crimelibrary.com/notorious_murders/celebrity/marilyn_monroe), but the site gives you a lot more than conspiracy theorizing, including in-depth biographical background, a photo gallery, an extensive Marilyn Monroe bibliography, the official

Some have alleged that Marilyn Monroe's death was due to a prescription from her psychiatrist Dr. Ralph Greenson, pictured here. (Photo source: www.crimelibrary.com/notorious_murders/celebrity/marilyn_monroe)

autopsy report, and even Marilyn's will. The discussion of the potential involvement of the Kennedys in Marilyn's life, and death, is logical, if speculative. As the site notes:

> There are a number of credible people who claim that Marilyn Monroe had affairs with one or both Kennedy brothers. John Kennedy, at least, was known to indulge himself in extramarital adventures. So it is not at all implausible that President Kennedy availed himself of the charms of one of the sexiest and most attractive women of that era … Was there an attempt on the part of the government to cover up John Kennedy's indiscretions with Marilyn Monroe? It would be very surprising indeed if there were not such an attempt.

However, as the site further notes, "Destroying phone records and personal journals and scraps of paper are not in the same league with murder."

It's a great site for someone looking to get acquainted with the main theories and the pros and cons of each individual theory about Marilyn's death.

Was it murder? According to several articles posted on WorldNetDaily (www.worldnetdaily.com), it was. Type "Marilyn Monroe" into the site's search engine and a number of articles come up, with titles like "Uncovered FBI documents link RFK to Monroe's death." In a piece titled "Blonde Bombshell," the site excerpts a book by Joe DiMaggio's niece, June, in which she alleges that her mother, speaking to Marilyn on the phone on the night of her death, overheard her blurt out the name of her killer as he stormed into her bedroom. According to the niece, her mother never revealed the name she heard. "I even asked her on her deathbed, 'Won't you tell me now?'" she writes. "And she just said, 'No, I want my family to live.'" June DiMaggio, who remained friendly with Marilyn even after her uncle's divorce, reveals that Marilyn was cheery and upbeat on the day of her supposed suicide: "When I saw her that fateful day, she went on and on about her new life and her plans for the future. She had a contract to fulfill, but she was hoping to cut back to perhaps a movie a year so that she could finally begin to enjoy life with her own family, in her cozy home." She claims Marilyn and Joe DiMaggio were planning to remarry on August 8, "the day that would instead be her funeral."

A thorough exploration of that day, and the events leading up it, can be found in the transcript of a broadcast of the TV show *48 Hours Mystery* on the CBS News Web site (www.cbsnews.com/stories/2006/04/20/48hours/main1524970.shtml). The show, which was hosted by correspondent Peter Van Sant, explores anew the controversy surrounding Marilyn's death. It also corroborates the rumors of a Marilyn–JFK liaison, citing a former secret service official who says the affair was "common knowledge" among those entrusted to protect the president. It also posits the idea that Marilyn was becoming a security risk for the president:

During a vacation in February 1962 in Mexico City, the movie star was mobbed by reporters. But away from the flashbulbs, she had a series of private, controversial meetings.

"She spent time socially, talked late at night with people who were American communists," says [biographer and journalist Anthony] Summers.

Most people didn't know it, but Summers says Marilyn was passionate about politics. "Marilyn Monroe wasn't a dumb blonde. She devoured books on politics. She liked to talk to people about politics," he says.

Marilyn's political talks in Mexico were being monitored, and the FBI had opened a file on the movie star.

According to newly released FBI documents, Monroe was considered a potential security risk. "Here you have a woman who is close to the President of the United States and to the attorney general who goes to Mexico and talks into the night with known communists," says Summers. "She was a security risk."

But for most Americans, Marilyn was a star of the screen, not a political figure. She was, for her generation, the original "It" girl. Those who want to glean some sense of Marilyn's impact on pop culture can visit her official site (www.marilynmonroe.com), which offers news, biography, photos, quotes, trivia, and anecdotes. The site immodestly promises "Everything Marilyn!" and pretty much fulfills that promise. For those who are new to the Marilyn Monroe cult of adoration, there are some helpful at-a-glance pages with information about Marilyn's life, career, and legacy. And for the truly devoted, there's a "Did you Know?" trivia section where you can learn, among other things, that in 1947, she was crowned "Miss California Artichoke Queen."

For a woman who found herself in frequently silly, or even demeaning, situations, it's somewhat surprising to discover evidence of a quick wit and genuine thoughtfulness. But that might be the conclusion many reach after reading many of her quotes, collected on the

Many researchers have suggested that Marilyn had a romantic liaison with both President Kennedy and his brother Robert. (Photo source: www.historyplace.com)

"Marilyn Monroe" page of Brainy Quote (www.brainyquote.com/ quotes/authors/m/marilyn_monroe.html). In retrospect, many of the quotes, probably uttered for a quick laugh, now take on the resonance of great sadness:

> Hollywood is a place where they'll pay you a thousand dollars for a kiss and fifty cents for your soul.

> I knew I belonged to the public and to the world, not because I was talented or even beautiful, but because I had never belonged to anything or anyone else.

> A career is wonderful, but you can't curl up with it on a cold night.

The iconic Marilyn Monroe. (Photo source: www.cbsnews.com)

Those who want to understand the roots of Marilyn's loneliness and sense of isolation should check out the Marilyn Monroe "biography" page on Ellen's Place (www.ellensplace.net/mmbio3.html). The site helpfully chronicles her early years and marriages, interspersed with quotes from the actress that really humanize the headlines of her life. As she noted about her time being bounced from foster family to foster family, "The world around me then was kind of grim. I had to learn to pretend in order to … I don't know … block the grimness. The whole world seemed sort of closed to me. I felt on the outside of everything, and all I could do was to dream up any kind of pretend-game."

A number of Marilyn Monroe sites link to the FBI report on her adult life—comprised mostly of summaries of television and print interviews she granted, as well as extensive notations of her travel arrangements and personal affiliations. You can find a link to that report, among many others, at the Marilyn Monroe Wikipedia entry (en.wikipedia.org/wiki/Marilyn_Monroe). Much more grim, but worth a read for Marilyn complete-ists, is the full autopsy report (www.marilynmonroepages.com/autopsy.html).

Good-Bye Norma Jeane

Would there continue to be worldwide interest in the life of Marilyn Monroe even if it weren't for the questions surrounding her death? She was a figure of inestimable impact in the post–World War II world, and her rise to stardom paralleled the growth of cinema as a potent pop cultural force. She was of her time, but also for all time. Her status as an icon (she was voted "Sexiest Woman of the Century" by *People* magazine) grows with each passing decade. The woman who started out as a charity case ended up having it all, yet she remained an enigma in life.

Sadly, her death seems likely to remain an enigma as well.

Protocols of the Elders of Zion

Some conspiracy theories seem to be more of an intellectual parlor game than a serious exploration of an issue. The stakes, the consequences of being right or wrong, are largely abstract. Make a good argument, retain bragging rights. But few minds will *really* be changed.

This is not the case with the *Protocols of the Elders of Zion*. This conspiracy theory can be said to have contributed, in part, to the deaths of millions of people during World War II in the death camps of Hitler's Germany. The pervasive campaign against the Jews—formalized and given credence by the believers of the *Protocols*—took root in the worldwide dissemination of this so-called master plan for Zionist world domination. The modern scourge of anti-Semitism leeches back to the century-old document, the reputed record of a meeting of a super-secret cabal of Jewish "elders" outlining their specific plan to take control of the world's wealth and political power.

Though widely acknowledged by most as a fraud, this spectacularly inflammatory document retains a certain, almost hypnotic power in the hands of those who wish to find a villain on the global stage. Whenever the explosive passions between the Jewish state and its detractors reignite, some autocrat somewhere is sure to be found quoting from the *Protocols*, stoking the flames of racial hatred and breathing life anew into the question of the document's authenticity.

121

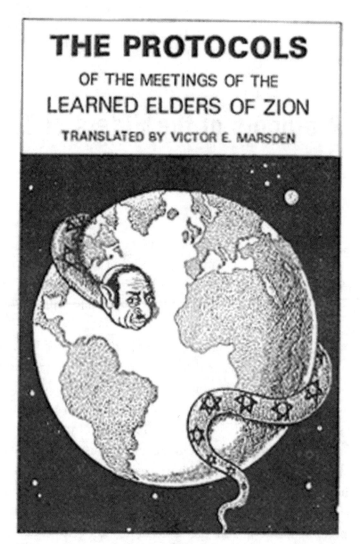

THE PROTOCOLS

OF THE MEETINGS OF THE
LEARNED ELDERS OF ZION

TRANSLATED BY VICTOR E. MARSDEN

This cover page of the *Protocols of the Elders of Zion* depicts a Jewish Snake embracing the globe. (Photo source: ddickerson.igc.org/protocols.html)

Kings of the World

There is some disagreement about the origin of the *Protocols* among those who have studied the document's strange development and dissemination. Most scholars agree that the basic text of the *Protocols* comes from a reworked version of a French political pamphlet from the

1860s, *Dialogue aux Enfers entre Montesquieu et Machiavel (Dialogue in Hell Between Montesquieu and Machiavelli)*, a text that offered a hypothetical debate between proponents of a liberal state and a despotic tyranny. In the reworking, many of the arguments reappear, this time in the form of statements reportedly made by Jewish elders at a meeting held to formalize a plan to seize control of the world's capital and governance. Scholars have also found bits and pieces of other works, both fiction and nonfiction, peppered throughout the *Protocols*.

Each of the "protocols," or instructions, outlines how the group will acquire the power it seeks. Relying on propaganda and campaigns of misinformation, the *Protocols*, which is divided into 26 chapters, calls for such things as attacking Christianity and replacing it with Judaism, acquiring control of the media, and using it to disseminate messages that will cause nations to distrust each other, ultimately leading to world war and the destruction of the current global social order (to be replaced by a single economic system controlled by Jewish financiers), and even introducing a "King of the Jews" who will be, in the words of the *Protocols*, "the real Pope of the Universe, the patriarch of an international Church."

Here are some excerpts, which provide a taste of the overall document:

> Today I may tell you that our goal is now only a few steps off. There remains a small space to cross and the whole long path we have trodden is ready now to close its cycle of the Symbolic Snake, by which we symbolize our people.

> Who and what is in a position to overthrow an invisible force? And this is precisely what our force is. Gentile masonry ["Freemasonry"] blindly serves as a screen for us and our objects. ...

> Throughout all Europe, and by means of relations with Europe, in other continents also, we must create ferments, discords and hostility.

> In the near future, we shall establish the responsibility of presidents. By that time we shall be in a position to disregard forms in carrying through matters for which our impersonal puppet will be responsible.

> God has granted to us, His Chosen People, the gift of the dispersion, and in this which appears in all eyes to be our weakness, has come forth all our strength, which has now brought us to the threshold of sovereignty over all the world.

It is widely believed that the *Protocols* was written in Paris around 1895 by an agent of the Russian secret police named Pytor Rachovsky. Historians suggest that Rachovsky was trying to discredit the attempt to move Russia away from the control of the ruling aristocracy. The argument goes that Rachovsky, a staunch traditionalist in the service of the czars, hoped to show that economic modernization was the result of a Jewish plot to destroy the country and create economic chaos. In other words, he was linking all those who were agitating for modernism with a secret, evil, foreign-controlled cabal. He further exploited this connection by suggesting in the *Protocols* that the Jews were working through the Freemasons—an organization of which many in Russia and Europe were already suspicious.

The *Protocols* was first published in 1905 by Sergei Nilus, another member of the Russian secret police. Several editions were circulated over the next decade, contributing to what scholars acknowledge as a widespread Russian anti-Semitism. Russian expatriates spread the *Protocols* all throughout Europe after the fall of the Czars in 1917, claiming that the Jews were behind the Russian Revolution. Copies of the *Protocols* showed up in newspapers throughout Europe and the U.S. during the 1920s.

Hitler and "The Jewish Menace"

The *Protocols* became "exhibit A" in Adolf Hitler's campaign against the Jews. Officials in the Third Reich widely distributed the *Protocols*, and Hitler himself spoke and wrote at length about the

Sergei Nilus was a member of the Russian secret police and publisher of the *Protocols*. (Photo source: ddickerson.igc.org/ protocols.html)

Jewish plot to take over the world. Hitler's vehemence in the *Protocols'* authenticity reaches its nadir in a chilling passage in his book, *Mein Kampf*:

> The important thing is that with positively terrifying certainty they [the *Protocols*] reveal the nature and activity of the Jewish people and expose their inner contexts as well as their ultimate final aims. The best criticism applied to them, however, is reality. Anyone who examines the historical development of the last hundred years from the standpoint of this book will at once understand the screaming of the Jewish press. For once this book has

become the common property of a people, the Jewish menace may be considered as broken.

That last sentence underlies the undeniable connection between Hitler's campaign against the Jews and the *Protocols*. As Marlon Kuzmick noted in the *Encyclopedia of American Conspiracy Theories*:

> In the end, the *Protocols* formed one of the pillars of the Nazi ideology. [N]ot only did the Nazis found their anti-Semitism on the *Protocols*, they also seemed entranced and profoundly *influenced* by the elders' conspiracy ... the tragic result of this ideology is well known—at least 6 million lives destroyed in the Holocaust.

Gaining Traction

The *Protocols* underwent several editions in several languages throughout Europe in the 1920s and 1930s and continued to win adherents, despite a series of articles that appeared in the *Times* of London arguing that the *Protocols* was only a pastiche of previously published political satires.

More popular, however, than the *Times'* exposé was the publication of the *Protocols* in American auto tycoon Henry Ford's newspaper, *Dearborn Independent*. The newspaper's series of 91 articles about the *Protocols* was eventually republished as *The International Jew*, a text that was itself published in newspapers throughout the U.S. and Europe, helping to spread the idea of a worldwide Jewish conspiracy.

The era of the 1920s and 1930s could not have been more fertile for the spread of a theory scapegoating one group for the woes of the civilized world: regional tensions presaging another world war, economic collapse and sustained depression, and the growing power of the mass media.

Despite the continued insistence of credible figures—historians, scholars, journalists, and human rights advocates—that the document is fraudulent, there are still those individuals and groups that cling to

Nazis searched for Jewish residents of the Warsaw Ghetto shortly before deporting them to a concentration camp. (Photo source: www.holocaust-history.org)

the belief that the *Protocols* remains an authoritative account of the plan for Jewish domination of the world. Contemporary commentators have noted, with alarm, that groups such as the Islamic Resistance Movement (Hamas) continue to refer to the *Protocols* in its official "covenant," as do white supremacist neo-Nazi groups and the Ku Klux Klan.

Those who find Jewish intrigue behind today's headlines are often as clever as they are convinced of their conspiracy theory. Faced with scholarly evidence suggesting the *Protocols* is a fiction, they've recast the argument to suggest that results—not authenticity—matter most. As one anti-Semitic Web site proudly notes:

> The ideas of power development depicted in it [the *Protocols*] move on our contemporary stage, play the parts foretold and produce the events foreseen. So even if you don't believe in the authenticity of this remarkable document, one thing you can't deny is their fulfillment.

You can toss the *Protocols* out the window if you want, but you can't deny the fact that everything they plotted, planned and predicted has either already happened, or is happening now.

For more than 100 years, the *Protocols* has given credence to those who see world history as a series of planned "accidents," orchestrated by malevolent forces who manipulate public officials like marionettes on a stage—an admittedly low-tech metaphor that still applies in our high-tech age.

Internet Protocols

There are dozens of Web sites that deal in various ways with the *Protocols*, with many of the advocates of the theory of Jewish world domination citing sources as disparate as the Bible, the United

Some believers in the *Protocols* see a Zionist plot to "substitute the sensual and material for spiritual fulfillment." (Photo source: www.savethemales.ca/000205.html)

Nations, and a century of global military conflict as evidence for their belief.

If you want to get a sense of the "true believers" in the *Protocols*, check out the unambiguously titled Jew Watch site (www.jew watch.com)—but be prepared for some provocative and blatantly racist claims. The site bills itself as a repository of "The Internet's largest scholarly collection of articles on Jewish history" (though such "scholarly" articles carry titles like "See How What the *Protocols* Said Has Been Done by the Jews Word-For-Word"). In a general overview to the *Protocols*, visitors will be informed that:

> We can see the *Protocols* being carried out word-by-word in the world-power the Jews at the top have achieved. These are the incredibly motivated schemers who were involved in the worldwide conspiracy to create Israel. They controlled the media to accomplish that, and they still own all of it.

The site also contains a link to a documentary film about the *Protocols*, a collection of arguments about the *Protocols*' validity "from many nations and scholars," and, of course, the full text of the *Protocols* itself.

Not to be outdone is the World Conquest Through World Jewish Government Web page (www.biblebelievers.org.au/przion1.htm), a site that finds Jewish denials of the *Protocols*' authenticity as evidence of their validity:

> The claim of the Jews that the *Protocols* are forgeries is in itself an admission of their genuineness, for they NEVER ATTEMPT TO ANSWER THE FACTS corresponding to the THREATS which the Protocols contain.

The site consists of a long introductory essay about the *Protocols*, a "Who Are the Elders?" overview of the super-secret cabal behind the *Protocols*, and the text of each of the individual *Protocols* linked to the site's homepage. The introductory material makes pretty clear the type of thinking that the site exhibits throughout. In a discussion of the history of the *Protocols*, the site's authors showcase several extracts from the diaries of the 19th-century "Father of Modern Zionism" Theodore Herzl, speeches from Jewish leaders in the first half of the 20th century, and the text of the *Protocols* to establish the following conclusion:

> The remarkable correspondence between these passages proves several things. It proves that the Learned Elders exist ... It proves that the desire for a "National Home" in Palestine is only camouflage and an infinitesimal part of the Jew's real object. It proves that the Jews of the world have no intention of settling in Palestine or any separate country ... It also demonstrates that the Jews are now a world menace, and that the Aryan races will have to domicile them permanently out of Europe.

For sheer chutzpah, it's hard to beat the "Protocols of Zion" section at the Save the Males Web site (www.savethemales.ca/000205. html), which aims at "exposing feminism and the New World Order." The Jews aren't really responsible for the *Protocols*, asserts the site, Satan is:

> The book is Satanic in character ... Idealistic-sounding principles are used to deceive and manipulate the goyim [gentiles] ... with the aristocracy gone, the Satanists form an invisible government by bribing politicians and cultural leaders with fame and fortune.

Casual Web surfers might be taken aback at the austere, alarmist pronouncements issuing forth from the site: "We are in the eleventh hour of a multi-generational conspiracy designed to first degrade and then enslave mankind." The *Protocols* is "a long term plan for world dictatorship" built upon an effort to degrade humanity; "this is why the media constantly appeals to our animal qualities with pornography, violence and immorality."

The Web site ThreeWorldWars.com reaches a similar conclusion in an essay posted at www.threeworldwars.com/protocols.htm: "The *Protocols* of the Learned Elders of Zion is the most blatantly Satanic document in world history!" The site's authors challenge the supposition that the document is fraudulent by pointing out that "there have been many attempts to discount the *Protocols* as a fraud, and the fact remains that there is no documentary proof … despite many opinions to the contrary, the documents have never been categorically proved to be fraudulent." The site offers a mostly recycled list of apparent correspondences between 20th-century world history and the *Protocols* itself.

One can well imagine the feeling of Jewish groups such as the Anti-Defamation League (ADL) upon encountering such sentiments. But Web surfers don't have to imagine—they can go to the ADL site for a thorough and comprehensive retort (www.adl.org/special_reports/protocols/protocols_intro.asp). The first line of the site offers a succinct rebuttal of the *Protocols*: "It is a classic in paranoid, racist literature." The ADL acknowledges the enduring belief in the *Protocols*' authenticity "in bigoted, frightened minds around the world." The site offers more than just an indignant and dismissive commentary on the conspiracy theory. Visitors will find a timeline of the *Protocols*' dissemination under an article titled "The Hoax Spreads," cautionary essays about the contemporary re-emergence of anti-Semitism, and links to the broader ADL site for more articles and alerts about anti-Semitic activities around the globe.

Some of the best and most comprehensive coverage of the *Protocols* controversy can be found at sites affiliated with Holocaust research, such as the Holocaust History Project (www.holocaust-history.org), which offers a series of short, reader-friendly essays about several aspects of the *Protocols*, from the paper trail that begins with similar anti-Semitic pamphlets from France in the late 19th century, through Hitler's appropriation of various sections of the *Protocols* for propaganda value, to the widespread use of the *Protocols* among groups such as the Ku Klux Klan. As the site notes:

> Even today the *Protocols* of the Elders of Zion is one of
> the principal propaganda weapons of anti-Semitism ...
> The Institute for Historical Review—the intellectual cen-
> ter of the movement denying the Holocaust—continues to
> see the *Protocols* and it is still used to attack Jews.

The online edition of the *Holocaust Encyclopedia* (www.ushmm.
org/wlc/en) offers short, wide-ranging articles about the *Protocols*,
from an introduction to the subject that acknowledges the power of
the digital age ("Its lies about Jews, which have been repeatedly discredited, continue to circulate today, especially on the internet") to a
bibliography of articles and books about the *Protocols*. The site has
entries about the first publication of the *Protocols* in Russia, the articles in the *London Times* exposing the *Protocols* as a "clumsy pla-
giarism," the Nazi-era spread of the *Protocols*, and excerpts from

Hate groups such as the Ku Klux Klan, shown here at a rally in 1923, have often
used the *Protocols* to justify their anti-Semitism. (Photo source: wikipedia.org/
wiki/KKK)

International courts, the U.S. Senate, and the U.S. State Department about the *Protocols*. The site also notes with alarm the widespread embrace of the *Protocols* in various parts of the world today:

> Many school textbooks throughout the Arab and Islamic world teach the *Protocols* as fact. Countless political speeches, editorials, and even children's cartoons are derived from the *Protocols*. In 2002, Egypt's government-sponsored television aired a miniseries based on the *Protocols*, an event condemned by the U.S. State Department. The Palestinian organization Hamas draws in part on the *Protocols* to justify its terrorism against Israeli civilians.

For general thoroughness, the *Protocols* site at ddickerson.igc.org/protocols.html is the gold standard, offering dozens of links to helpful, thorough, and informed commentaries on all aspects of the *Protocols* controversy. Site author and watchdog David Dickerson links to general interest sites, online encyclopedias, public research organizations, academic institutions, newspapers, and book excerpts. The site's perspective is one of complete disdain for those who think there is something to the idea of a Jewish worldwide conspiracy. In the interest of complete disclosure, Dickerson offers a link to the *Protocols* itself, but he draws the line at generating traffic for those who find credence in the various theories of Jewish manipulations: "Although I have misgivings about providing this document [the *Protocols*], I refuse to link to the anti-Semitic sites that host copies of it."

There's not much about the *Protocols* that would seem to inspire laughter or song, but that didn't stop someone from trying. An animated video, setting the *Protocols* to pop music, can be found on the Web site of Pajamas Media (www.pajamasmedia.com/2006/11/thought_the_protocols_of_the_e.php). The three-minute video features a guitar-strumming cartoon Orthodox Jew bragging about his standing as a member of the Learned Elders and of his plans for world domination. The whole thing is quirky, bitingly satirical, and, musically, quite catchy. In the often rhetorically intense world of debate about the *Protocols*, it's a welcome, if slightly disorienting, respite.

Respecting Your Elders

While many conspiracy theorists often hang their beliefs on unseen, missing, or destroyed documents, those who believe in a master plan for Jewish domination continue to argue that there is an actual document to support their beliefs. The history of anti-Semitic suspicion certainly predates the *Protocols of the Elders of Zion*, but for a variety of reasons it is *that* document—no matter how well refuted—that has become the "proof" for many who wish to blame a Jewish conspiracy for the often-dire events of the modern world. And no amount of "debunking" seems likely to change their minds. For believers, the *Protocols* is too sophisticated—and too predictive—to be ignored.

Pearl Harbor

Yesterday, December 7, 1941—a date which will live in infamy—the United States of America was suddenly and deliberately attacked by naval and air forces of the Empire of Japan ... I believe that I interpret the will of the Congress and of the people when I assert that we will not only defend ourselves to the uttermost but will make it very certain that this form of treachery shall never again endanger us.

So said President Franklin D. Roosevelt to a still-stunned nation in perhaps the most famous presidential address of the modern era. The phrase "a date which will live in infamy" has become, for most Americans, as familiar and stirring as the preamble to the Constitution or the verses of the Pledge of Allegiance. And while there's no denying the "infamy" of the attack, some critics and researchers have argued that it's Roosevelt himself who engaged in an act of infamy.

These skeptics have concluded that the president was the principal figure in a conspiracy to entice the Japanese into the attack. In fact, this chorus of conspiracy theorists suggests that Roosevelt and members of his cabinet were well aware of Japan's plans to attack the Pearl Harbor naval base in Oahu, Hawaii, but they sat on the intelligence reports that would have allowed America to prepare for the attack. As proof of their theory, historians, researchers, and just plain

Some conspiracy theorists blame President Roosevelt, shown here signing a declaration of war in December 1941, for instigating the attacks at Pearl Harbor. (Photo source: wikipedia.org/wiki/FDR)

skeptics offer lots of official memos, records of meetings, telegrams, and recently disclosed material from the U.S. Archives.

Is there truly any proof that this horrific attack unfolded with the knowledge—even approval—of the U.S. government? And could such a conclusion ever find acceptance among a populace whose embrace of Roosevelt's call to action rallied "The Greatest Generation" to its finest hour?

You don't need to travel to Pearl Harbor to investigate the incident. The latest and best research is as close as your home computer.

A New Era Dawns

On a brilliant Sunday morning, just after sunrise, the first wave of what would eventually comprise 350 Japanese fighter planes began an assault on the Pearl Harbor naval base at Oahu, Hawaii. The planes had taken off from a small fleet of aircraft carriers of the Imperial Japanese Navy and arrived with almost no resistance. In a smothering attack that took less than 90 minutes, the Japanese destroyed five U.S. Navy battleships, three destroyers, and more than 180 aircraft. More than 2,300 American servicemen and civilians were killed in the attack, and more than 1,139 were wounded. Losses on the Japanese side were minimal.

The attack led to a declaration of war by the U.S. against Japan. Three days later, Adolf Hitler's Germany declared war against the U.S., and the stage was now set for America's full-scale entry into World War II. What had been, according to historians of the period, a largely isolationist posture on the part of the American public was replaced overnight by a patriotic rush toward war. There's no doubt that the attack on Pearl Harbor changed the balance of power in what

The USS *West Virginia* was one of the ships destroyed during the Japanese attack on Pearl Harbor. (Photo source: www.history.navy.mil/photos/events/wwii-pac/ pearlhbr/pearlhbr.htm)

had so far been a "European War." The entry of the U.S. into the conflict resulted in, among other things, an eventual allied victory, crushing defeats for the nascent military powers of Japan and Germany, and the rise of the U.S. as a formidable superpower. Pearl Harbor, it can be argued, recalibrated the balance of global power. One of the enduring ironies of the attack is that it was such a spectacular victory for the Japanese as well as the first step toward their eventual defeat.

Conspiracy theorists say this is exactly what Roosevelt was hoping for. Aware that most Americans opposed U.S. entry into the European theater of war, the president, they allege, needed a reason, a provocation that would justify it. The Pearl Harbor conspiracy theory suggests that Roosevelt engineered a series of actions—primarily a series of embargoes and blockades that prevented Japan from acquiring raw materials to sustain its recently expanded operations in China (which Japan had invaded). Then, he moved much of the U.S. fleet to Pearl Harbor, despite the objections of several of his military advisors, who argued that the base was too "exposed." Conspiracists argue further that U.S. diplomats made demands during negotiations with the Japanese in the wake of Japan's invasion of China that Roosevelt knew would be unacceptable to the Japanese and would provoke a response.

As historian Robert Stinnett put it in his widely discussed 1999 book, *Day of Deceit: The Truth About FDR and Pearl Harbor*, "Roosevelt believed that his countrymen would rally only to oppose an overt act of war on the United States. The decision he made, in concert with his advisors, was to provoke Japan through a series of actions into an overt act: the Pearl Harbor attack." Stinnett claims Roosevelt accepted the eight-point plan of his Naval Intelligence Office (the so-called McCollum Memo), which included the recommendation that the president "keep the main strength of the U.S. Fleet in the vicinity of the Hawaiian islands."

And most explosively, conspiracy theorists claim Roosevelt possessed the specific intelligence reports that detailed the attack on Pearl Harbor, but instead of informing base commanders, he chose to let the attack proceed as planned—all the way up to America's declaration of war on December 8, the day after the day "of infamy."

Tales from the Cryptographer

Much of the "evidence" used to establish the case of Roosevelt's foreknowledge derives from the U.S. military's efforts to break the secret code used by the Japanese navy. For more than a year prior to the attack on Pearl Harbor, U.S. military cryptographers in Hawaii and at intercept stations around the Pacific Rim had been monitoring, recording, and attempting to decode transmissions from the Japanese fleet. Though the U.S. was not at war with Japan, the tension between the two countries was high. In 1931, Japan's conquest of Manchuria and its withdrawal from the League of Nations ratcheted up the diplomatic friction. In 1937, Japan attacked China and, four years later, it moved into northern Indo-China. The U.S. responded by freezing all of Japan's assets in the U.S. and initiating an oil embargo. In the summer of 1941, Japanese Prime Minister Fumimaro Konoe proposed a summit meeting with Roosevelt to discuss the contentious relationship, but Roosevelt declined, stating that any such meeting could only take place after Japan withdrew its forces from China.

According to some researchers, the U.S. code breakers succeeded in deciphering Japan's complex "Purple Code," and by the late spring or early summer of 1941, U.S. officials had access to Japanese plans—including, they argue, the detailed plan of attack on Pearl Harbor. There is a body of evidence that supports the argument that Roosevelt was receiving regular dispatches and briefings from the senior military officials involved with code breaking. Where historians and conspiracy theorists differ is on what, specifically, many of those dispatches contained. As some researchers have noted, many of the intercepted messages contain general information but nothing that should have raised red flags among military experts. As one Web site on the subject argues, "The U.S. civil and military intelligence had … good information suggesting additional Japanese aggression throughout the summer and fall before the attack. At the time, none specifically indicated an attack against Pearl Harbor, nor has any doing so been identified since."

However, that view is dismissed as erroneous and even naive by a growing number of skeptics and conspiracy theorists who argue that there's no way Roosevelt wouldn't have been aware of what one researcher called "a flurry of Japanese communication" picked up by U.S. transmission stations around the Pacific Rim in the week preceding the attack. In addition, one of the intercepted messages, known as the "Bomb Plot" message (and recently made available to researchers through the Freedom of Information Act), featured a communication between Japanese naval officials and a Japanese spy in Hawaii, requesting specific information about the locations and types of ships guarding Pearl Harbor.

While historians can't seem to agree on just what, precisely, Roosevelt knew, and what he should have done with that information, there's widespread agreement that he was in fact looking for the U.S. to take a more active role in the war. It's not unfounded to suggest that Roosevelt given his close relationship with Britain's Winston Churchill and his trepidation about Nazi advances throughout Europe, was planning, as a contingency, for a U.S. war effort. Some scholars of the period have a tough time, however, making the leap that many conspiracy theorists do—that the Commander in Chief of the U.S. Armed Forces would have allowed the wholesale slaughter of 2,400 Americans without lifting a finger to stop it.

Though more than half a century has passed since the event, new information and new theories continue to sprout on the Web. If the events of December 7, 1941, seem like ancient history, it might be time to sign on for a refresher course in what happened—or at least, what most people have been *told* that happened.

War of Words

The mix of patriotism, finger-pointing, dispassionate historical interest, and gut-level anger has created an eclectic, even explosive, landscape on Pearl Harbor Web sites. Those who feel betrayed by the government have set up sites that, quite naturally, have an indignant tone. One of the more extensive sites endorsing the conspiracy theory is the Pearl Harbor: Mother of All Conspiracies site (www.geo cities.com/Pentagon/6315/pearl.html). This site offers an extensive timeline of events leading up to the attack, including excerpts from

Some believe that Roosevelt's close relationship with Winston Churchill led the U.S. president to provoke an act of war by Japan, generating public support for the U.S. to join Great Britain in the war effort. (Photo source: wikipedia.org/wiki/FDR)

many memos, diplomatic reports, and minutes of meetings focusing on the growing tensions between the U.S. and Japan. There's a wealth of "background" on everything from American code-breaking efforts to a list of messages that Roosevelt was likely to have received from his own intelligence officers and diplomats from other countries involved in the war, as well as discussions, essays, and commentary about Roosevelt's concerns regarding Nazi Germany, and his growing desire to enter the war effort. There's no doubt, however, where the authors of this site stand:

> Conclusion: Roosevelt was a *traitor* [in red]. The US was
> warned by, at least, the governments of Britain, Netherlands,

Australia, Peru, Korea and the Soviet Union that a surprise attack was coming. All important Japanese codes were broken. FDR ... and others knew the attack was coming, allowed it and covered up their knowledge.

The site also makes much of the fact that the ships that were destroyed in the attack were "old and slow," and would not have constituted a serious blow to American naval might (the site alleges Roosevelt sent the "A-list" ships to join the Atlantic fleet months before the attack). Finally, the site blasts the government for continued "cover-up by secrecy" for its refusal to release a number of still-classified coded messages that were received and deciphered in the months before the attack.

The debate about the extent of U.S. deciphering capabilities comprises a good portion of a fascinating Web site, sponsored by a think tank known as the Independent Institute, called The Truth About Pearl Harbor: A Debate (www.independent.org/issues/article.asp?id=445). This site features a lengthy point-counterpoint debate between author Stinnett and journalist Stephen Budiansky. Not surprisingly, Stinnett repeats the claims in his book, *Day of Deceit*, that the U.S. had adequately deciphered the Japanese code and was in possession of the details of the coming attack. His opponent in the debate paints a different picture. Here's a taste of the lively back-and-forth exchange:

Robert Stinnett: Two questions about the Japanese attack on Pearl Harbor have ignited a controversy that has burned for 60 years: Did U.S. naval cryptographers crack the Japanese naval codes before the attack? Did Japanese warships and their commanding admirals break radio silence at sea before the attack? If the answer to both is "no," then Pearl Harbor was indeed a surprise attack described by President Franklin D. Roosevelt as a "Day of Infamy." The integrity of the U.S. government regarding Pearl Harbor remains solid. But if the answer is "yes," then hundreds of books, articles, movies, and TV documentaries based on the "no" answer—and the integrity of the federal government—go down the drain.

Stephen Budiansky: Historians who have reviewed Mr. Stinnett's book have been rightly critical of his work on several grounds. David Kahn, whose classic book *The Codebreakers* is widely acknowledged as the definitive work on cryptologic history, reviewed Mr. Stinnett's book in the *New York Review of Books* and called it the "most irrational" of the many Pearl Harbor conspiracy books yet written. Archivists at the National Archives and Records Administration who have tried to locate documents Mr. Stinnett cites in his book have been unable to do so. His method of citing archival records is indeed so obscure that it is unlikely anyone who sought to verify Mr. Stinnett's claims as to these documents' content and context would be able to do so in most instances …

Robert Stinnett: Stephen Budiansky fails to answer the newest evidence that drastically alters the three main questions of Pearl Harbor: (1) Prior to December 7, 1941, did the U.S. break the Japanese operations code known as Code Book D, (2) did the Japanese fleet commanders break radio silence and (3) reveal their locations to U.S. Navy radio direction finders? Mr. Budiansky responds with 1950-era media cover stories and assures his readers that the answer is "no" to all three questions.

The lack of critical consensus about exactly what was known and whether FDR was really trying to provoke the Japanese has opened the door to a wide variety of interpretations—with no shortage of theories regarding what *really* happened before and during the attack on Pearl Harbor. For instance, the "Pearl Harbor" page of the Federal Debt Relief System (FDRS) Web site (www.fdrs.org/attack_on_pearl_harbor.html) blames the Council on Foreign Relations for the attack. The Council—often linked by conspiracy theorists to another quasi-governmental group called the Trilateral Commission (see Chapter 12)—is seen, in the eyes of the FDRS, to be responsible for fomenting the attack. "The Pearl Harbor conspiracy is another in a long line of New World Order schemes thought up as part of the larger Council on Foreign Relations conspiracy." The thinking behind such an assertion is that the defeat of Germany and Japan would exacerbate the move toward "one-worldism," which would ultimately make control of the world's wealth and political power much easier. Quoting the work of noted conspiracy author Jim Marrs, the site asserts, "CFR members were interested in exploiting the Second World War—as they had the first—as a justification for world government."

Those who like their history firsthand should check out the so-called McCollum Memo—the eight-point plan designed to provoke Japan into a military response—which is the subject of its own

Aerial view of the U.S. fleet at Pearl Harbor seven months before the fateful attack. (Photo source: www.history.navy.mil/photos/events/wwii-pac/prelim/phbr-1.htm)

Wikipedia entry (en.wikipedia.org/wiki/McCollum_memo). The article situates the memo in the context of the prewar tensions with Japan and also offers a facsimile and transcription of its major points.

Much more firsthand material is available on the comprehensive Pearl Harbor site maintained by the Naval Historical Center (www.history.navy.mil/photos/events/wwii-pac/pearlhbr/pearlhbr. htm). Interested readers will find in-depth articles on most aspects of the attack (though precious little on the conspiracy angle). Mostly, the site features historical essays, articles, illustrations, a photo gallery, and an FAQ page that ought to satisfy even the most curious naval gazer. Similarly, there's a lot of good information about Pearl Harbor, then and now, available through the Navy's Web site, Naval Station Pearl Harbor (www.cnic.navy.mil/pearlharbor/ index.htm). And for complete-ists, check out the full text of Roosevelt's December 8 Pearl Harbor speech to the U.S. Congress (ww2homefront.com/fdr speech12-8-41.html), complete with his condemnation of the "surprise offensive" and his stirring call to remember "the character of the onslaught against us."

A worthwhile site, whether or not one has firm conclusions about what Roosevelt and his cabinet knew, is the online version of the USS *Arizona* National Memorial Museum (www.nps.gov/usar). The actual memorial building rises above the site where the USS *Arizona* was sunk in the attack, and both the physical facility and the Web site offer visitors a chance to learn more about the ships that were harbored there.

Some researchers, conspiracy theorists, and amateur historians have tried to draw parallels between the attack on Pearl Harbor and the 9/11 attacks. For a quick but thoughtful exploration of the link between those two events—especially the idea that the government possessed some foreknowledge of the attacks—take a look at the article "Pearl Harbor: History Whitewashed?" by Ian Woods, posted on the Web site of the online think tank Centre for Research on Globalisation (www.globalresearch.ca/articles/WOO203A.html). As the author of the piece concludes:

Is it possible that history is repeating itself now? I only raise the question, because there are so many questions that remain unanswered concerning the events of September 11. In the words of philosopher and poet George Santayana, "Those who cannot remember the past are condemned to repeat it." The evidence presented by [author and researcher] John Toland suggests that Pearl Harbor was a crisis created by the U.S. government on December 7, 1941 to manipulate public opinion and sway the American people into going to war.

For those who like a little less speculation in their historical overview and a little more content (actually, a *lot* more content), a great site is National Geographic's Remembering Pearl Harbor page (plasma.nationalgeographic.com/pearlharbor). The site is extremely

The destroyer USS *Shaw* explodes during the Japanese bombing raid on December 7, 1941. (Photo source: www.history.navy.mil/photos/events/wwii-pac/pearl hbr/pearlhbr.htm)

interesting and includes video presentations, a thorough rundown of the specifications of the ships and planes that were involved in the attack (on both sides), and a searchable archive of survivors' stories. For those who want to capture some of the history for themselves, there's a Pearl Harbor museum store as well.

Dredging Up the Past

For a generation of Americans, and for many who have seen the movies, read the books, and heard the recordings of FDR's speech, the Japanese attack on Pearl Harbor will never be replaced as the single worst incursion in the history of the Republic. Time, and a host of other unexpected terrors, have perhaps blunted the immediacy and the horror of the event, but it stands nonetheless at the apex of 20th-century dislocation. The fascination with Pearl Harbor probably resides as much in the mystery of what the government knew as in the fascination of considering what would have happened had there been *no* Pearl Harbor. World War II reshaped the world in ways that were unimaginable, yet now seem inevitable. The attack at dawn that Sunday in December shook the civilized world to its core, a seismic tremor whose aftershocks continue to echo through our time.

The Trilateral Commission

If you were going to start a super-secret group whose aim was to run the world, which of the following would you do?

a. Establish a Web site so everyone could see what you do and who your members are

b. Meet regularly in world capitals with high-profile politicians and academics giving speeches covered by the global media

c. List your organization in the Manhattan phone directory, one of the most regularly used references in the U.S.

d. All of the above

If you said "d," you could conceivably be speaking of the Trilateral Commission. According to some, this organization—despite a public goal of forging greater cooperation among the U.S., Western Europe, and Japan—has a hidden agenda: namely, to create an all-encompassing world government. Conspiracy theorists view the group's high profile as something of a ruse—a false front of sorts. Behind all the talk about enhancing relationships among economic superpowers is the implicit goal of "one worldism." Or, as the conspiracy-minded put it, total world domination.

So the Trilateral Commission (which derives its name from the three regions of the globe it represents) "bands together to protect its interests, and to ensure, in the developed nations, that political leaders were brought to power who would ensure that the global financial interests (of the Rockefellers and the other ruling elites) would be protected over the hoi poloi." At least, that's the claim of some of its critics, who often refer to the group as the "World Shadow Government."

What kinds of decisions do the members of the Trilateral Commission make that could be seen as evidence of a far-flung plot to rule the world? Conspiracy theorists will tell you that, for starters, they decide who heads the governments in their respective regions. They get presidents and prime ministers elected and are responsible for filling positions at the very highest level in the military and civilian government. And, of course, they control the banks.

The conspiracy theories about the Trilateral Commission have prospered not because of what's unknown but because of what's *known*. There is an immense amount of information available about the group: its history, stated objectives, position papers, roster of members, etc. This makes all the conspiracy theorizing seem pretty counterintuitive. The Trilateral Commission members themselves would, ostensibly, be among the first people to share information

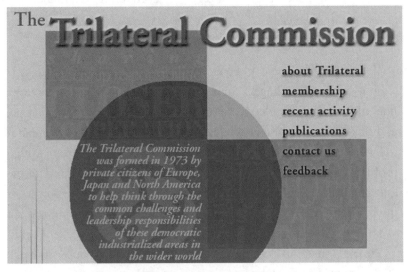

The homepage of the Web site for the Trilateral Commission—proof of openness or simply a public ruse? (Photo source: www.trilateral.org)

about the group (most are public figures, including several major media figures, such as newspaper editors and news anchors). So if there's no secrecy, what has aroused the suspicion of so many individuals and groups?

To begin with, there's the concentration of power. Take a look at the roster of members and you will see the most influential social, political, and economic titans on the planet.

Then there's the group's founder, international financier David Rockefeller, chairman of the Chase Manhattan Bank and head of his family's world financial empire. Lots of conspiracy theories are due simply to the disproportionate wealth of certain families, such as the Rockefellers (money might not be the root of all evil, but it certainly seems to be the root of most conspiracy theories).

Perhaps most convincing to those who look askance at the group are its successes. A couple of years after its founding in 1973, the group invited a fairly obscure Southern governor, Jimmy Carter, to join its ranks. His rapid rise through the political system and his unlikely presidency are evidence, conspiracy theorists say, of the group's power and influence. As one critic has noted:

> Carter, of course, campaigned as a "populist"—as a "man of the people"—as an "outsider" with no ties to the Establishment. The fact is, however, Carter, who said he'd never lie, was an elitist, an insider, the Trilateral Commission's "man on a white horse."

Several other presidential candidates and dozens of cabinet officers have also been members of the Trilateral Commission. And the Columbia University professor Zbigniew Brzezinski, who wrote the book in the early 1970s advocating the creation of such a commission, became Carter's National Security Adviser.

A Foreign Situation

One wouldn't think that such an organization, comprised of the most powerful bankers, politicians, academics, and media moguls,

Zbigniew Brzezinski advocated creating the Trilateral Commission and became the National Security Adviser to President Jimmy Carter. (Photo source: wikipedia. org/wiki/Zbigniew_Brzezinski)

would need much help ruling the world. But die-hard conspiracy theorists argue that the Trilateral Commission has been working in tandem for the past 30 years with another quasi-public, highly influential group called the Council on Foreign Relations.

Originally founded at the end of World War I as a sort of unofficial governmental study group, the Council is comprised of many of the same people who sit on the Trilateral Commission (its members have included Rockefellers, Henry Kissinger, George H. W. Bush, and Bill Clinton, as well as Supreme Court justices and the editor of the *New*

York Times). The Council on Foreign Relations, some argue, serves as a think tank for originating some of the ideas that are then promoted by the Trilateral Commission. The ideas promulgated by the Council, some say, all tend to argue for the creation of a New World Order, the end of national sovereignty, and the creation of an all-powerful global government. People suspicious of such consolidation point to global trade agreements like the North American Free Trade Agreement (NAFTA) and General Agreement on Tariffs and Trade (GATT) and the creation of the World Trade Organization (WTO) to bolster their arguments that the political power structure in the Western world is tilting toward "one worldism."

As Melvin Sickler, a critic wary of this worldwide realignment, puts it, "There are two groups of elite men and women in particular that most people do not know about, but which are a clear threat and danger to the freedom of the American people. These are the Council on Foreign Relations (CFR) and the Trilateral Commission."

Sins of Commission

What is it that the members of the Trilateral Commission actually *do* when they get together for their annual meeting? Mostly they make lots of recommendations, usually in the form of "draft reports" that suggest some course of action that Western governments ought to take. The Commission's Web site (www.trilateral.org) alludes broadly to issues of "partnership." Critics see such benign language as a smokescreen for its more insidious agenda, from promoting bank loans to impoverished Third World countries to dismantling trade barriers and creating global "free trade" zones. Some conspiracy theorists claim that the U.S. Congress does the bidding for the Trilateral Commission, rubber-stamping its New World Order agenda. As one commentator has noted:

> Few Americans really understood back in 1993 what would happen under GATT because few ever heard of it— too many simply bought the propaganda from politicians and the rest were more interested in sports, porn, drugs,

booze or fun times. Guess how many members of the
entire Congress read GATT? One—former Senator Hank
Brown. He's the only senator who read this 28,000 page
treaty and stated emphatically that no way would he vote
for it. Yet, the rest of the Senate ratified this insidious
treaty *without ever reading it.*

Those who warn of the commission's power and its disproportionate influence say the seeds of the Commission's destructive impact
were sown by the group's architect, Brzezinski, in his book *Between
Two Ages*, where he wrote: "Resist as it might, the American system
is compelled gradually to accommodate itself to this emerging international context, with the U.S. government called upon to negotiate,
to guarantee, and to some extent, to protect the various arrangements
that have been contrived even by private business."

That notion that the U.S. government is beholden to private, or
even foreign, interests is what really rankles the Commission's critics, who point with alarm to the growth of military alliances (enlarg-
ing the North Atlantic Treaty Organization [NATO, www.nato.int],
for example) and to diplomatic agreements that bind all nations into
a common economic or political cause. While such arrangements are
often defended as necessary in a world shrinking because of advances
in telecommunications and the free-flow of capital, conspiracy theorists see the situation quite differently. They see the Trilateral
Commission's work as an inexorable move toward a United Nations-
dominated world government, with the U.S. losing its clout as a
superpower and its citizens surrendering their constitutional rights in
favor of "global partnerships." They see the tentacles of the Trilateral
Commission choking capitalism and U.S. sovereignty. As one commentator has argued, if you understand the "one world government"
movement, then you can "connect the dots as to why Congress
refuses to abolish the unconstitutional, privately owned Federal
Reserve, immediately withdraw from the United Nations and the continuing passage of these devastating trade treaties," adding "Our
Republic is perilously close to being destroyed."

Conspiracy theorists see the expansion of groups such as NATO (headquarters pictured here) as evidence of a move toward "one worldism." (Photo source: www.nato.int)

Between the Lines

The fact that so much of what the Trilateral Commission does is so public puts this conspiracy theory into a special class, rather like a magician who explains the trick *before* his performance. This seems to really enrage some of the Internet-based critics of the Commission, who seem disheartened in their inability to get people to look at what the Trilateral Commission is doing. Can it be called a cover-up if a group issues press releases trumpeting its plans for greater global cooperation? If meetings are held every year in high-profile places with advanced news coverage and a Web site linking to the group's own policy statements? If you can get names and addresses of all the group's acknowledged members? How can this be a conspiracy when it's happening in the most public, brightly lit corridors in the Western world?

Well, there's the *official* purpose of the group, theorists say, and the *real* purpose. And though those two are closely related, the difference is significant, they argue. Who, after all, can be against "greater cooperation" among the countries of the world? But if that cooperation comes at the loss of self-determination, then what officially looks like a blessing becomes, in reality, a curse. And the Internet watchers who ride herd over the Trilateral Commission will tell you they certainly know the difference.

In Their Sites

In the continuing effort to perhaps disguise its conspiracy by being as public as possible, the Trilateral Commission itself offers an extensive Web site (www.trilateral.org), featuring links to a roster of current members and a wealth of publications, as well as a detailed history of the organization and the philosophy behind the group:

> When the first triennium of the Trilateral Commission was launched in 1973, the most immediate purpose was to draw together—at a time of considerable friction among governments—the highest level unofficial group possible to look together at the key common problems facing our three areas. At a deeper level, there was a sense that the United States was no longer in the singular leadership position as it had been in earlier post World War II years, and that a more shared form of leadership—including Europe and Japan in particular—would be needed for the international system to navigate successfully the major challenges of the coming years.

For the non-suspicious, the site offers a fascinating glimpse into the workings of an alpha group of global movers and shakers. For the less convinced, phrases like "a more shared form of leadership" leap off the page as a warning about what this group wants to do to the formerly independent United States of America.

A good introductory overview of the perceived dangers of the group can be found at WorldNetDaily (www.worldnetdaily.com/news/article.asp?ARTICLE_ID=44965), in an analysis by columnist Devvy Kidd, who has also written about the "treasonous operation" of the Council on Foreign Relations, a group of "elitists out to destroy our constitutional republic … and merge all nations into a 'one world government.'" Regarding the Trilateral Commission, Kidd notes unequivocally that "The Trilateral Commission is another little known entity that is diligently and methodically working to destroy the sovereignty of this nation and put the United States under foreign rule—it is the twin monster of the CFR." WorldNetDaily hosts a variety of news articles, opinion pieces, and an archive of stories about the dangers of global cabals.

The article "Is the Trilateral Commission the Secret Organization that Runs the World?" from the Web site The Straight Dope (www.straightdope.com/classics/a2_295.html) would seem to promise another of those none-too-subtle exhortations that the Internet is increasingly known for. However, the article's overview of the conspiracy theory offers a thorough, even skeptical critique of the Trilateral Commission's reach:

> Among true believers, opinions about what the Trilateral Commission is up to fall roughly into two categories: the merely dubious and the totally insane. The John Birch Society and its conferees see the commission as the latest manifestation of the international conspiracy that is trying to create a one-world totalitarian state, or at least a New World Economic Order … the less extreme view is that while the Trilateralists may be well intentioned, the clubby atmosphere tends to create a climate of opinion (either socialist or fascist, depending on whether you're on the far right or far left) that is inimical to America's real interests.

No such skepticism exists on the Thirst for Justice Web site (www.prolognet.qc.ca/clyde/cfr.html). Calling the Trilateral Commission and the CFR "the two organizations that run the United States," the site's author, Melvin Sickler, provides Web surfers an extensive, if subjective, history of both organizations: "The Council on Foreign Relations was founded in 1921 by Edward Mandell House, who had been the chief advisor of President Woodrow Wilson … House was a Marxist whose goal was to socialize the United

States." Here's his take on the Trilateral Commission: "The Trilateral Commission was founded to work for the same goal: a one-world government." The site makes much of Jimmy Carter's ascension to the presidency as an example of the Commission's power and of the triumph of Brzezinski's social philosophy: "To think that the teacher in this relationship praised Marxism, and wanted to form a one-world government. And the student became the President of the United States."

Some good, general background about the Commission—free of the doom-and-gloom prophesying of many other sites—can be found on the "Trilateral Commission" page of SourceWatch (www.sourcewatch.org/index.php?title=Trilateral_Commission), a self-described "encyclopedia of people, issues and groups shaping the public agenda." The page mimics the look of Wikipedia and

Jimmy Carter's ascension to the presidency was due, some skeptics claim, to his involvement with the Trilateral Commission. (Photo source: www.jimmycarter library.org)

offers a comprehensive history, a section on the funding of the Commission, and four pages listing the group's officers and executive committee. The page also lists contact information for the Commission, including addresses, phone numbers, fax numbers, and email addresses.

One of the most intriguing and well-presented overviews of the Trilateral Commission is available through the Web site of an organization called the American Institute for Economic Research (www.cooperativeindividualism.org/aier_on_conspiracy_06.html). Taking as its jumping-off point the notion that "The degree to which secrecy—or conspiracy—plays a part in it cannot be reasonably ascertained. But there is much about it that ought to invite closer scrutiny," the site soberly assesses in think-tank-style prose the status and influence of the group:

> The Trilateral Commission has no official standing, in spite of the appearance of "commission" in its name. To the contrary, the Trilateral Commission membership may breach U.S. law for some of its members. This is not because, as some assert, the Trilateral Commission is an "illegal super-secret political party." But neither is it, as David Rockefeller claimed, merely a group of "private citizens of Western Europe, Japan and North America to foster a closer cooperation among these three regions on common problems."

The site raises some legitimate-sounding concerns about whether the Trilateral Commission is even a legal organization:

> Crucial to the question of American legality is the membership of many officials of foreign governments in Europe and Japan ... The Logan Act explicitly prohibits U.S. Citizens not in appropriate government positions from attempting to deal with foreign government officials on aspects of foreign relations. Yet this is precisely what the Trilateral Commission focuses on.

The site even offers a percentage breakdown of what types of people make up the Trilateral Commission:

- Think-tank academics: 40 percent

- Bankers and related legal executives: 25 percent

- Multinational corporate executives: 25 percent

- Labor union representatives: 5 percent

- Mass media representatives: 5 percent

Although the site labels the CFR as the "mouthpiece" of the Trilateral Commission, interested readers might want to seek out the CFR official Web site (www.cfr.org) to see what the group has to say for itself. The site "is designed to be an online resource for everyone in these turbulent times who wants to learn more about the complex international issues challenging policy-makers and citizens alike." Among its features are a history of the group's founding and development, lots of serious sounding, heavily researched articles about various regions of the globe, and a "mission statement" detailing the council's efforts to "better understand the world and the foreign policy choices facing the United States and other governments."

Is that a sincere declaration of intent or an understated masterpiece of propaganda? Don't ask the people at the Conspiracy Archive (www.conspiracyarchive.com/NWO/Council_Foreign_Relations. htm)—they see right through this sort of thing:

> CFR members in the mass media, education, and entertainment push their propaganda of "humanism" and world brotherhood. We should all live in peace under a world government, and forget about such selfish things as nationalities and patriotism. We can solve our own problems. We don't need God, or morals, or values: it's all relative, anyway, right? Because if we actually had some moral character and values, we might be able to discern that these people are actually EVIL.

So, the CFR is not just sneaky, but evil? The Conspiracy Archive notes that it's not only global domination, big-picture stuff, but "there are also allegations of involvement in gun running, drug smuggling, prostitution and sex slaves; and many mysterious assassinations and 'suicides' of witnesses and others who got too close to the truth." The Web site also provides links to an extensive array of articles connecting the Trilateral Commission to everyone from European Unionists to international Zionists.

An Elite Theory

Trying to prove a link between the Trilateral Commission and the structures of power in Western society has never been the challenge for conspiracy theorists. Nothing could be simpler, or more self-evident. President Ronald Reagan once hosted a reception for Commission members at the White House! That's a pretty clear indication that the group holds considerable sway in the corridors of

Are the Founding Fathers (shown here in a famous depiction of the signing of the U.S. Constitution) being subverted by the secret agenda of the Trilateral Commission? (Photo source: wikipedia.org/wiki/US_constitution)

power. But are they using that access to subvert the U.S. Constitution and realign the powers of the modern world into one all-powerful entity—one that would trump the autonomy of any of the member republics?

Commission members would no doubt dismiss such speculation as much paranoid nonsense, and they would refer interested persons to the lines of their precisely worded policy statements. Doubters have already read those lines, and everything in between.

The Hindenburg

The breathtaking spectacle of the massive, lighter-than-air zeppelins that once cruised the world's skies in the 1920s and 1930s is now the stuff of newsreels and coffee-table books. Heralded as one of the great advances in transcontinental transportation, dirigible flight seemed poised to displace ocean cruising as the preferred mode of travel for well-heeled globetrotters. That hope was accelerated—and then incinerated—by the mighty German airship *Hindenburg*.

Named after the president of Germany, Paul Von Hindenburg, the fabled airship stretched more than 800 feet from nose to tail—almost as long as the *Titanic*. Made of an aluminum-alloy metal frame, the ship was held aloft by a collection of hydrogen-filled bags. (The German engineers who designed the *Hindenburg* wanted to use the non-flammable gas helium, but the U.S. had enacted a military embargo on helium, so the engineers modified the ship to use hydrogen.) It contained cabins for 50 passengers and carried a crew of 61. It made its first flight on March 4, 1936, and after a year of transatlantic crossings, was refitted with an additional 10 cabins.

After its first full year of service, the *Hindenburg* was famous worldwide, having made more than a dozen round-trips across the Atlantic, with several well-publicized trips to the U.S. and Brazil helping to stir interest in the dirigible. But it was to be the airship's first voyage of its second year that would ensure it an ignominious place in the annals of aviation.

The *Hindenburg* was almost as long as another ill-fated vessel: the *Titanic*. (Photo source: www.unmuseum.org/hindenburg.htm)

Fire in the Sky

The golden age of zeppelins happened to coincide with the beginning of the golden age of broadcasting—a confluence that resulted in the *Hindenburg* becoming immortalized through perhaps the most famous radio news report ever recorded.

On May 6, 1937, as the *Hindenburg* was preparing to complete its first voyage of the new season, almost a thousand onlookers—and dozens of newsmen and cameramen—milled about the grounds of the Naval Air Station at Lakehurst, New Jersey, where the airship was headed to dock. The zeppelin had been delayed several hours by strong headwinds over the Atlantic Ocean, and its arrival was now being pushed back again because of an earlier series of slow-moving thunderstorms. As the weather cleared around 6 PM, the *Hindenburg*—which had been making long, languorous loops in the sky over the Jersey Shore—received the following message from the station:

Conditions now considered suitable for landing. Ground crew is ready. Thunderstorm over station, ceiling 2000 feet, visibility 5 miles to Westward, surface temperature 60. Surface winds west-northwest 8 knots, gusts under 20 knots, surface pressure 29.68.

As the flying behemoth approached the station, its arrival was chronicled by radio reporter Herb Morrison, who was taping a report for WLS radio in Chicago:

> Here it comes, ladies and gentlemen, and what a sight it is, a thrilling one, a marvelous sight. The sun is striking the windows of the observation deck on the Westward side and sparkling like glittering jewels on the background of black velvet ... Oh, Oh, Oh! ... It's burst into flames! Get out of the way, please, oh my, this is terrible, oh my, get out of the way, please! It is burning, bursting into flames, and is falling ... Oh, this is one of the worst ... Oh, it's a terrific sight. Oh, the humanity!

In just a matter of minutes, the *Hindenburg* had ignited in a fire that began with a tremendous explosion near its tail section and then quickly spread to enmesh the rest of the lumbering, sinking giant. Some passengers and crew members who had realized what was happening jumped several hundred feet to the ground, while others appeared to simply cling to the vessel as it became awash in smoke and flames. Burning debris rained from the sky on the ground crew and those who had gathered to meet the airship's passengers. Newsreel photographers captured the horrific scene on film, documenting the blistering speed at which the zeppelin immolated. Moments after the ship exploded, what was left of it crashed into the ground. Thirty-six people—roughly one-third of those aboard the ship—died in the accident. Several dozen others were seriously injured and burned.

Headlines and photographs in newspapers around the world the next day told the story of the great airship's conflagration but were unable to answer the main question: What caused the explosion?

Seventy years later, the search for that answer continues.

A Static Situation

Within days of the crash, a board of inquiry—conducted by the U.S. Department of Commerce—was convened. Its month-long investigation saw almost 100 witnesses, from scientists to onlookers, testify about the explosion. Representatives of the German government observed the proceedings and prepared their own report for the commission. The board ultimately concluded that the "most probable"

The *Hindenburg* burst into flames and crashed to the ground on May 6, 1937, killing 36 and injuring dozens more. (Photo source: www.unmuseum.org/hindenburg.htm)

cause of the explosion was a buildup of static electricity along the skin of the zeppelin, which ignited a leak from one of the hydrogen cells. But even the board of inquiry seemed to undercut its own findings, stating "In spite of thorough questioning of all witnesses [and] thorough inspection and search of the wreckage ... no completely certain proof can be found for any of the possibilities."

From the very beginning, sabotage had loomed as a real possibility. More than 20 years after the explosion, the airship's surviving captain, Max Pruss, was telling interviewers that he believed sabotage was the cause. Researcher Michael Mooney, in his 1972 book, *The Hindenburg*, revealed the existence of a cache of documents in the National Archives that seem to give credence to the sabotage theory. Mooney writes:

> Among these materials were letters forwarded from the Secretaries of Commerce and Interior reminding Solicitor South Trimble, Jr. that "a finding of sabotage might be cause for an international incident, especially on these shores." But while the Board of Inquiry did its best to avoid the discovery of sabotage in its public hearings, almost every dirigible man (including Captain Pruss, [et al.]) in private agreed that sabotage was the cause. Over the weeks while the Board of Inquiry conducted meetings during the day, both the German and the American commissioners and advisors held meetings at night to discuss, off the record, the inescapable evidence of sabotage before them.

Those who endorse the sabotage theory—and the governmental conspiracy to cover it up—make an interesting argument. The huge, internationally recognized airship, with its imposing swastikas on the tail fins, had come to symbolize the growing power and influence of the Nazi regime. Anyone who brought down the *Hindenburg* could, ostensibly, be seen as striking a blow against the German fatherland and its fervent leader, Adolf Hitler. What better time and place to destroy this symbol, they argue, than in front of the world press, with newsreels spooling and flashbulbs popping? Such an attack, they argue, might be a signal to the German resistance of the vulnerability of the Nazi power structure.

The advocates of sabotage suggest that the *Hindenburg* was not supposed to explode while still in flight, but shortly after the passengers and crew had safely disembarked (they argue the detonation was caused by a time bomb planted in the tail section). But for the delay caused by the thunderstorms, the bomb would have exploded just after the last passengers had disembarked but while the international media was still present to record the explosion, theorists maintain.

In the decades since the accident, a number of other possible causes have been put forward, from the suggestion that a bolt of lightning struck the zeppelin to the notion that someone might have shot at the airship from the ground. Recent scientific investigations have come to focus on the paint that coated the fabric wrapping the *Hindenburg*, noting its highly flammable qualities. But the idea of sabotage clings tenaciously to the historical wreckage of the downed airship.

Interest in the *Hindenburg*'s inglorious fall from grace continues unabated. There have been several nonfiction books, dozens of articles in scientific journals and popular magazines, novels, Hollywood movies, and a *National Geographic* special about the disaster. The *Hindenburg* was the last of the great airships, responsible for both generating worldwide interest in dirigible flight and singlehandedly ending the era of lighter-than-air passenger travel. In a century that saw humanity soar at jet speed, and set foot on the surface of the moon, the *Hindenburg* remains the totem of mankind's aerial aspirations. But the real tragedy of the *Hindenburg*, conspiracy theorists argue, is that airship travel became extinct as a result of governmental collusion and bureaucratic backroom dealing, rather than for any logical, scientific reason. If the board of inquiry had really done its job, they argue, then public fears about the safety of zeppelin travel would never have been stoked, and these wondrous, mammoth airships would be as common today as cruise ships in the Caribbean.

The *Shenandoah*, built in 1922, was the first American zeppelin, beginning the short-lived era of lighter-than-air travel in the U.S. (Photo source: www.cider presspottery.com/ZLA/greatzeps/american/Shenandoah.html)

But it *is* possible to return to the golden age of zeppelin travel—through the Internet and the many sites dedicated to zeppelin travel in general and the *Hindenburg* in particular. And for those who feel the truth has never come out, you need only sign on to your home computer to read the *real* story.

A Fly-by of the Best Sites

A good, general overview of the *Hindenburg*—its construction, destruction, and the various theories seeking to explain the tragedy—can be found at The Museum of UnNatural Mystery site (www.un museum.org/hindenburg.htm). The site features a quick, comprehensive account of zeppelin travel, from the first dirigible in 1852 to the start of World War II. The amount of background information is just right for someone who wants to learn about the *Hindenburg* but not immerse himself in the engineering or historical minutia of the period. The site reproduces the text but not the audio of the Herb Morrison broadcast, and it features still pictures but no video of the explosion. The various theories behind the explosion are dealt with quickly and efficiently, with no one theory being endorsed by the site's authors. The explanation for the electrostatic spark is offered in clear, reader-friendly prose, and the suggestion of sabotage is dealt with in equal measure, with the site pointing out, rather obviously, "If a saboteur was at work, it must have been one of the crew or passengers." To their credit, the site's authors identify the most likely candidates: a surviving passenger named Joseph Spah and a crewman named Eric Spehl (who is the favored candidate of most book-length studies endorsing the sabotage theory). Though the site doesn't take a position, it does note wistfully that after that fateful day in Lakehurst, "The zeppelin, once thought to be the wave of the future, was suddenly a thing of the past."

But zeppelins continue to evoke an almost sentimental attachment to those who admire their grace as well as their girth. A great site to learn more about the classic zeppelins—both German- and American-built—is The Great Zeppelins page (www.ciderpresspottery.com/ZLA/greatzeps/german/Hindenburg.html). The site offers a short catalog of the most noteworthy zeppelins, from, of course, the *Hindenburg* to that ship's most important precursor, the German-made *Graf Zeppelin*, the largest of its day in the decade before the *Hindenburg*. The roster of American-built airships is impressive, beginning with the *Shenandoah*, the first American-made zeppelin (which has secured its place in zeppelin annals because it was the first airship ever filled with helium, rather than hydrogen). Clicking on any of the links to the individual ships mentioned takes you to additional pages of history, trivia, and mechanical specifications. There's very little information about the actual explosion that felled the *Hindenburg* but quite a lot of background about the construction of the ship and the tension between its principle designer, Dr. Hugo Eckner, and the Nazi authorities. The site also provides information on the small but innovative line of zeppelins built by the British during the 1920s, reminding readers of the truly international character of the mid-1920s zeppelin craze.

Nothing fanned the fire of global interest in zeppelins like the massive *Hindenburg*, and few sites can claim the depth and breadth of the entry on the fabled airship in Wikipedia (en.wikipedia.org/wiki/Hindenburg_disaster). The site provides a daunting amount of historical and technical information, including the chemical makeup of the paint that coated the skin of the vessel ("iron oxide and cellulose acetate butyrate impregnated with aluminum powder") and the cost of a ticket from Germany to Lakehurst, New Jersey ($400). The site provides intriguing details about the various theories of the ship's destruction, including the American-German sabotage cover-up theory, noting, "proponents of the sabotage theory point out that any finding of sabotage would have been an embarrassment for the Nazi regime. Thus they speculate that such a finding was suppressed for political reasons." The site is also one of the few that also mentions the possibility that Hitler himself might have been behind the destruction of the *Hindenburg* because of the anti-Nazi views of its designer, Dr. Eckner. The site provides a thoughtful and scientifically grounded discussion of other theories, such as the static electricity theory, the lightning theory, the flammable paint theory, structural failure, the puncture theory, and even the Lugar Pistol theory (which suggests that someone on board the *Hindenburg* fired a shot at the hydrogen cells; a spent Lugar shell was reportedly found among the wreckage at the site).

Was it sabotage? (Photo source: en.wikipedia.org/wiki/Hindenburg_disaster)

Because interest in the *Hindenburg* remains active, history buffs might want to pay a visit to the place where the event unfolded. But if you can't make it to Lakehurst, you can check in with a couple of Web sites that provide lots of information about the *Hindenburg's* ground zero. The Navy Lakehurst Historical Society (NLHS) has an exhaustive site (www.nlhs.com) aimed at "preserving the heritage of Naval Air Station Lakehurst," which remains active today as the Naval Air Engineering Station. The site offers lots of photos, articles, and reference materials about the *Hindenburg*, as well as many other airships that frequently docked at the base. There are dozens of photos of the interior of the *Hindenburg* as well as the base's other hangars and former airships, and a history of the base's connection to airship travel (the zeppelins *Shenandoah*, the *Los Angeles,* and the *Akron* were all based at Lakehurst). If you still have questions after visiting the site, there are links to contact historians and researchers at the NLHS.

A less comprehensive but decidedly quirkier site dedicated to the *Hindenburg* crash site can be found at RoadsideAmerica.com (www.roadsideamerica.com/ attract/NJLAKhinden.html). Among the odd facts readers will discover here are that the Lakehurst Motel "has a big, blue blimp on its neon sign" and that "where the *Hindenburg* crashed is now a vast, empty expanse of crumbled asphalt mixed with occasional scrubby weeds." (The precise spot of the crash is marked by a little zeppelin that sits "atop a wind vane on a pole," while "the original giant Hangar No. 1 still stands, voluminous enough to hold a zeppelin.") There is also practical information for potential tourists, from where to get a "special *Hindenburg* pass" to visit the base to mention of the nearby Air Ship Tavern and hours of operation for the Lakehurst Historical Society Museum.

After the crash, the American government undertook an investigation into the cause of the disaster. Although conspiracy theorists largely discount the findings, the report—complete with the testimony of dozens of witnesses—is available online through the Federal Bureau of Investigation (FBI) Web site (foia.fbi.gov/foiaindex/ hindburg.htm). The four-part report, totaling 337 pages, can be accessed through downloadable PDF files.

Visitors to Lakehurst Naval Air Station can visit the exact spot where the massive zeppelin crash landed. (Photo source: www.roadsideamerica.com/attract/NJLAKhinden.html)

Those who have never seen the footage of the *Hindenburg's* spectacular immolation can watch a three-minute video of the approach, explosion, and brief, chaotic aftermath at the British Newsfilm Online site (newsfilm.bufvc.ac.uk) (just type "Hindenburg" into the search box). The raw, unedited footage is grim but undeniably compelling.

Audiophiles and radio history buffs should check in with www.otr.com/hindenburg.html, a comprehensive site dedicated to the radio report filed by Herb Morrison, whose famous firsthand account remains one of the most chilling and remarkable reports ever broadcast. The site provides lots of behind-the-scenes and technical information about Morrison's broadcast: "Engineer Charles Nehlsen was manning the Presto recorder. The recorder includes a large turntable with a 16-inch platter, a heavy-duty lathe, which would actually cut into the wax disc, and an amplifier." As the site notes, the *Hindenburg*'s explosion marked a turn not just in aviation history but also in mass media. "This event reflected the potential power of radio broadcasting immediately before and during World War II as the Murrow Boys and others would bring the war home to America via the airwaves."

It's important to remember that the *Hindenburg* saga unfolded against the backdrop of the rise of the Third Reich in Germany. Web surfers can reacquaint themselves with this critically important chapter of modern world history with a terrific Web site dedicated to German history (www.germanculture.com.ua). This massive site is divided into subject areas (business/economy, food, literature, philosophy, etc.) and historical periods. The lengthy but readable essay titled "The Third Reich: Consolidation of Power" provides an essential overview of the intellectual and militaristic currents in the air during the period of the *Hindenburg*'s ascension. Complex social movements and the growth of Nazi-ism are rendered clear and comprehensible, as when the site notes: "Many Germans supported it, some out of opportunism, some because they liked certain aspects of it such as full employment, which was quickly achieved. The regime also brought social order, something many Germans welcomed after 15 years of political and economic chaos." Against this backdrop, the *Hindenburg* can be seen as a symbol of Germany's rising power.

The Future, Adrift

The *Hindenburg* remains a potent and cautionary emblem of the birth of the modern world, from its technological innovations to its enigmatic end. It foretold, in both its splendor and its ignominy, the grace and horror of the unfolding century. And the exact cause of its annihilation is just as likely to attract the curious as the mighty dirigible itself did as it passed in awesome beauty through the world's skies.

The Philadelphia Experiment

In the early years of World War II, German U-boats possessed a distinct advantage over the ships they targeted: maneuverability. In 1942, enemy submarines torpedoed and sank more than 1,000 Allied ships, causing the British and U.S. navies to rethink the design of their so-called destroyer, which played the vital role of defending larger vessels. Within a year, the U.S. Navy built and launched new, smaller ships—christened "destroyer escorts"—that could better protect the fleet from enemy subs due to much improved maneuverability.

But would that be enough? These destroyer escorts would still be susceptible to magnetically guided torpedoes and magnetically triggered mines. The U.S. Navy, using a process invented by a Canadian chemist and widely employed by its British counterpart, experimented with "degaussing"—a procedure that neutralized a ship's magnetic field by wrapping its hull in electrical cables carrying a specified current. "It could be said that degaussing, correctly done, makes a ship 'invisible' to the sensors of magnetic mines," the Naval Historical Center noted.

The U.S. Navy, however, pushed scientific possibilities even further, contend some conspiracists, in the hopes of achieving true invisibility for its ships and, as a result, an unmatched military trump card. Pursuing such a project in 1943 on a destroyer escort in the Philadelphia Naval Yard, the Navy actually succeeded, according to the claims of a persistent conspiracy theory. While the "Philadelphia Experiment" supposedly rendered the ship invisible to the naked eye, another unintended outcome—along with unanticipated "side effects" on the crew—caused the Navy to scrap its research, forever classifying what conspiracy theorists have dubbed "Project Rainbow" *above top secret.*

A Strange and Mysterious Berth

The story of the alleged Philadelphia Experiment remained unknown for more than a decade, until amateur astronomer Morris Jessup published *The Case for the UFO* in 1955. In his book and subsequent publicity tour, Jessup argued that the U.S. space program ought to pay more attention to Albert Einstein's Unified Field Theory, arguing that antigravity and electromagnetism (which he theorized UFOs utilized for flight) rather than rocketry would "establish effective and economical space travel." Then, in January 1956, Jessup received a letter from Carlos Miguel Allende, who wrote that the U.S. Navy had indeed researched Einstein's theories. In fact, Allende claimed, it had applied them in an experiment on the USS *Eldridge*, providing the first account of what has become known as the Philadelphia Experiment.

According to the conspiracy theory known as the Philadelphia Experiment, the U.S. Navy rendered the destroyer escort the USS *Eldridge* invisible during tests in 1943 and even caused it to teleport several hundred miles before reappearing seconds later. (Photo source: www.softwareartist.com/philexp.html)

Retrofitted with special equipment, the destroyer escort supposedly underwent a test on October 28, 1943, at the Philadelphia Naval Yard. An electromagnetic field enveloped the ship—accounting for a "greenish fog"—and forced light to bend around the massive hulk. The *Eldridge* vanished. As it began to reappear, a sudden flash of blue light preceded the ship's second disappearance. This time, however, the *Eldridge* simultaneously appeared in the naval yard in Norfolk, Virginia—300 miles away. Then, in a matter of minutes, it reappeared in a green fog at the dock in Philadelphia. The experiment resulted in an unplanned effect: teleportation.

Without Carlos Allende (also known as Carl Allen), it seems there would have been no Philadelphia Experiment. Did he really witness successful invisibility tests? Was he an alien with knowledge of the experiment and how it might work? Or was he the mastermind of an elaborate hoax? (Photo source: web.archive. org/web/20020601165207/http://www.parascope.com/en/articles/allen de.htm)

Allende, in his letter to Jessup, claimed to have witnessed parts of the extraordinary event from aboard the SS *Andrew Furuseth*. Though the experiment was successful, he claimed the crew suffered horrific fates. Some went insane; others caught fire. Sailors vanished into thin air. Even worse, several sailors became fused to the ship, body parts bonded to bulkheads and the deck. Allende, referencing an article in an unnamed newspaper about a bar fight involving survivors of the experiment, claimed that crew members instantaneously disappeared from sight. The Navy terminated the experiment.

Skeptical but curious, Jessup sent a postcard to Allende asking for evidence. He received a response later that spring from Allende, now calling himself Carl M. Allen, who failed to provide any corroboration or details. Jessup lost interest. But a year later, in 1957, the Office of Naval Research (ONR) in Washington, D.C., was mailed, anonymously, a copy of *The Case for the UFO* and invited Jessup to its facility to have a look. The paperback contained extensive annotations—apparently written by three different "people" in a conversational manner, as if they were passing the book back and forth. "Mr. A," "Mr. B," and "Jemi"—who presented themselves as otherworldly beings—each used a different color ink, and the annotations included references to the knowledge of the Philadelphia Experiment as well as seemingly well-informed commentary on Jessup's theories about UFOs, force fields, space travel, and the like. Jessup recognized the handwriting as that of Allen.

The Varo Corporation, a military research firm, soon reprinted a handful of the annotated versions of the book and included the correspondence from Allen to Jessup. It has become know as the Varo Edition.

On April 20, 1959, Jessup committed suicide—attaching a hose from the exhaust pipe to the interior of his car, while running, at a Florida park. In 1969, Allen confessed to the Aerial Phenomena Research Organization that it was all a hoax, wrote Robert Goerman in an article, "Alias Carlos Allende: The Mystery Man Behind the Philadelphia Experiment," which appeared in the October 1980 issue of *FATE* magazine. Ten years later, however, Allen recanted—though Goerman revealed that Allen (often described as a drifter from a small

Pennsylvania town and not an alien) sent copies of the annotated book to his parents asserting that he co-wrote it.

Nonetheless, conspiracy theories still abound purporting that the Navy did indeed achieve optical invisibility and teleportation that fall day in 1943 at the Philadelphia Naval Yard. Several books have propelled that notion through the years, including 1979's *The Philadelphia Experiment: Project Invisibility*, by William L. Moore and Charles Berlitz. Criticized as speculative at best, the authors have also been accused of plagiarizing parts of the novel *Thin Air*, by George E. Simpson and Neil R. Burger, published the year before, which tells the story of a fictional investigation into an experiment gone awry aboard the *Eldridge* in 1943. Yet it remains an oft-cited source among conspiracy theorists. Then came the sci-fi/fantasy film *The Philadelphia Experiment* in 1984, which added time travel to the invisibility/teleportation mix.

Why then, if the birth of the Philadelphia Experiment story originated from one unreliable source as an apparent hoax, do the conspiracy theories persevere?

Invisible Proof

While the available evidence seems to suggest no such experiment—on the *Eldridge* or any other ship—ever took place, conspiracy theorists conjecture that the lack of proof is the consequence of a massive cover-up.

The Navy has repeatedly and categorically denied the claims of the Philadelphia Experiment conspiracists. In fact, its review of the *Eldridge*'s records—deck log and war diary—reveal the ship was never in Philadelphia between its August 27 commissioning and December 1943. Conspiracy theorists respond to this "fact" by arguing that these documents could have easily been altered. And why did the ONR take so much interest in the annotated copy of *The Case for the UFO*? The official response is that it didn't but that individual officers used their own time and money to produce the Varo Edition, according to an "Information Sheet" released by the agency in 1996:

Two officers, then assigned to ONR, took a personal interest in the book ... [and] personally had the book retyped
and arranged for reprint ... The officers and their personal
belongings have left ONR many years ago, and ONR does
not have a file copy of the annotated book.

Spurred on by this interest, Jessup began to investigate the possibility that the Navy actually did perform the experiment. According
to many conspiracists, his suicide—on the same day he was supposedly scheduled to meet with Dr. Mason Valentine (known for his
research into Atlantis and the Bermuda Triangle) and share his discoveries—was no suicide but a murder perpetrated by the government. But even Jessup's own daughter, interviewed in a History
Channel special on the Philadelphia Experiment, suspected he killed
himself when she was first told he was dead.

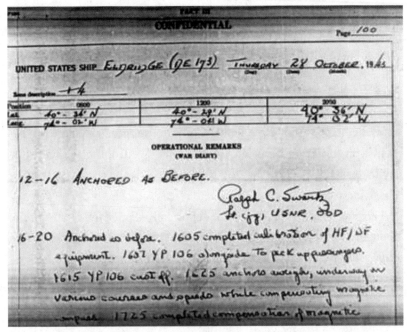

The official log entry for October 28, 1943—the supposed date of the
Philadelphia Experiment—places the ship in New York. While the records from its
August commissioning to the end of 1943 reveal the USS *Eldridge* was never in
Philadelphia, conspiracists argue that the entries could have been doctored as part
of a cover-up. (Photo source: www.softwareartist.com/philexp.html)

Conspiracy theorists also point to Einstein's involvement with the U.S. Navy at the time. The Naval Historical Center acknowledges that "During 1943–1944, Einstein was a part-time consultant with the Navy's Bureau of Ordnance, undertaking theoretical research on explosives and explosions." Skeptics allege—despite "no indication that Einstein was involved in research relevant to invisibility or to teleportation"—the physicist's "official" role served as a cover story for his *real* work: the application of his Unified Field Theory.

In 1999, at the first reunion of the *Eldridge*'s crew, the case for the conspiracy theory seemed to suffer a major blow. "The *Eldridge*, they said yesterday, may well have been invisible to Philadelphia because it was never in Philadelphia," reported Lacy McCrarey for the *Philadelphia Inquirer*. The sailors were "laughing at reports that their ship was involved in a top-secret World War II experiment," according to the article. "I think it's somebody's pipe dream," one said; "I have not the slightest idea how these stories got started," another added; "It never happened," yet another sailor said. The conspiracy theorists, however, have an explanation, or two, for the crew's dismissal of the alleged experiment: The government brainwashed the experiment's survivors, or the Navy employed a "special" crew during the experiment.

These numerous speculative claims have found a home on the Internet, helping to keep alive a conspiracy theory that might otherwise have faded as nothing more than a fabulous hoax. But the opposing arguments are just as prevalent on the Web (if not more so), making for some interesting online debates about whether the Navy achieved—or even attempted—the most remarkable feat in human history.

Traveling Through (Cyber) Space and Time

The Varo Edition of *The Case for the UFO* played a key role, along with the two letters from Allende to Jessup, in originating the Philadelphia Experiment conspiracy theory. With a very limited number of copies printed by the military research company in the late 1950s, nearly all of which remained in the hands of some officers

Along with official ship logs, the crew of the USS *Eldridge* emphatically claim that it never docked in the Philadelphia Navy Yard, shown here from the air in the 1940s. (Photo source: www.softwareartist.com/philexp.html)

within the ONR and the author of the original book, reading the annotated version was all but impossible. Now, however, anyone with Internet access can scroll through its pages. A PDF of a facsimile, produced by Saucerian Press in 1973 from an original copy (www.cassiopaea.org/cass/Varo-Jessup.pdf) provided by a close friend of Jessup, offers some background information on Jessup himself, as well as a brief discussion regarding ONR and Varo's involvement in reprinting the annotated version. The 165-page document also contains the all-important Allende letters—a glimpse into the genesis of a conspiracy theory and an opportunity to compare Allen's writing with the annotations by "Mr. A," "Mr. B," and "Jemi." As "Mr. A" notes:

U.S. NAVYS FORCE-FIELD EXPEIRIMENTS 1943 OCT. PRODUCED INVISIBILITY OF CREW & SHIP. FEARSOM RESULTS. SO TERRIFYING AS TO, FORTUNATELY, HALT FURTHER RESEARCH.

Did these characters have inside knowledge of experiments at the Philadelphia Naval Yard? Were they extraterrestrials? Or were they all really one person—a human—intent on constructing an elaborate hoax?

Robert Goerman, for one, argues the latter in his article on Allende first published in *FATE* magazine more than 20 years ago and now archived on the Web (web.archive.org/web/20020601165207/http://www.parascope.com/en/articles/allende.htm). After beginning an investigation in an attempt to figure out the true identity of Allende and his story of the vanishing ship, Goerman realized his neighbors were the parents of the mystery man, leading to revealing clues. In the end, the writer makes a compelling case "that the legend of Carl Allen/Carlos Allende is mostly fiction." As Goerman writes:

> Think about this for a moment. Here we have an extraordinary experiment to determine the feasibility of creating an invisible, invincible naval fleet; the experiment, conducted under security-conscious wartime conditions, is so sensitive that it is above top secret.
>
> If we are to believe Allen, our naval hierarchy abandoned sanity and historical precedent by conducting an experiment of enormous importance in broad daylight using a badly needed destroyer escort vessel which at the moment was supposed to be guarding a convoy of merchant supply ships from Axis torpedoes; not only that, but naval authorities conducted this test so dangerously close to the S.S. *Andrew Furuseth* that Allen claims that he was able to insert his arm "INTO THAT TERRIFIC FLOW."

The Naval Historical Center's Philadelphia Experiment Web page (www.history.navy.mil/faqs/faq21-1.htm) is worth a quick visit in that it provides a summary of the *Eldridge*'s movements during the time frame in question, further injecting doubt into the conspiracy theory: "*Eldridge* was never in Philadelphia." Die-hard researchers can purchase the ship's entire World War II records. The page also offers specific information regarding the whereabouts of the SS *Andrew*

Furuseth, from which Allen claims to have witnessed the *Eldridge*'s teleportation to Norfolk. Its conclusion: "*Eldridge* and *Andrew Furuseth* were not even in Norfolk at the same time."

The Skeptic's Dictionary entry on the Philadelphia Experiment (skepdic.com/philadel.html) presents an overview of the conspiracy theory, filled with useful links, from a decidedly debunking point of view ("The simple truth is that Allen made it all up"). The site also excerpts an interview of Edward Dudgeon, who claims he was aboard a ship harbored next to the *Eldridge*, by UFO investigator Jacques Vallee, and provides a link to the full interview.

In Vallee's "Anatomy Of A Hoax: The Philadelphia Experiment 50 Years Later" (www.rense.com/ufo/philahoax.htm), Dudgeon argues that the degaussing process probably started the rumors of "invisibility" and that a common electrical storm (known as St. Elmo's fire) accounted for the green glow. He also claims to be one of the two soldiers who, according to Allen and others, vanished during a bar fight:

> Two of us were minors. I told you I cheated on my enlistment papers. The waitresses scooted us out the back door as soon as trouble began and later denied knowing anything about us. We were leaving at two in the morning. The *Eldridge* had already left at 11 p.m. Someone looking at the harbor that night [might] have noticed that the *Eldridge* wasn't there any more and it did appear in Norfolk. It was back in Philadelphia harbor the next morning, which seems like an impossible feat: if you look at the map you'll see that merchant ships would have taken two days to make the trip. They would have required pilots to go around the submarine nets, the mines and so on at the harbor entrances to the Atlantic. But the Navy used a special inland channel, the Chesapeake-Delaware Canal, that bypassed all that. We made the trip in about six hours.

In a strongly worded "Rebuttal" posted on the same page, however, "Special Civilian Investigator" Marshall Barnes challenges Vallee's credibility and Dudgeon's story, calling the interview "a deliberate, premeditated, disinformation work executed using the foreknowledge of propaganda, disinformation and counter-intelligence tactics."

The most intriguing, and most bizarre, character involved in the debate over whether the Philadelphia Experiment actually occurred is Al Bielek. After seeing the movie *The Philadelphia Experiment*, Bielek (who has a doctorate in physics) began recalling things about his past, namely that while aboard the *Eldridge* during the experiment, he jumped ship during teleportation and time-traveled to the year 1983—to another government-sponsored project in Montauk, Long Island. There, in the future, he was brainwashed and forgot that his real name was actually Ed Cameron. His Web site, The Philadelphia Experiment & Montauk Survivor Accounts (www.bielek.com), is a wild ride and a must visit. Here's an excerpt from a description of Al's "brother," Duncan Cameron (who, by the way, is responsible for the creation of Bigfoot):

> Al Bielek says that before the USS Eldridge rematerialized, Duncan jumped back off the ship and returned back to 1983.
>
> He was used extensively as a psychic in the Montauk project. During one of the experiments, Duncan Cameron lost his "time lock" and began to age one year for every hour that passed.
>
> The time engineers at Montauk went back in time (to 1950) and convinced Duncan's original father, Alexander Cameron to sire another son. When done, they removed Duncan's soul and put it into the new child. This person is who we know today as Duncan Cameron.

The site features dozens of interviews with these "survivors" available for download in audio files, as well as a CD and DVD for sale. "Because these projects are so secretive, gaining hard evidence is nearly impossible," the site's author states on the homepage. "However, that doesn't mean the projects never happened." As one might expect, there's also a site that goes to great lengths to debunk the self-proclaimed time traveler (www.bielek-debunked.com).

The Philadelphia Experiment from A–Z Web site (www.soft wareartist.com/philexp.html) by Andrew Hochheimer—often interviewed when the conspiracy theory is the subject of a television program—is a more comprehensive online destination, not just concerned with Bielek. From a robust, annotated list of Web sites and other reference materials to a brief overview of the legend and a gallery of *Eldridge* photos, the site serves as a valuable portal into the corners of cyberspace occupied by discussion of "Project Rainbow."

Not Fade Away

"If someone were to write a book telling the *real* story," concluded Goerman, "its title might be *The Philadelphia Hoax: Project Gullibility*." While many tend to agree it was a hoax—mainly because the story originates from a single unreliable source with no evidence to back it up—the story of the *Eldridge*'s magical mystery tour in

Despite being given to the Royal Hellenic Navy during this ceremony in 1951 and rechristened the *Leon* by the Greek Navy, the legend of the USS *Eldridge* lives on. (Photo source: www.history.navy.mil/faqs/faq21-1.htm)

1943 persists. And the Philadelphia Experiment conspiracy theory, fascinating and fantastical, isn't likely to disappear any time soon. In part, that's a direct result of the lack of proof in support of the claims. As one Web site noted:

> [T]he government has been known to cover up because of national security before. An example of such a situation would be the Manhattan project … and no word was ever said about it until it was obvious that we had an atomic bomb.

But more than any other reason, it's the idea that invisibility and teleportation are possible that keeps the Philadelphia Experiment alive. We wish it were true; we want it to be true. It's why the words science fiction and fantasy are often interchanged. After all, who wouldn't want the power to disappear from sight or travel hundreds of miles instantaneously without ever having to pay for airfare? But when it comes to how these phenomena might be applied by those with power, perhaps science fiction is better than reality.

Freemasonry

The oldest "secret society" still in existence today, the Order of Free and Accepted Masons, is also the largest. A fraternal organization with more than 5 million members throughout the world, the all-boys club requires belief in a "Supreme Being," though not necessarily the God of any organized religion. Instead, religious tolerance, according to members, is one of the important precepts of Freemasonry, as are the principles of liberty, equality, and fraternity. Masons say participation in the organization—which entails first filling out a petition, garnering sponsorship from two members, and obtaining the votes of members via secret ballot—is simply a means to better oneself (through introspection and intellectual discussion) and better the communities in which one lives (through charity and philanthropy). The fraternity facilitates, members say, social and professional networking opportunities.

And although much of the public typically associates Masonry with secrecy, members often argue that "the Craft" (as it is often called) isn't even a true *secret society* but more a *society with secrets*. "Their grand secret is that they have no secret," said Steven C. Bullock, author of *Revolutionary Brotherhood: Freemasonry and the Transformation of the American Social Order*, echoing the sentiments once expressed by one of the more famous Masons, Benjamin Franklin. Richard E. Fletcher, executive secretary of the Masonic Service Association of North America, thinks privacy is often mistaken for secrecy: "While he is being challenged to look inward at himself as a person, he is going to have to self-reflect, contemplate, think. This can't be done in a public forum."

There are, however, esoteric traditions: secret handshakes, closed meetings, rituals, symbols and signs, and an oath of secrecy (supposedly enforced by severe penalties). Couple that with its august roster of members—Founding Fathers, presidents, prime ministers, and elected and appointed government officials, among other influential and powerful members of society—and Freemasonry becomes ripe for speculation by the conspiracy-minded. The theorizing about Freemasonry's powerful role in orchestrating some of history's most significant events, as evidenced by the prevalence of Web sites alleging the Craft's objective of worldwide dominance, ranges from the American Revolution and the 9/11 attacks to the staging of the Moon landing and the assassination of JFK. Some "anti-Masons" see the group as part of a Zionist plan to control the world; other conspiracists point to its connections to the Bavarian Illuminati as one clue of Freemasonry's effort to create a New World Order; some assert that Freemasonry is an occult society that worships Lucifer. No matter the conspiracy theory, Masonry—which has been subject to both political and religious opposition throughout its history—is time and again cast in the role of villain.

A Mysterious Foundation

"Ask five different people for the origins of the Freemasons and you may get five different explanations," one Web site notes.

Some trace Freemasonry roots back to the ancient Egyptian civilization. Others say Masons embrace a different mythology—the murder of Hiram Abiff, architect of King Solomon's Temple (built in Jerusalem in 967 BC), when he refused to reveal the secret of the temple and Masonry to three assailants. The fraternity's initiation rituals, it is believed, involve the re-enactment of this murder. The Freemasons have also been linked to the Knights Templar, an order of crusading monks arrested by King Philip IV of France and outlawed by the pope in the early 14th century; they worked "underground" for

The Square and Compass—one of the most recognizable Freemasonry symbols—represents not only the organization's origin as a trade guild, but also its code of conduct: "square their actions by the square of virtue" and "circumscribe their desires and keep their passions within due bounds toward all mankind." (Photo source: www.freemasonry.bcy.ca)

more than three centuries, some say, before resurfacing in the 1700s as the Freemasons.

The actual origins of Freemasonry, according to neutral historians, can be found during the Middle Ages, when skilled stone workers—traveling throughout England, Scotland, and France for jobs building the great cathedrals of the time—formed guilds, or unions, with secret handshakes and passwords to prove their status when they arrived in a new place. The official logo of Freemasonry, in fact, is an interlocked square and compass (tools of the trade, yes, but also symbolic of the group's philosophy). Eventually, the trade guilds evolved, as non-craftsmen were allowed membership, from an "operative" group to a "speculative" (or philosophical) fraternity known as Freemasons. The combining of four lodges in London in 1717 into the first Grand Lodge gave birth to modern Freemasonry.

The Cornerstone of Controversy

Freemasonry has a long history of attracting criticism and, in some instances, persecution, as well as charges of conspiracy.

Stephanie Watson, in an article titled "How Freemasons Work" for HowStuffWorks.com, provides a synopsis of just how deep the early suspicions of the society ran:

> In 1737, King Louis XV banned the Freemasons in France. A year later, Pope Clement XII forbade Catholics from becoming Freemasons on penalty of excommunication, and the Portuguese government made Freemasonry punishable by death.

In 1798, John Robison only furthered misgivings about Freemasonry when he published his exposé, *Proofs of a Conspiracy against All Religions and Governments of Europe*. In it he asserted that Adam Weishaupt—a Jesuit priest and founder of the Illuminati (an atheistic secret society formed in Germany in 1776 in an effort to create a New World Order)—had joined the Freemasons in 1777 to carry on with his plan when the Bavarian government put a stop to his former organization. Robison led the charge, which would gain in popularity through the years, that Freemasons were responsible for the French Revolution.

Many conspiracy theorists have also come to see the hand of Freemasonry in the American Revolution—with good reason. George Washington, Benjamin Franklin, John Hancock, Paul Revere, and a third of the signers of the Constitution were Masons. Washington actually wore his Mason apron while dedicating the U.S. Capitol. The reverse side of the Great Seal of the United States, which is full of Masonic symbolism and perhaps even a New World Order message, appeared for the first time when Franklin D. Roosevelt (a Mason) authorized its placement on the back of the $1 bill in 1935. The theorizing associated with the seal, as well as the symbolism found in the layout of Washington, D.C., is a more modern development in the conspiratorial world. At the time of the Revolutionary War and its aftermath, however, Masonry did not warrant much significant inquiry or protest. But that all changed in 1826, when William Morgan (a former Freemason from the town of Batavia, New York) announced he would pen a tell-all, exposing the society's secrets to

George Washington, depicted here wearing his Masonic apron (which he wore to the dedication of the U.S. Capitol), is perhaps the most famous Freemason and among a group of Masons in leadings roles of the American Revolution. (Photo source: people.howstuff works.com/freemason.htm)

the world. The print shop was set ablaze, and Morgan was abducted and never found (dead or alive). The Freemasons who kidnapped him received light sentences from Mason-filled juries, triggering outrage among a public that assumed Morgan had been murdered. An anti-Masonry movement commenced, spurring the creation of the Anti-Masonic Party that, though short-lived, ran a presidential candidate in 1828 and 1832.

A century later, a different type of anti-Masonry took root in Nazi Germany. Hitler viewed Freemasonry as a tool of the Jewish people to fulfill what he saw as the prophecy of the *Protocols of the Elders of Zion* (see Chapter 10), as he notes in this excerpt from *Mein Kampf*:

> To strengthen his political position he tries to tear down the racial and civil barriers which for a time continue to restrain him at every step. To this end he fights with all the tenacity innate in him for religious tolerance—and in Freemasonry, which has succumbed to him completely, he has an excellent instrument with which to fight for his aims and put them across. The governing circles and the higher strata of the political and economic bourgeoisie are brought into his nets by the strings of Freemasonry, and never need to suspect what is happening.

Deemed political prisoners by Hitler, an estimated 80,000 to 200,000 Freemasons died as a result of the Nazi philosophy and regime. The notion that Freemasonry is part of a larger Zionist plot to control the world survived the Hitler years: Under Saddam Hussein, the Ba'ath Party of Iraq considered it a felony to "promote or acclaim Zionist principles, including Freemasonry," and Hamas continues to take this anti-Masonry stance.

Some supporters of Freemasonry have argued that the rhetoric of its critics today mirrors that of the Nazis. And while modern conspiracy theories of Freemasonry's role in the world run rampant, most focus on the political, especially involving the American government (more than a dozen U.S. presidents were Masons). Most conspiracy theorists even argue that the majority of Freemasons know little about their own organization. As Terry Melanson, in an article titled "Freemasonry, Conspiracy Within, Initiation and the Brotherhood" (available at www.conspiracyarchive.com), notes:

> The majority of Masons today don't have a clue as to the true meaning of their rituals and symbols. And they certainly cannot be called bad people. Misled, yes, and most really are the good natured philanthropists helping their community, that we see outwardly. You see it is not

required of initiates to ascend any higher than that of the third degree Master Mason. They know there are another 30 degrees if one wished to continue, but the initiation process is a tedious and drawn out affair (it might take a year to reach the third degree), which the participants, for the most part, are happy it's over with. For them it is good that they not continue. And that's just the way higher initiates, or adepts, like it.

It's this secret society within the secret society, conspiracists argue, that spreads the influence of Freemasonry, controlling government and manipulating events to achieve its aims of world domination. As one respected Mason put it, the *real* Freemasonry is "a fraternity within a fraternity ... an outer organization concealing an inner Brotherhood of the elect."

The Masonic Temple in Washington, D.C., is where much of the Freemasonry lore originated. (Photo source: wikipedia.org/wiki/Image:WashDCMasonic 2007.jpg)

Keeping a Watchful Eye

Much of the information on the Web pertaining to Freemasonry is marked by the passionate rhetoric of staunch defenders and by the myriad fascinating claims of zealous conspiracy theorists. But one's online search should really begin with at least some neutrality in an attempt to understand the many facets of Freemasonry. The series of articles maintained on Wikipedia (en.wikipedia.org/wiki/free masonry) provides just that, along with an unmatched comprehensiveness on the topic. This main entry for Freemasonry offers a tutorial on its convoluted history and complex organizational structure, as well as an overview of the group's principles and activities (from rituals to signs to charitable efforts) and a summary of the anti-Masonic opposition and criticism. There are also separate entries for anti-Masonry (en.wikipedia.org/wiki/anti-masonry) and Masonic conspiracy theories (en.wikipedia.org/wiki/masonic_conspiracy_theories). Especially on the latter page, be sure to check out the "Notes and References" section, which serves as a spectacular portal to sites that attempt—some more convincingly than others—to "connect the dots" between Freemasonry and crop circles, a NASA conspiracy, Satan, corporate logos, the Illuminati, American presidents, the Denver International Airport, the assassination of JFK, New World Order, and the infiltration of the American government. The Wikipedia series also provides a list of members, which seems revealing on its own—though the site does offer a disclaimer that "Masonic membership can sometimes be difficult to verify."

Another useful, and a bit more concise, overview of Freemasonry is the "How Freemasons Work" article at HowStuffWorks.com (people.howstuffworks.com/freemason.htm). The author traces the evolution of Freemasonry from its origins to its modern incarnation. The site also includes the "33 Degrees of Freemasons"—the various levels a member can progress through—and several images. The article does, however, dismiss entirely any notion of nefarious activity. "In reality, there is no factual basis to any of the conspiracy theories against the Freemason—from the suggestion that the Masons designed the Washington, D.C., street grid in the shape of a pentagram (a sign of the occult), to the idea that they were somehow involved with the Jack the Ripper murders in 19th century London," the author writes.

The author of the "Freemason" page of the Freedom Domain site (www.freedomdomain.com/freemasons/freemason.html) would beg to differ, as evidenced by the eye-catching headline at the top of the page: "FREEMASONS CONTROL THE WORLD!!" Though it won't win any design or writing awards, this Web page offers some quintessential conspiracy thinking on Freemasonry:

> Freemasonry itself is not evil but it is used in evil ways by people with evil intentions. The symbols and knowledge and the pursuit of knowledge for philosophical and religious purposes itself is not evil. What IS EVIL is how FREEMASONRY IS USED TO PROMOTE AND MAINTAIN POWER!! We would all be better off if the Freemasons stopped trying to control the world.

The site provides a primer on the meaning and use of Masonic symbols and numerology, from the use of the pentagram and an intersecting square and compass in the layout of the nation's capital (a map is provided) to the supposed importance of the numbers 3, 13, 32, and 33. Providing images of several flags from countries throughout the world that contain certain symbolism ("some more obvious than others"), the author of the site argues that Masonic influence is not limited to America: "The Freemasons are a WORLDWIDE BROTHERHOOD. They do not follow any particular religion as Freemasonry itself is a religion to it's initiates." At the bottom of the page, links to sites dealing with some other prominent Freemasonry conspiracy theories are listed, including its involvement in the JFK assassination and the cover-up of the discovery of UFOs.

Another site worth checking is www.masonicinfo.com. While the banner on the top of the homepage reads "Anti-Masonry: Points of View," this is a site fiercely dedicated to debunking the claims against Freemasonry, as the author notes on the "Site Facts" page:

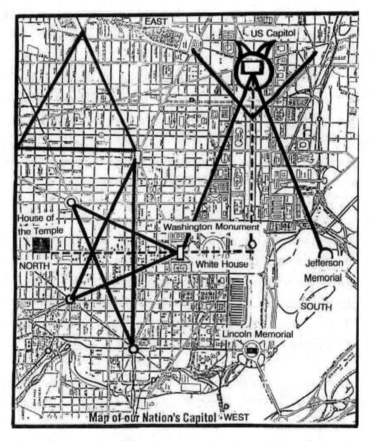

Some theories assert that Masonic and occult symbols, including the pyramid and pentagram, can be found in the layout of the street grid of Washington, D.C. (Photo source: www.freedomdomain.com/ freemasons/freemason.html)

This site was created by a Mason in hopes he would more fully "appreciate" the thinking of those who—either as an avocation or on a "lark"—chose to defame Masons and Masonry. While many online Masons had addressed Masonry ... we found no single place where the many facets of anti-Masonic activity were addressed. This web site is the result.

The site is so massive that the best way to navigate through it is from the "Site Map," which is divided into four main categories:

"Objections," "Objectors," "Freemasonry," and "Charities." Dozens of subsections listed under these categories address every imaginable conspiracy theory and complaint about Masonry. There are also pages that attempt to explain the philosophy and workings of the Masons, with a mix of seriousness and sarcasm. For example, on the "What Masons Believe" page, the author begins with a list that includes belief in a "Supreme Being" and that "Chocolate ice cream is better than strawberry." While it's certainly a bit flippant, the author repeatedly stresses that "Masonry/Masons has/have no pre-defined belief system: one's beliefs and opinions are their own!" The site also provides a wealth of information about becoming a Mason.

For an equally comprehensive but distinctly more critical look at Freemasonry, log on to Freemasonry Watch: Monitoring the Invisible Empire, the World's Largest Secret Society (www.freemasonry watch.org). Those familiar with the popular news site "The Drudge Report" will recognize the format of the bottom half of the homepage—hundreds of headlines linking to news articles and videos (some "breaking news" mixed with archived reports) on mostly credible, mainstream news sites. Not all of the information provided on the site is directly connected to Freemasonry, though there's no shortage of Masonry news and most of the content deals with some aspect of the secret society's role in and impact on the world. Clicking the banner at the top of the page opens the main site, which features an amazing amount of content on Freemasonry: a list of "Breaking Masonry News," an extensive video and audio archive (this alone makes this a worthwhile site), a well-attended message board, a comprehensive listing of links, and hundreds of essays and photos.

The Web site of the Grand Lodge of British Columbia and Yukon (freemasonry.bcy.ca/grandlodge.html) contains 2,600 pages of information and is an impressive source for researching Freemasonry. Hundreds of essays are posted on wide-ranging topics: anti-Masonry, history, charity, famous Freemasons, customs, ritual, symbolism, book reviews, references in popular culture, and more. Read *Thomas Paine's Origin of Free-Masonry*, published in 1818, scroll a list of Masonic references in modern cinema, or learn about the meaning of the "all-seeing eye." Though this site obviously approaches things with a pro-Masonic tone, its presentation of information is extremely thorough.

Don't have a dollar bill on hand? Log on to The Masonic Seal of America Web page (www.geocities.com/endtimedeception/seal.htm). A large image of both sides of the Great Seal of the United States (found on the $1 bill) graces the top of the site followed by an interpretation—popular among conspiracy theorists—of the symbolism displayed within it, which the author argues is clear evidence of Masonic influence and the proclamation of a "New World Order."

Throwing Stones

Is there a covert cabal of elite powerbrokers within Freemasonry—essentially a well-intentioned social club formed to protect this *real*

According to some conspiracy theorists, the Great Seal of the United States, found on the back of the $1 bill, is evidence of the influence of Freemasonry. It's chock-full of Masonic symbolism—the pyramid, the Eye of Providence, and the announcement of a "New World Order." (Photo source: www.geocities.com/endtime deception/seal.htm)

Brotherhood—working to control the world? Well, that depends on who you ask. It is clear that there's no middle ground here: Masons and their supporters are steadfast in the denial and dismissal of such claims as ridiculous; conspiracy theorists, however, are equally resolute in arguing that Freemasonry is seeking to create, if they haven't already, a dangerous, anti-democratic New World Order.

Look at the charity Freemasonry supports and the good it does in communities across the globe, defenders say.

Look at the secrecy, the Masonic symbolism, and its list of members, conspiracists say.

The fierce debate—only intensified by the Web—won't be settled any time soon. Freemasonry, like other secret societies, will always be treated with suspicion by outsiders. As one Web site notes, "[A]s long as the Freemasons continue to cloak themselves in a veil of secrecy, the questions—and accusations—about them will likely continue."

The JFK Assassination

Is there one single event in American history that has generated more debate, discussion, and speculation than the assassination of President John F. Kennedy? After four decades, the tide of articles, books, and Web sites proposing theories about the murder of the iconic president shows no signs of abating. Want to start an argument at your next family gathering or informal backyard get-together? Mention the words "magic bullet." Or "lone gunman." Or "Warren Commission." Or "grassy knoll." The vocabulary of the assassination has been codified into a lexicon of national doubt.

Often referred to as "the mother of all conspiracy theories," the various scenarios that purport to explain the assassination range across several countries (Cuba, Vietnam, Russia) and professional disciplines (politics, the military, the Mafia). The list of suspects seems to grow with each passing year but so does the weight of "evidence," which has been used to indict (at least in the court of public opinion) everyone from Vice President Lyndon Johnson to Supreme Court Justice Earl Warren, as well as Nikita Khrushchev, Fidel Castro, and Chicago mobster Sam Giancana. Some theorists even link all of the aforementioned in a sort of master global conspiracy.

The event was so horrific—and such an electroshock to the body politic—that it's almost inconceivable that the assassination has taken on an aspect of, well, entertainment. But the wealth of movies, documentaries, TV specials, books, and lectures testifies to the abiding, if disquieting, interest in JFK's untimely demise. His assassination has been a career-maker for some researchers and writers and a reliable ratings-generator for anxious publishers and television producers. Freeze-frames from the Zapruder film—the home movie of the assassination as it unfolded—regularly grace the covers of national newsweeklies. The public's appetite for new theories about the former president's murder seems as limitless as the media's willingness to exploit the widespread obsession.

In the final analysis, the abundance of clashing theories and acknowledged "experts" lead only to an insoluble equation. Do not be persuaded by book titles that proclaim the case "closed" or the mystery "finally solved." The mystery is no closer to being solved today than in the first few days after November 22, 1963, when the presidency—and an era of unfettered confidence in the "American Century"—was shattered by sniper fire.

A freeze-frame from the Zapruder film of the JFK assassination. (Photo source: www.whatreallyhappened.com/RANCHO/POLITICS/JFK/jfk.html)

The Known and the Unknown

For every known and widely accepted fact of the assassination, there are multiple interpretations and disagreements hanging on each. For instance, JFK was shot—but was it from behind, in front, or from multiple locations? Lee Harvey Oswald, the man who was arrested for the assassination, was almost certainly a triggerman—but was he the only one? And was he working for the KGB? The CIA? The Mafia? (Each has been frequently alleged.) Jack Ruby, the man who killed Oswald when he was being transferred from the Dallas police headquarters, performed the act—on live television no less—but there are still a dizzying number of suggested motives: Did he hope to silence Oswald before he could reveal who had employed him as assassin? Did he act out of pure outrage at the crime itself? Was he mentally deranged? And although JFK's wounds were thoroughly examined by doctors at both Parkland Hospital in Dallas (where he was rushed immediately after the incident) and Bethesda Naval Hospital, why is there such wide disagreement about such

"Lone gunman" Lee Harvey Oswald at a news conference after his arrest. (Photo source: mcadams.posc.mu.edu)

basic matters as whether the bullet hole in his throat is an entrance wound or an exit wound?

The assassination happened in Dallas's Dealey Plaza, in front of hundreds of witnesses—many of whom have testified to hearing shots from a "grassy knoll" in the plaza. But the alleged "lone gunman" supposedly fired from the sixth floor of the plaza's Book Depository building. Some witnesses even claim to have seen a gunman fleeing the scene—a scenario that was refuted in the official Warren Commission report on the assassination.

The Zapruder film shows the president's motorcade passing through the plaza moments before the fateful shots, but experts disagree on whether Oswald had time to fire the three shots recorded on the film in a space of just a few seconds with his bolt-action Italian rifle. Further, many experts strongly dispute the official explanation that the same bullet that purportedly struck JFK in the back of his neck exited through his throat, and then entered Governor John Connally's back, near his armpit, exiting below his nipple, and then shattering the bone in his wrist and finally wounding him in the thigh (this is the so-called magic bullet theory).

Adding to the intrigue of all the unreconciled questions is the specter of motive: Why would Oswald do it? Those who accept the Warren Commission report's conclusion that Oswald acted alone see him as an isolated, rejected loner with a record of erratic behavior and questionable associations. Conspiracy theorists point to Oswald's established ties to many of America's acknowledged enemies at the time; he had defected to the Soviet Union, married a Russian woman, moved to New Orleans, and started a pro-Castro organization. Even more intriguingly, Oswald, a former U.S. Marine, was able to return from Russia a declared communist and establish his life in the U.S. with little interference from the FBI or CIA. As one author noted, "Oswald returned to the United States in 1962 … and the State Department facilitated his journey. They returned his passport quickly, made no difficulties about his citizenship, exempted his wife from immigration restrictions and loaned him money." Theorists speculate that the former marine Oswald must have been working for the CIA or FBI as a spy to have been able to renounce his U.S. citizenship, move

Members of the Warren Commission present a copy of its final report to President Johnson. (Photo source: mcadams.posc.mu.edu)

to Russia as an avowed Communist, and then re-enter the U.S. with the active support of the U.S. government.

The Guilty Party

Why would the CIA, FBI, or any branch of the U.S. government want to facilitate the assassination of JFK? Conspiracy theorists argue that he had incurred the wrath of the so-called Military-Industrial Complex (the Pentagon, defense contractors, and others with an interest in sustained military conflict) with his plan to end American involvement in Vietnam. No more war meant no more war-profiteering or lucrative, multiyear supply contracts. So, the theory goes, sources in the Pentagon, working with certain "rogue" elements of the CIA, arranged for the assassination. The CIA, as many critics have noted, was actively involved in many assassination schemes in the 1960s and had the experience and personnel to call upon for such an undertaking. Also, it's been alleged that the CIA was still stinging from what was seen as JFK's betrayal of the agency during the disastrous Bay of Pigs invasion.

Other theories have centered on the Mafia, suggesting that JFK's attorney general (and brother) Robert Kennedy's aggressive campaign against organized crime was a threat to their continued existence. In addition, there was a widespread feeling among some crime syndicates that the Mafia had helped JFK get elected in 1960 and that his failure to reign in his brother Robert represented a betrayal of the mob's earlier, critical support.

Castro is often alleged to have had a hand in the assassination, ostensibly in retaliation for the many failed CIA-sponsored plans to assassinate him. There are theorists who claim the Soviet Union was responsible, with Nikita Khrushchev still stewing over the humiliation of having to back down during the American Naval blockade during the so-called Cuban Missile Crisis. Oswald's many ties to both the Soviet Union and Cuban governments have helped sustain these theories.

Some critics have even accused then-Vice President Lyndon Johnson of masterminding the assassination, arguing that his hatred of the Kennedys, along with his fear of being dropped from the ticket

Some see the hand of the Soviet Union's Nikita Khrushchev in the JFK assassination. (Photo source: wikipedia.org/wiki/John_F._Kennedy)

in 1964, pushed him to the brink. Johnson was well connected to Big Oil and the Military-Industrial Complex, and conspiracy theorists note that the assassination took place in Johnson's home state of Texas, alleging that Johnson had a hand in changing the route of the motorcade and even selecting the personnel in the president's vehicle. As for motive, Johnson obviously had a great deal to gain from JFK's abrupt departure from the political landscape. And many conspiracy theorists point to LBJ's reversal of JFK's withdrawal of troops from Vietnam in favor of a sharp escalation of U.S. involvement in the conflict as evidence of Johnson's being beholden to the Military-Industrial Complex.

Each one of these theories—and many others with only slightly lesser claims on credibility—has found a home in the increasingly crowded universe of JFK conspiracies. And it would be difficult to overestimate the role the Internet has played in promulgating the theories about JFK's assassination and the various cover-ups. The breadth and depth of the Web sites that deal in some way with the assassination could certainly fill several books, not just one chapter in a broader study like this one. There's an impressive amount of effort—and some truly groundbreaking scholarship—being expended by theorists, amateur and credentialed. Spending time burrowing through the mountain of information—accurate, speculative, or just plain bizarre—dealing with the JFK assassination can be a disorienting experience. One could emerge better informed, irredeemably suspicious, exasperated by the volume of unsupported claims, or, more likely, feeling some measure of each.

Rifling Through the Web

There are so many Web sites dedicated to the JFK assassination that many of the better sites now also include guides to the hundreds of other sites available to help newcomers acclimate themselves to the landscape of JFK conspiracy theories. That's the case with the Kennedy Assassination Home Page (mcadams.posc.mu.edu), an impressively comprehensive site that includes a useful "Best of Kennedy Assassination Web Sites" page. The site is the work of

Marquette University Political Science Professor John McAdams, who makes no bones about his endorsement of the lone gunman theory. And while he is openly dismissive of much of the conspiracy theorizing, his site is so expansive and so well organized that even die-hard conspirators will find something interesting there. As McAdams usefully explains:

> This web site is dedicated to debunking the mass of misinformation and disinformation surrounding the murder of JFK. If you are a believer in Oswald as a lone gunman, you are likely to enjoy this web site, since most of that misinformation and disinformation has come from conspiracists. But if you are a sophisticated conspiracist, you likely understand that the mass of silly nonsense in conspiracy books and documentaries does no service to the cause of truth in the assassination, and simply buries the "case for conspiracy" under layers of bunk.

The site provides links to everything from schematics of Dealey Plaza to audio interviews with eyewitnesses, and, of course, dozens of newspaper and magazine articles, as well as book reviews, movie reviews (McAdams dismisses Oliver Stone's *JFK*: "We expect Hollywood movies to take some liberties with the historical record. But what do we think when Hollywood turns history on its head?"), and lots of arcane but fascinating trivia. Newcomers might be a bit overwhelmed, but readers with the time and interest will find their poking around amply rewarded.

Another extensive but well-organized site—this one generally supportive of the idea of a conspiracy—is the Kennedy Assassination for the Novice (pages.prodigy.net/whiskey99), put together by researcher E. C. Dorsch Jr. The site provides a basic overview of the facts of the case for beginners and extensive essays on all aspects of the conspiracy. Web surfers will probably learn as much from the questions Dorsch asks as they will from his answers. Here's a sampling:

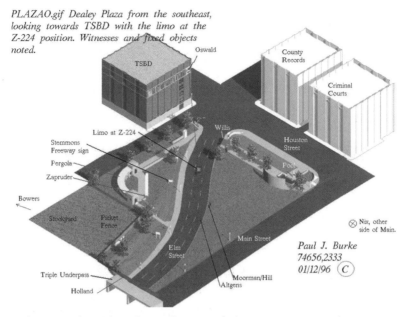

PLAZAO.gif Dealey Plaza from the southeast, looking towards TSBD with the limo at the Z-224 position. Witnesses and fixed objects noted.

Oswald

County Records

TSBD

Criminal Courts

Limo at Z-224

Willis

Houston Street

Stemmons Freeway sign

Pergola

Pool

Zapruder

Bowers

Stockyard   Picket Fence

⊗ Nix, other side of Main.

Main Street

Paul J. Burke
74656,2333
01/12/96 Ⓒ

Elm Street

Triple Underpass

Moorman/Hill
Altgens

Holland

A diagram of Dealey Plaza, the site of the assassination. (Photo source: mcadams.posc.mu.edu)

Can you believe that, accidentally, the president was hung out to dry, virtually under the window of a man who brought a rifle to work that day, just in case such a scenario happened?

Can you believe that the soon to be assassin would carelessly show himself with rifle in hand prior to the motorcade showing up and yet go unmolested because, accidentally, there happened to be no security assigned as there usually should have been?

Can you believe that a bullet which transversed two human beings, penetrated eight different fabrics and broke or shattered two different bones could be found on a stretcher without the slightest hint of ever hitting anything solid, nor contain any blood or tissue which could tie it to either victim?

Can you believe that multiple federal agencies and Dallas police could mishandle and/or misidentify multiple clues in a major murder because they were simply inept? Can you believe the same about the three pathologists?

That's the tenor of much of the information on the site, which offers lots of links and an extensive bibliography for those who want to go further in their exploration.

There's nothing quite like the visceral thrill of participating in a major news event as it unfolds, and for those who were too young or simply can't recall the events of November 22, 1963, a great site to visit is the "JFK Assassination Conspiracy" page at the Soundboard Web site (www.soundboard.com/sb/JFK_assassination_conspir. aspx). One can download local radio and television bulletins as they were first broadcast moments after the shooting, as well as interviews with eyewitnesses in Dealey Plaza—including a radio interview with amateur film buff Abraham Zapruder. (There are also the live, "on-the-scene" reports from the basement of the Dallas Police Headquarters as Oswald was being transferred to the county jail but was suddenly shot by Jack Ruby.) It's hard not to feel a chill as one

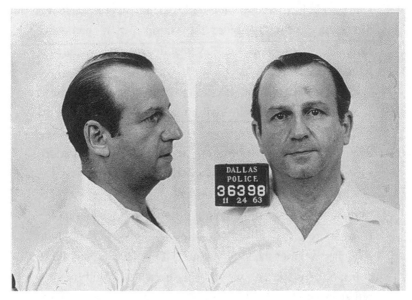

The mug shot of Jack Ruby, killer of Lee Harvey Oswald. (Photo source: wikipedia.org/wiki/Jack_Ruby)

listens to that horrific moment in 1963 that caused professional news-casters to waver in their composure as the nation listened in shock to the reports of the president's killing.

A slightly less scholarly but clear and helpful look at the assassina-tion and subsequent controversies can be found at the "Kennedy Assassination" page on the site The Fifties Web—Your Retro 50s, 60s and 70s Source (www.fiftiesweb.com/kennedy/kennedy-assassination. htm). The site offers a day-by-day link menu from November 22 to November 25, giving readers information about the event, as well as other major events happening in the world at that time (and even local weather reports). There is an extensive "Kennedy Family Tree" page, a transcript of JFK's inaugural address, personal accounts from those who knew the president, and sound files from Walter Cronkite's announcement on CBS that the president had been shot. Perhaps most interesting is the article and series of photos of the so-called magic bullet, which the site notes "is in near perfect condition" (as the close-up photos seem to confirm), even though it "hit Kennedy in the back, exited his neck and then continued on to hit Connally in the back, wrist, and leg, and onto his stretcher at Parkland Hospital." But the tone of the site is reflective, not prosecutorial, more a lament of the tragedy than a search for truth: "Many people feel that the Fifties actually ended on November 22, 1963. No more feel good days. Our sense of invincibility had changed to vulnerability."

Most JFK assassination sites don't seek that kind of poignancy, which often leaves them sounding somewhat encyclopedic—which is to say, dull. An exception is the engaging but fair-minded JFK page on the truTV Crime Library Web site (www.crimelibrary.com/terrorists_ spies/assassins/jfk/1. html). The site contains a lengthy feature story examining the conspiracy-theory controversies, highlighted by inter-views with true believers on both sides of the issue. As the site notes, once the Warren Commission weighed in with its report on September 24, 1964, "the whodunit debate has roiled ever since."

There are certainly lots of writers and researchers who seem "roiled up" as well. A good example of the kind of passion that one often finds on these kinds of sites is displayed on the JFK page at the Web site What Really Happened? (www.whatreallyhappened.com/

RANCHO/POLITICS/JFK/jfk.html). The site is shorter than most dedicated to the assassination, but it's long on indignation at those who have helped foment the cover-up, including former President Gerald Ford (who, according to one prominently displayed link, "Admits Fictionalizing the Warren Report"). The site also goes after the complacent news media, which has abetted the cover-up, singling out one of America's most prominent journalists for special censure:

> Dan Rather, at the time an unknown newscaster from a small market Texas TV station, viewed the Zapruder film, then described it to America on the CBS Network. As this recording [audio link] of that broadcast shows, Rather lied to all of America in claiming that the head shot pushed John F. Kennedy's head forward. Rather's meteoric rise to network status and stardom soon followed. When the Zapruder film was finally shown publicly, during Jim Garrison's trial of CIA agent Clay Shaw, Rather's lie was revealed for all to see.

Perhaps the most aptly named JFK assassination Web page is Notes on a Strange World, available at the site maintained by the Committee for Skeptical Inquiry (www.csicop.org/si/2005-01/strange-world.html). As the author of the article "Facts and Fiction in the Kennedy Assassination" notes, in what could be the only truly indisputable conclusion about the assassination: "Investigators must guard against preconceived ideas before starting an investigation. Before you know it, you start twisting facts and discarding evidence that contradict those ideas, making you draw unfounded solutions."

The Search for a Verdict

The JFK assassination remains one of those historic moments that people often anoint, retrospectively, as a tipping point from one era into the next. Maybe because it was so shatteringly unexpected, or maybe because it revealed something long suspected but seldom uttered about the presence of evil in the world, the assassination seemed to kill something in the idealistic American psyche. But it also created something: skepticism—a growing distrust that would soon be fueled by an increasingly unpopular war with a justification that became problematic and a presidency destined to be toppled by deceit. The nascent doubt that took root among a handful of amateur skeptics in Dallas in 1963 mushroomed into epic proportions within a decade of the assassination.

Die-hard doubters are unlikely to ever accept the government-sanctioned explanation that Oswald acted alone. There are simply too many questions—many of which seem unresolvable. And for those who accept the report of the Warren Commission—a minority among the public, many surveys continue to find—the conspiracy theorists represent the triumph of paranoia over clear thinking. The facts speak for themselves—no need to invent theories, they argue. And the fault line of suspicion that once ran through the country has, thanks to the Internet, now circled and divided the globe.

September 11, 2001

The events of September 11, 2001, are unforgettable.

Images of airplanes slamming into the sides of the sleek sky-scrapers, footage of those iconic buildings that punctuated the famous New York City skyline crumbling to the streets below in a plume of dust and debris, the large flag draped over the side of the burning Pentagon are all etched forever into the collective American consciousness.

When the dust had finally settled, the death toll exceeded 3,000. Almost immediately, the U.S. government attributed the attacks—which President George W. Bush would describe as "the Pearl Harbor of the 21st century" in his diary entry that night—to Osama bin Laden. Nineteen terrorists with links to al-Qaeda were identified as hijackers of the four commercial passenger jets that wreaked havoc on that clear September morning. It was the worst attack on American soil in history. The president quickly vowed revenge: "We will make no distinction between the terrorists who committed these acts and those who harbor them," Bush said, addressing the nation in primetime and announcing what would become the dogma of his administration.

"America is united," wrote reporters for *USA Today*, highlighting the results of a poll conducted in the aftermath of the attacks. "Like no other event in recent history … last week's terrorist attacks have forged a common sense of purpose among Americans."

This picture shows a jet—allegedly United Airlines Flight 175—moments before it barrels into the World Trade Center's South Tower at 9:03 AM on September 11, 2001. The North Tower had already been hit by another airliner 17 minutes earlier. (Photo source: 911research.wtc7.net)

That patriotic passion persisted for some time—not only among the citizenry but also in much of the mainstream media. By January 2002, however, the unity began to dissipate, as some people began to raise questions regarding the official account of the attacks. Why was bin Laden immediately accused, without any consideration of other suspects? What is the relationship between the bin Laden family and the Bush family? Why did fighter jets fail to respond to and intercept the hijacked planes?

The list of concerns didn't stop there. But what these early skeptics really wanted was a Congressional inquiry. When Bush and Vice President Dick Cheney persuaded Senate leaders to limit the scope of such an investigation to failures of the intelligence community, suspicions increased. Pressure for an independent investigation would eventually result in the formation of the 9/11 Commission in November 2002. The White House's initial resistance and its subsequent reluctance to cooperate with the commission stoked claims of conspiracy and cover-up. When its final report was issued in the summer of 2004, skeptics of the official 9/11 story included not only the usual suspects but also families of victims, journalists, academics, and even a congresswoman.

Thanks largely to their use of the Internet, 9/11 conspiracy theorists have attracted a remarkable number of adherents. According to a variety of recent credible polls, 42 percent of Americans believe the U.S. government has engaged in a cover-up and 36 percent believe it is likely (either somewhat or very) that "federal officials either participated in the attacks ... or took no action to stop them."

As Lev Grossman wrote in *Time* magazine as the fifth anniversary of the attacks approached, "Thirty-six percent adds up to a lot of people. This is not a fringe phenomenon. It is a mainstream political reality."

A New Pearl Harbor

Already aware that a plane crashed into the side of one of the World Trade Center's Twin Towers at 8:46 AM, Bush entered a second-grade classroom at Emma E. Booker Elementary School in Sarasota, Florida, for a photo-op to promote his education plan. At about 9:06 AM, as Bush sat in front of the class, his chief of staff Andrew Card whispered something into his ear, reportedly that a second plane plummeted into the other tower and that "America is under attack." The president showed no overtly noticeable reaction (though descriptions in the press varied from "the color drained from the president's face" to he "wore a bemused smile"); he continued to listen to the children read aloud from *My Pet Goat* for another seven minutes or so, not leaving the classroom until about 9:16 AM.

This scene, made infamous by Michael Moore in his scathing documentary film *Fahrenheit 9/11*, has been used as ammunition by those conspiracy theorists who believe high-level government officials knew the attack would occur and did nothing to prevent it.

Many see more than mere incompetence on display, arguing that the president's behavior—his inaction—suggests he wasn't surprised by the events as they unfolded and knew he was in no danger. More than a few skeptics have wondered why the Secret Service did not immediately move to protect Bush, whose appearance at the school had been publicized since September 7 (the same day two of the hijackers visited Sarasota). The school, only about three miles from Sarasota-Bradenton Airport, was less than a half-mile off the

President Bush continued reading *My Pet Goat* to school children for more than seven minutes after being told by his chief of staff that a second plane flew into the other tower, raising suspicions among conspiracy theorists. (Photo source: wikipedia.org/wiki/The_Pet_Goat)

approach path to that airport. "Hijackers could have crashed a plane into Bush's publicized location and his security would have been completely helpless to stop it," argued the authors of an article chronicling Bush's day. The country was, by this point, clearly under attack—by hijacked airplanes converted into missiles.

But the Secret Service never hurried Bush from the scene. Instead, Bush—even after the reading lesson concluded—lingered, chitchatting with the students. Because the agency seemed in no hurry to hustle Bush from his known and apparently vulnerable location, some conspiracists suggest it either "acted with extreme incompetence," was overruled by the president, or possessed insider knowledge of the attack. Finally, after delivering a brief speech in the originally scheduled time slot, the motorcade departed for the airport at about 9:35 AM. With Air Force One now thought to be a target, some skeptics wonder why no fighter jets escorted it on takeoff and only joined it about an hour later.

Many theorize that, when scrutinized in light of intelligence reports and the conduct of government officials in the weeks and months prior to September 11, 2001, the cumulative weight of circumstantial evidence adds up to prior knowledge of the attacks and purposeful failure to protect the country—echoing charges leveled against President Franklin D. Roosevelt in the decades since the attacks on Pearl Harbor.

While top officials claimed no one could have predicted that terrorists would use airplanes as missiles, even a cursory scan of the official record seems to point to the contrary: German, British, Russian, Israeli, and even Taliban officials warned in the summer of 2001 of planned hijackings and imminent attacks on American targets; federal authorities had knowledge for years that suspected terrorists linked to al-Qaeda were taking flight lessons from schools in the U.S. (one was even convicted in the mid-1990s for plotting to crash a plane into CIA headquarters); a 1999 National Intelligence Council report concluded that terrorists could attempt to crash-land aircraft into the Pentagon and other federal buildings; and, of course, the now-infamous August 6, 2001, Presidential Daily Briefing titled

"Bin Laden Determined to Strike in U.S.," which mentioned the possibility of hijackings.

Conspiracy theorists also point to a number of other oddities that they claim suggest insider foreknowledge: an usually high amount of activity (including a surge in the purchase of "put" options, which "allow investors to profit from the decline in value of stocks") involving the stocks of United and American airlines, insurance companies, and financial institutions—all of which plummeted as a result of 9/11—the week before the attacks; the FBI recommendation months before the attack that Attorney General John Ashcroft not fly on commercial airliners (because, officials claim, of threats on his life, and on September 10, according to a *Newsweek* report, "a group of top Pentagon officials suddenly cancelled travel plans for the next morning, apparently because of security concerns"); and Secretary of Defense Donald Rumsfeld's announcement in a press conference the day before the attacks that the Pentagon "cannot track $2.3 trillion in transactions."

Dov Zakheim, comptroller of the Pentagon at the time, also happened to participate in the creation of a report titled *Rebuilding America's Defenses: Strategy, Forces and Resources for a New Century*. Published in September 2000 by the Project for a New American Century—a highly influential neoconservative think tank that has counted among its members Rumsfeld, Dick Cheney, Richard Armitage, I. Lewis Libby, Paul Wolfowitz, Richard Perle, and a host of other hawks in the Bush administration—the report argues for a doctrine of increased defense spending, aggressive foreign policy, and renewed military strength (especially in the form of a "substantial American force presence in the [Persian] Gulf"). "Further, the process of transformation, even if it brings revolutionary change, is likely to be a long one," the report states, "absent some catastrophic and catalyzing event—like a new Pearl Harbor."

On September 11, 2001, the Project for a New American Century got its "new Pearl Harbor"—coincidence, or something much more nefarious?

Sifting Through the Rubble

While one set of conspiracy theorists argues top government officials had the foreknowledge of an attack but allowed it to happen because they wanted "some catastrophic and catalyzing event" to achieve their agenda, another group adds to that theory, claiming the U.S. government orchestrated (or at least assisted in coordinating) the events of 9/11.

There is no single "inside job" conspiracy theory, as many within the "9/11 Truth Movement"—a loosely aligned group of organizations and individuals who vehemently question the official 9/11 explanation—disagree on the details of how the government carried out the attacks. Each of the incidents—the crash of American Airlines Flight 11 into the North Tower, the crash of United Airlines Flight 175 into the South Tower, the collapse of both towers, the collapse of World Trade Center Building 7, the crash of American Flight 77 into the Pentagon, the crash of United Flight 93 into a remote field in Pennsylvania—has generated a variety of conspiracy theories on its own.

In general, some of the central tenets of theories purporting U.S. government involvement and a subsequent cover-up include:

- Several "war games" and military training exercises, conducted by the North American Aerospace Defense Command (NORAD), U.S. Air Force, National Reconnaissance Office (NRO), Federal Emergency Management Agency (FEMA), and other federal agencies on or around September 11, 2001, redeployed defense aircraft from normal Northeast patrols, restricted response capabilities, and caused confusion among officials as to whether the attacks were "real world or an exercise."

- The collapse of the Twin Towers and Building 7 (which was not hit by a plane and did not fall until 5:20 PM) resulted from controlled demolition, as theorists point out that no steel-framed high-rise or skyscraper ever collapsed due to fire or localized damage before or since 9/11.

- Though hotly debated even among conspiracy theorists, damage to the Pentagon does not support the notion that a Boeing 757 barreled into the building and the alternatives vary from a missile to bombs inside the building to military aircraft modified to look like Flight 77.

- Flight 93 was shot down by U.S. fighter jets and did not crash as a result of passengers fighting to regain control of the cockpit.

- Three of the four black boxes *were* discovered in the rubble at Ground Zero (despite government claims that none were found).

- The removal of debris from the World Trade Center site equated to the largest destruction of criminal evidence in American history.

Among the slough of additional hypotheses circulating online include Israeli government involvement, the use of computer systems and remote control to guide the planes to their targets, the implausibility of cell phone use aboard Flight 93, "plane swapping" prior to the attacks, missiles

According to many conspiracists, World Trade Center Building 7, which was not struck by a jet, exhibited the features of a controlled demolition when it collapsed nearly eight hours after the Twin Towers had been reduced to rubble. (Photo source: 911research.wtc7.net)

attached to the bellies of the planes, and even "video fakery" to create the scenes of planes impacting the Twin Towers.

With so many varying theories being proposed, sometimes in the guise of concrete fact, it might seem difficult to know which, if any, carry at least some credibility. The Web has never before played a more significant role in fermenting a debate between supporters of a government-sanctioned account and believers in some alternative theory. With the equivalent of dozens of volumes of research available with the click of the mouse, a bit of online exploration will position even those previously unaware of a 9/11 conspiracy theory to decipher what's plausible and what's not.

A Virtual Battleground

A quick Web search for "9/11 conspiracy theories" or "9/11 conspiracy" spits back millions of results. Where to begin one's quest, and where to go from there, is at first glance a daunting task.

A useful starting point is Wikipedia's entry on the September 11, 2001 attacks (en.wikipedia.org/wiki/9-11), which provides a reader-friendly overview the various aspects of the day's horrific events with sections detailing "The attacks," "Responsibility," "Reactions," "U.S. Government response," and "Long-term effects." Discussion of the conspiracy theories that have arisen in the aftermath comprises only two sentences on the page, though a link to a more detailed Wikipedia article, "9/11 conspiracy theories," is provided (en. wikipedia.org/ wiki/9/11_conspiracy_theories). The page offers readers a comprehensive summary of the vast number of theories proposed in an effort to explain what "really" happened. It also serves as an invaluable portal into the online resources—news articles, official documents and reports, photographs, and informative sites—available on the topic. Be sure to check out the nearly 250 links in the "References" section, as well as the "External links" (separated into "supporting" and "debunking" categories).

Perhaps the most notable of all the Web sites dealing in some way with the alleged 9/11 conspiracy is Loose Change (www.loosechange 911.com)—home to the independent documentary, produced by amateur filmmakers on a laptop, that has popularized the arguments against the official story unlike any other effort. Those who log on are able to watch the entire second edition through Google Video free of charge, and a DVD version is available for purchase. As one review noted, "*Loose Change* covers a great deal of material, moving from one point to another in rapid succession. It presents a long list of claims supporting the conclusion that 9/11 was engineered by insiders, but does so with a mixture of strong and flawed arguments." Nonetheless,

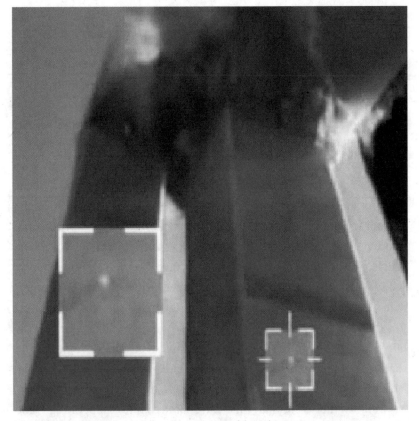

Many conspiracy theorists allege that the World Trade Center towers came crumbling down as a result of a planned demolition. The producers of the documentary *Loose Change* claim puffs of air and debris—explosions—can be seen immediately before the floors above collapse. (Photo source: www.loose change911.com)

the film is recommended viewing for anyone wanting to sink his or her teeth into the debate.

Screw Loose Change (www.lolloosechange.co.nr) offers a rebuttal by inserting criticism via subtitles into the video. Another site, 9-11 Loose Change Second Edition Viewer Guide: And Debunking of Various 9/11 Conspiracy Theories (www.loosechangeguide.com/ LooseChangeGuide.html), provides a transcript of the video interspersed with "analysis," criticism, and sarcasm. Both attempt to debunk not parts of *Loose Change* but all of it. The Web site Sifting Through Loose Change (911research.wtc7.net/reviews/loose_ change)—a detailed critique by 9-11 Research—takes a much more nuanced approach: "to foster an understanding that, despite its many errors, the film raises questions that urgently demand serious scrutiny." Using an illustrated transcript, the authors provide their take on each assertion made throughout the video, adding symbols (coins, of course) to denote which claims have value and which are without merit. Most of the disagreement tends to come when *Loose Change* suggests that Flight 77 did not crash into the Pentagon. The counterpoints offered by 9-11 Research are essential reading for anyone who feels persuaded by the compelling documentary.

9-11 Research's main site (911research.wtc7.net) presents one of the strongest cases against the official explanation. "There are numerous red flags in the official story, which requires a long series of highly improbable coincidences," the site announces on the homepage. Detailed research, sober arguments, and reasoned analysis are hallmarks of this compelling site.

The Web site of the 9/11 Truth Movement (www.911truth.org) serves as a sort of catch-all for the theories that claim "elements within the US government and covert policy apparatus must have orchestrated or participated in the execution of the attacks for these to have happened in the way that they did." Expansive and a bit untamed, 911Truth.org does manage to appeal to newcomers with articles such as "Top 40 Reasons to Doubt the Official Story of September 11th, 2001" and "Beginners' Guide to 9/11 Truth." Die-hard skeptics won't be disappointed either, with a voluminous cache of articles on just about every possible detail and angle. Most impressive is the number of links provided throughout the site.

But for those who cry foul when it comes to the 9/11 conspiracy theories—the debunkers—the efforts of *Popular Mechanics*, first published in its March 2005 issue (now available at www.popular mechanics.com/technology/military_law/1227842.html), are most important, matching the popularity of *Loose Change*, just at the other end of the philosophical spectrum. "Healthy skepticism, it seems, has curdled into paranoia," write the editors. A team of researchers and reporters investigated what the magazine deemed "16 of the most prevalent claims made by conspiracy theorists." The claims—several of which had already been disavowed by segments of the conspiracy theorists—focus on "The Planes," "The World Trade Center," "The

Popular Mechanics argues that this photo is "proof that a passenger plane, not a missile, hit the building." Even many within the 9/11 Truth Movement believe a large commercial jet struck the Pentagon, although they still do not see it as the work of the accused terrorists. (Photo source: www.popularmechanics.com/technology/military_law/1227842.html)

Pentagon," and "Flight 93." Through nine Web pages, the group provides a response (called "Fact") to each claim, using photographs in
several instances as evidence to back their reasoning. "In the end, we
were able to debunk each of these assertions with hard evidence and
a healthy dose of common sense," they write.

Conspiracy theorists and their debunkers are not the only groups in
this debate that maintain an online presence. For official accounts of
what happened on 9/11, three Web sites are worth exploring. First, the
9/11 Commission's final report (www.9-11commission.gov/report/
index.htm) is available for download, section by section. Second, the
National Institute of Standards and Technology, which was responsible for determining the cause of the World Trade Center's collapses,
offers a summary of its findings (the report consists of 43 volumes)
on a useful page titled "Answers to Frequently Asked Questions"
(wtc.nist.gov/pubs/factsheets/faqs_8_2006.htm). Lastly, the U.S.
Department of State attempts to refute "The Top September 11
Conspiracy Theories" (usinfo.state.gov/xarchives/display.html?p=
pubs-english&y=2006&m=August&x=20060828133846esnamfua
K0.2676355), which links to lengthier and more detailed articles produced by the State Department in response to certain claims.

For history buffs perhaps less concerned with conspiracy theories,
the September 11 Digital Archive (911digitalarchive.org) enables
users to explore the "stories, images, emails, documents, sounds, and
videos of September 11." Part oral history project, part time capsule,
part news vault, the site—which offers a valuable list of links—
reminds one all too well what that tragic day felt, sounded, and
looked like.

Motive and Means

Who had the will? Who had the motive? Who had the means?
These are the questions that 9/11 conspiracists say should be asked.
Their answer: the U.S. government. As for the will, they often point
to Operation Northwoods—a proposal by leaders of the Department
of Defense in 1962 (made public in 1997) to create simulated or real
acts of terrorism on American soil and against U.S. interests. By

accusing Cuba, the plan suggested, the government would have the public support needed for military action against Fidel Castro; President Kennedy, however, rejected the plan. As for a motive, conspiracy theorists point to the aftermath of 9/11: Bush's approval rating jumped an astounding 34 percent to the fourth highest level ever recorded; the neocons running the administration got their "new Pearl Harbor" and, as a result, military footing in the Middle East; the attacks provided the impetus for the invasion of Iraq, which the Bush administration began discussing eight months before 9/11; a variety of increased domestic powers resulted as well, from the USA PATRIOT Act to warrant-less eavesdropping authority; and the Military-Industrial Complex reaped a financial windfall from 9/11.

As for the means, however, some conspiracy-theory critics contend the Bush administration and the U.S. military are simply too incompetent to pull off such a feat. "The same people who are making a mess of Iraq were never so clever or devious that they could stage a complex assault on two narrow towers of steel and glass tucked alongside the Hudson River," wrote Michael Sheldon in the *Daily Telegraph*. Others, like MIT engineering professor Thomas W. Eager, say the conspiracists "cherry-pick" the information they use to form their theories: "They determine what happened, throw out all the data that doesn't fit their conclusion, and then hail their findings as the only possible conclusion."

But as long as the events of 9/11 continue to wield such sway over America's domestic agenda and foreign policy, and there's no reason to expect otherwise, the conspiracy theories surrounding the supposed terrorist attacks will continue to appeal to increasing segments of the population.

Bodies of Evidence:
The Lindbergh, Lincoln, Hoffa,
and Morrison Mysteries in Brief

Certain events throughout history have played out in a way that gives rise to questions, even in the face of "official" explanations. Many of the names, dates, and places that comprise the menu of historical memory are incontrovertible, but an examination of the fuller record often reveals lacunae—gaps in what can be stated, with certainty, to have happened.

This is the space conspiracy theorizing inhabits.

Sometimes those gaps are large, providing the room for extensive speculations. When several witnesses reported hearing the sound of gunfire coming from the grassy knoll in Dealey Plaza, a space opened up for shadowy gunmen working in concert with Lee Harvey Oswald. When Princess Diana's sedan entered a Parisian tunnel, out of sight of the paparazzi's prying eyes, a space opened up for government assassins working on behalf of her Majesty, the Queen. As the years between Will Shakespeare's departure from Stratford-upon-Avon and his arrival in London remain unaccounted for, a host of possible playwrights-in-training rushes in to fill the space where Shakespeare's apprenticeship should have been.

How large these gaps are often determines the longevity, and viability, of a conspiracy theory. When most of the facts are known, there's not much room for the theorists to maneuver or construct plausible counter-histories. But when there remain serious, unanswered questions, even after decades of investigation, the vacuum of uncertainty inevitably gets filled with the informed speculation known as conspiracy theory.

But not all conspiracy theories are created equal. The following mysterious disappearances and suspicious deaths have generated lots of speculation, with varying degrees of success among researchers, historians, and amateur sleuths in providing answers to those questions that continue to haunt the imagination and tease the intellect.

The Lindbergh Baby Kidnapping

Once upon a time, it was known as "the crime of the century." On March 1, 1932, 20-month-old Charles Augustus Lindbergh, son of the world-famous aviator, was kidnapped from the family's weekend home in Hopewell, New Jersey. The crime was front-page news all around the world, with readers transfixed by the kidnapping, investigation, trial, and aftermath of this bizarre and gripping saga. And although the police arrested a suspect—who was later convicted and, despite mounting questions about his guilt, executed in the electric chair—this case continues to transfix historians and researchers. Some conspiracy theorists have doggedly pursued the case, convinced that the convicted man, Richard Bruno Hauptmann, a German immigrant from the Bronx, could not possibly have committed the crime.

Many unanswered questions continue to plague historians and investigators, some of whom remain actively committed to uncovering "the real kidnapper." Skeptics point to a number of seemingly inexplicable components of the case against Hauptmann. For instance, the kidnapping took place on a Tuesday night, but the Lindberghs normally never stayed in Hopewell past the weekend (little Charles had a cold and the family decided to wait until Wednesday to return to their mansion in Englewood, New Jersey). If someone had planned to kidnap the Lindbergh baby, skeptics argue, he would not have planned to commit the crime at the Hopewell location—because the Lindberghs would not have been expected to be there. No one could have known of the family's last-minute decision to remain in Hopewell.

Also troubling to skeptics: Why would someone attempt a kidnapping during a time when all the lights were on, the domestic staff was in residence, and the family was at home having dinner?

Many are also bothered by the lack of physical evidence. Hauptmann's footprints were not found at the scene. And the ladder

WANTED
INFORMATION AS TO THE WHEREABOUTS OF

CHAS. A. LINDBERGH, JR.
OF HOPEWELL, N. J.
SON OF COL. CHAS. A. LINDBERGH
World-Famous Aviator

This child was kidnaped from his home in Hopewell, N. J., between 8 and 10 p. m. on Tuesday, March 1, 1932.

DESCRIPTION:

Age, 20 months	Hair, blond, curly
Weight, 27 to 30 lbs.	Eyes, dark blue
Height, 29 inches	Complexion, light

Deep dimple in center of chin
Dressed in one-piece coverall night suit

ADDRESS ALL COMMUNICATIONS TO
COL. H. N. SCHWARZKOPF, TRENTON, N. J., or
COL. CHAS. A. LINDBERGH, HOPEWELL, N. J.

ALL COMMUNICATIONS WILL BE TREATED IN CONFIDENCE

COL. H. NORMAN SCHWARZKOPF
March 11, 1932   Supt. New Jersey State Police, Trenton, N. J.

The FBI poster soliciting information about "the crime of the century"—the kidnapping of the Lindbergh baby in 1932. (Photo source: wikipedia.org/wiki/Lindbergh_kidnapping) that police allege was used to climb up to the shuttered, second story window of the nursery contained more than 400 sets of fingerprints. Not one belonged to Hauptmann.

The case remains one of the more actively pursued by Internet investigators. The best place on the Web for updated research on the case is www.lindberghkidnappinghoax.com, a massive collection of research and links to facts about the kidnapping, trial, and aftermath of Hauptmann's execution. As the page's title suggests, there is little regard for the official version of events, with the site's author claiming "The true Crime of the Century was not a kidnap/murder but rather, the execution of an innocent man—the murder of Richard Hauptmann."

Another great site that offers a thorough review of the trial of Hauptmann, which journalist H. L. Menken called "The greatest story since the resurrection," is the Richard Hauptmann Trial site (www.law.umkc.edu/faculty/projects/ftrials/Hauptmann/Hauptmann. htm). Also worth a look is the transcript of the PBS *American Experience* episode on Lindbergh, and specifically the discussion of the kidnapping (www.pbs.org/wgbh/amex/lindbergh/sfeature/crime. html). And browsers seeking a historical perspective should check out the archive of Lindbergh articles from *Time* magazine (www.time. com/time/archive/collections/0,21428,c_lindbergh_kidnapping,00. shtml).

The Lincoln Assassination

Most people can recite the basic facts of the assassination of President Abraham Lincoln, a watershed event in the history of the republic: Lincoln was shot by John Wilkes Booth while attending a performance at Ford's Theatre in Washington, D.C. Booth was later found hiding out in a farmhouse, where he was killed by a gunshot to the neck.

But how many people realize that Lincoln was killed as part of a conspiracy? In fact, Booth's co-conspirators were put on trial, convicted, and several of them executed (including Mary Surratt, the first woman to be hanged by the U.S. government).

THE ASSASSINATION OF PRESIDENT LINCOLN.
AT FORD'S THEATRE WASHINGTON D.C APRIL 14ᵗʰ 1865.

John Wilkes Booth shot President Lincoln—the culmination of a real conspiracy. Who was behind it, however, remains subject to debate. (Photo source: wikipedia.org/wiki/Lincoln_assassination)

So, in the case of Lincoln's assassination, it's not a question of whether there was a conspiracy but rather *who*, exactly, was behind it. Most historians believe that the mastermind of the conspiracy was Booth, an itinerant actor and devoted son of the South who sought to find a way to undue the Union and restore the Confederacy in the waning weeks of the U.S. Civil War.

But others have raised the specter of a wider and more nefarious conspiracy. Some researchers have questioned the role of Vice President Andrew Johnson in the assassination. These researchers have seized on a mysterious note that Booth left for Johnson at a Washington hotel where Johnson was staying the day of the assassination. "Don't wish to disturb you. Are you at home? J. Wilkes Booth," the note read. These theorists speculate Johnson was involved in the planning of the attack: A supposition Mary Todd Lincoln embraced, as she once wrote to a friend "that miserable inebriate Johnson had cognizance of my husband's death. Why was that card of Booth's found in his box? Some acquaintance certainly existed."

Others have claimed Booth was part of a larger Confederate plot to cripple the government. Still other researchers have also implicated the Catholic Church, the Freemasons, a cabal of international bankers, and even Lincoln's Secretary of War Edwin Stanton.

A helpful overview of the many theories surrounding the assassination can be found at the Abraham Lincoln's Assassination site (home.att.net/~rjnorton/Lincoln74.html). The site dissects a half-dozen of the most enduring theories, concluding, "It seems certain that the controversy will continue into the current century. Future studies and interpretations are a surety."

To get an idea of the breadth of information available about Lincoln in general, or the assassination in particular, check out the Abraham Lincoln Online site (showcase.netins.net/web/creative/lincoln/education/assassin.htm). Consisting mostly of annotated links, the site directs viewers to everything from the official autopsy report to the playbill from the fateful performance. The National Archives and Records Administration maintains a Web site about the Lincoln Assassination (www.archives.gov/exhibits/american_originals/lincoln.html). The site includes lots of official documentation about the assassination, including a reproduction of the District of Columbia police blotter logging the assassination among the other crimes of the day: "At this hour, the melancholy intelligence of the assassination of Mr. Lincoln, President of the U.S., at Ford's Theatre was brought to this office and information from the following persons goes to show that the assassin is a man named J. Wilks [sic] Booth."

The Disappearance of Jimmy Hoffa

For a number of years, the disappearance of American labor leader Jimmy Hoffa was treated as a sort of uncomfortable running gag, with late-night television comics relying on the uncertain circumstances of his disappearance to generate laughs. Was he buried in the end zone at Giants Stadium? Underneath the parking lot of a suburban shopping mall? In some poor, unsuspecting Detroit homeowner's backyard? Or could he be (as has been suggested) on ice, his body preserved in, of all places, Fort Knox?

The serio-comic end to Hoffa's life (if it really *did* end; some theorize he is alive and well) stands in sharp contrast to the hardscrabble life that took him from rural Indiana to the limelight of the presidency of the International Brotherhood of Teamsters. Although admired for his tenacity in dealing with titans of industry and well-placed political officials, it was his dealings with those who inhabit a more shadowy stratosphere that often got him into trouble. Consorting with a variety of figures from organized crime might have lead to his elevation as the nation's most formidable labor leader but it also led to convictions for attempted bribery—and perhaps even to his death.

To this day, no one has discovered where Hoffa ended up after he left the parking lot of the Machus Red Fox restaurant in Bloomfield

Jimmy Hoffa became Teamsters president, in part, because of his relationships with members of organized crime, which also resulted in legal trouble and perhaps even his disappearance in 1975. (Photo source: www.coverups.com/hoffa.htm)

Hills, Michigan, a suburb of Detroit, on July 30, 1975. There has certainly been no shortage of speculation, often revealed in tell-all memoirs of former Mafia hit men or by close associates of Hoffa's during his Teamster reign. A host of other books by police officials, private investigators, and independent researchers has turned up dozens of proposed burial sights. As recently as 2006, Michigan officials, acting on a tip, spent a week digging up a field near a farmhouse in Milford Township, Michigan. No body was discovered.

But there are lots of discoveries, and theories, being put forward on the Web. A good place to start is the Jimmy Hoffa page on CoverUps.com (www.coverups.com/hoffa.htm). The site synthesizes in a brief and reader-friendly style the many theories regarding his disappearance, even including the possibility that "Hoffa had run off to Brazil with a black go-go dancer."

An excellent piece of reportage, which chronicles Hoffa's life, disappearance, and legacy, can be found in the archives of the *Detroit News* (info.detnews.com/history/story/index.cfm?id=42&category=people). The article, titled "The Day Jimmy Hoffa Didn't Come Home," is an excellent introduction to the influence wielded by the labor icon. A slightly less objective but equally compelling read can be found on the Web page Dead Men Do Tell Tales (www.prairie ghosts.com/hoffa.html). This illustrated review of Hoffa's life and career includes a rundown of possible final resting places, including being buried in a gravel pit in Highland, Michigan, ground up at a meat processing plant and then dumped in a Florida swamp, or crammed into a 55-gallon steel drum and deposited in a toxic waste site in Jersey City, New Jersey. After running through all the possibilities, the site's author concludes:

> Hoffa was declared legally dead in 1982, but his case remains open. A special agent at the FBI's Detroit field office is still assigned to it. The investigation has generated over 16,000 pages of documents gathered from interviews, wiretaps, and surveillance, but despite the government's best efforts to get to the bottom of Jimmy Hoffa's disappearance, what really happens to him remains a mystery.

The Death of Jim Morrison

At about 5 AM on July 3, 1971, the legendary front man of the 1960s psychedelic band The Doors died at the age of 27. Jim Morrison—who was found by his longtime companion, Pamela Courson, in the bathtub of their Paris apartment—died of a heart attack, according to the French medical examiner who signed the death certificate.

Or did he?

Many of his fans and conspiracy theorists don't think so.

Rumors about what really might have happened began to spread without much delay—and continue to this day. From a drug overdose in a seedy nightclub (sometimes attributed to heroin, sometimes cocaine) to a political assassination (either by the FBI or French intelligence) to faking his death (there have been numerous Morrison sightings in the years since), the theorizing runs the gamut of nearly every possible scenario.

The conspiracy theories have no doubt been fueled by the strange state of affairs that comprise the official story. Morrison, according to the initial comments made by Courson to the press, wasn't dead, just "very tired and resting in a hospital." She continued to claim he was alive for days, even after the death certificate had been signed. She would eventually claim that the couple went to bed together but that Morrison awoke feeling ill and decided to take a bath. Only Courson, a Parisian doctor or two, and perhaps a few police officers, ever saw the body—as the coffin was sealed before Morrison's family or the American embassy was informed of his death. An autopsy was *not* performed. Nearly a week later, The Doors' manager announced the death of Mr. Mojo Risin', who had already been buried in a Paris cemetery.

"Why Morrison Death News Delay?" read a headline in the newspaper of record in Morrison's adopted city of Los Angeles, sparking the notion of a possible cover-up.

Perhaps that's because there was. In July 2007, the topic of Morrison's death resurfaced in mainstream media outlets, including *Time* (www.time.com/time/world/article/0,8599,1643884,00.html)

and *Rolling Stone* (www.rollingstone.com/rockdaily/index.php/2007/
07/10/jim-morrisons-death-may-be-reinvestigated). Sam Bernett,
who at the time was 21 and managing a Parisian hot spot (a club
called the Rock 'n Roll Circus), revealed that he found the rock star
in the club's bathroom with "foam coming out of his lips." According
to a doctor at the nightclub, Morrison was dead, overdosed on heroin.
Morrison's two drug dealers, according to Bernett, snuck the body
outside and brought it to the bathtub at Morrison's apartment.

Case closed. Well, not exactly.

Many conspiracy theorists accuse Bernett of fabricating the story
to sell copies of his book about Morrison. Despite being the most visited grave in the famous Le Pére Lachaise cemetery, Morrison's resting place, according to legions of fans and conspiracists, is empty.
For an excellent overview on the various theories surrounding
Morrison's demise, check out the Seize the Night Web site
(www.carpenoctem. tv/cons/lizard.html). When drummer John
Densmore first visited the grave, he said it was too short. And
Morrison had joked with his band mates in the months before his
"death" that he planned to flee from the spotlight to Africa. Even Ray
Manzarek, keyboardist for The Doors, once said:

> If there's one guy who would have been capable of stag-
> ing his own death—getting a phony death certificate or
> paying off some French doctor … and putting a hundred
> and fifty pounds of sand into a coffin and splitting to some
> point on this planet—Africa, who knows where—Jim
> Morrison would have been the guy to pull it off.

Gerald Pitts, a photographer and documentary filmmaker,
announced in 2005 that Morrison did, indeed, fake his own death "in
order to avoid being bumped off by the French government, which
had already sent Jimi Hendrix and Janis Joplin to their graves," as a
RollingStone.com news brief reported the claim. How does Pitts
know? Because he claims Morrison is living the cowboy life on a
ranch in rural Oregon. He says he's got the photos to prove it, a few
of which are posted on his Web site, Jim Morrison: A Living Legend

(www.rodeoswest.com/RM_JM_DOORS.html). Pitts claims that Densmore and Manzarek have confirmed his "discovery." And for just $24.95, you can buy his evidence—a video titled *Jim Morrison Discovered Living in the Pacific Northwest.*

But wait. Rock-and-roll journalist/historian Brett Meisner says he has proof that Morrison is indeed dead. In a photo of Meisner taken

Brett Meisner, pictured here in a photograph taken at Morrison's grave by Tom Petty, claims the rock legend's ghost (his torso and outspread arms) was captured in the frame (to the right of Meisner, between the two headstones behind him). (Source: www.rockandrollbadboy.com)

at Morrison's grave, he noticed something: the Lizard King's ghost. The "untouched" photo is posted on Meisner's site (www.rockand rollbadboy.com/hollywood_diaries/ghost_of_jim_morrison).

So which is it? Did Morrison break on through to the other side on July 3, 1971? Or was that not really the end? French officials are considering the possibility of reinvestigating the rock legend's death. Perhaps we'll even find out who or what is really in that grave.

The Search Continues

For those hoping for closure in any of these conspiracies—or, in fact, any of the ones detailed in this book—such an objective is elusive. Conspiracy theories are, by their nature, unproved (that's why they're *theories*). But such knowledge doesn't—and shouldn't—keep the inquisitive from pursuing the truth, however bizarre or unlikely it might seem. And the Internet provides a portal to the bizarre, the unlikely, and the dubious—as well as to the serious, the informed, and the scholarly. Because actual conspiracies have been shown to exist, this search is not pointless, nor limited: As history continues to unfold, so too will theories about what really happened.

Or at least what people *think* happened.

Featured Web Sites

Chapter 1: Roswell/Area 51

UFO Evidence, www.ufoevidence.org/topics/government.htm
The Roswell Incident,
   www.subversiveelement.com/roswell1_home.html
The Skeptic's Dictionary—Roswell, skepdic.com/roswell.html
CoverUps.com—Roswell, www.coverups.com/roswell
Crystalinks—Area 51, www.crystalinks.com/area51.html
Wikipedia—Roswell UFO Incident,
   en.wikipedia.org/wiki/Roswell_UFO_incident
Wikipedia—Area 51, en.wikipedia.org/wiki/Area_51
Armageddon Online, www.armageddononline.org
Welcome to Roswell, www.roswellnm.org

Chapter 2: The Death of Princess Diana

Diana, Princess of Wales, www.londonnet.co.uk/ln/talk/news/diana_
   conspiracy_theories.html
CoverUps.com—Princess Diana's Death, www.coverups.com/diana
ConspiracyPlanet.com, www.conspiracyplanet.com
The Murder of Princess Diana, www.dianamurder.com
WeThePeople—Diana Forum, www.wethepeople.la/diforum2.htm
"The Operation Paget inquiry report into the allegation of conspiracy
   to murder, " www.direct.gov.uk/en/Nl1/Newsroom/DG_065122

Time magazine—Princess Diana, www.time.com/time/daily/
  special/diana
The Work Continues, The Diana, Princess of Wales Memorial Fund,
  www.theworkcontinues.org

Chapter 3: TWA Flight 800

NTSB—TWA Flight 800 Accident Investigation,
  www.ntsb.gov/events/twa800/default.htm
YouTube—"Flight TWA-800 (mid-air explosion),"
  www.youtube.com/watch?v=w581BiSBzQA
YouTube—"TWA Flight 800 Shot Down by Surface-to-Air
  Missile," www.youtube.com/watch?v=L6BUXu0AEpg
TWA Flight 800 Articles by Jack Cashill,
  www.cashill.com/twa800/index.htm
TWA Flight 800: The Impossible Zoom Climb,
  raylahr.entryhost.com
Goddard's Journal—TWA 800, users.erols.com/igoddard/TWA800
Flight 800 Independent Researchers Organization (FIRO),
  www.flight800.org
Associated Retired Aviation Professionals—The Flight 800
  Investigation, www.twa800.com

Chapter 4: AIDS

SourceWatch: A Project of the Center for Media and Democracy—
  AIDS Conspiracy, www.sourcewatch.org/index.php?title=AIDS_
  conspiracy
ConspiracyPlanet.com—AIDS, www.conspiracyplanet.com/
  channel.cfm?ChannelID=34
Dr. Boyd E. Graves, www.boydgraves.com
AIDS Conspiracy—AIDS Biowarfare,
  sonic.net/~doretk/ArchiveARCHIVE/Aids/Aids.html
Flying Saucer Review—The AIDS-ET Connection Hypothesis,
  www.fsr.org.uk/fsrart37.htm

Totse.com—AIDS Conspiracy: Just a Theory,
www.totse.com/en/conspiracy/the_aids_conspiracy/aids.html
PubMed, www.ncbi.nlm.nih.gov/pubmed
AVERT—The Origins of HIV, www.avert.org/origins.htm

Chapter 5: The Shakespeare Authorship Question

Sir Francis Bacon's New Advancement of Learning,
www.sirbacon.org
Marlowe Lives! Association, www.marlovian.com
HenryNeville.com (Brenda James), www.henryneville.com
PBS: *Frontline*—The Shakespeare Mystery,
www.pbs.org/wgbh/pages/frontline/shakespeare
PBS: *Frontline*—Much Ado About Something,
www.pbs.org/wgbh/pages/frontline/shows/muchado
The Shakespeare Fellowship, www.shakespearefellowship.org
"Shakespeare" By Another Name, www.shakespearebyanother
name.com
The Shakespeare Authorship Page, www.shakespeareauthorship.com
Mr. William Shakespeare and the Internet, shakespeare.palomar.edu
Internet Public Library's Shakespeare Bookshelf,
www.ipl.org/div/shakespeare

Chapter 6: The Order of Skull and Bones

Conspiracy Theory Research List—The Boodle Boys,
www.ctrl.org/boodleboys
The Good Shepherd, www.thegoodshepherdmovie.com
Central Intelligence Agency (CIA), www.cia.gov
CIA—*The Good Shepherd*, https://www.cia.gov/library/center-for-
the-study-of-intelligence/csi-publications/csi-
studies/studies/vol51no1/the-good-shepherd.html
Propaganda Matrix—Skull and Bones,
www.propagandamatrix.com/archive_skull_and_bones.html
YouTube, www.youtube.com

Freedom Domain—Skull and Bones, www.freedomdomain.com/
Secretsocietes/Skullbones/skullbones.html
Bilderberg.org—Skull and Bones,
www.bilderberg.org/skullbone.htm

Chapter 7: The Jesus Controversy

Dan Brown, www.danbrown.com
Seize the Night—The Jesus Conspiracy,
www.carpenoctem.tv/cons/jesus.html
Bloodline of the Holy Grail, graal.co.uk/bloodlinelecture.html
TheTruthAboutDaVinci.com, www.thetruthaboutdavinci.com
The Priory De Scion & Secret Societies, www.scottbruno.com/
priory-de-scion.htm
Museum of Science–Boston—Leonardo, www.mos.org/Leonardo
Voice of Reason—*The Da Vinci Code*,
www.thevoiceofreason.com/Conspiracy/DaVinciCode.htm
AboveTopSecret.com, www.abovetopsecret.com
Discovery Channel—The Lost Tomb of Jesus,
dsc.discovery.com/convergence/tomb/tomb.html

Chapter 8: The Moon Landing

Was the Apollo Moon Landing Fake?,
www.apfn.org/apfn/moon.htm
The Faked Apollo Landings, www.ufos-aliens.co.uk/cosmic
apollo.html
CNN.com—NASA Debunks Moon Landing Hoax Conspiracy,
archives.cnn.com/2001/TECH/space/02/19/nasa.moon
Goddard's Journal—Are Apollo Moon Photos Fake?, www.ian
goddard.net/moon01.htm
Bad Astronomy—Fox TV and the Apollo Moon Hoax, www.bad
astronomy.com/bad/tv/foxapollo.html
MoonMovie.com, www.moonmovie.com
NASA—The Moon Landing Hoax,
liftoff.msfc.nasa.gov/News/2001/News-MoonLanding.asp

Chapter 9: The Death of Marilyn Monroe

truTV's Crime Library—The Death of Marilyn Monroe,
www.crimelibrary.com/notorious_murders/celebrity/
marilyn_monroe

WorldNetDaily, www.worldnetdaily.com

48 Hours Mystery—The Marilyn Tapes, www.cbsnews.com/
stories/2006/04/20/48hours/main1524970.shtml

MarilynMonroe.com, www.marilynmonroe.com

Brainy Quote—Marilyn Monroe quotes,
www.brainyquote.com/quotes/authors/m/marilyn_monroe.html

Ellen's Place—Marilyn Monroe biography,
www.ellensplace.net/mmbio3.html

Wikipedia—Marilyn Monroe,
en.wikipedia.org/wiki/Marilyn_Monroe

Marilyn's Autopsy, www.marilynmonroepages.com/autopsy.html

Chapter 10: Protocols of the Elders of Zion

Jew Watch, www.jewwatch.com

World Conquest Through World Jewish Government, www.bible
believers.org.au/przion1.htm

Save the Males—Protocols of Zion,
www.savethemales.ca/000205.html

ThreeWorldWars.com—The Protocols of the Learned Elders of
Zion Explained, www.threeworldwars.com/protocols.htm

Anti-Defamation League (ADL)—A Hoax of Hate,
www.adl.org/special_reports/protocols/protocols_intro.asp

The Holocaust History Project, www.holocaust-history.org

Holocaust Encyclopedia, www.ushmm.org/wlc/en

The Protocols of the Elders of Zion,
ddickerson.igc.org/protocols.html

Pajamas Media—Thought the Protocols of the Elders of Zion
  Couldn't Be Set to Music? Think Again!, www.pajamasmedia.
  com/2006/11/thought_the_protocols_of_the_e.php

Chapter 11: Pearl Harbor

Pearl Harbor: Mother of All Conspiracies,
  www.geocities.com/Pentagon/6315/pearl.html
The Independent Institute—The Truth About Pearl Harbor: A
  Debate, www.independent.org/issues/article.asp?id=445
Federal Debt Relief System (FDRS)—The Attack on Pearl Harbor
  Was a Set-up, www.fdrs.org/attack_on_pearl_harbor.html
Wikipedia—McCollum Memo,
  en.wikipedia.org/wiki/McCollum_memo
Naval Historical Center—Pearl Harbor, www.history.navy.mil/
  photos/events/wwii-pac/pearlhbr/pearlhbr.htm
Naval Station Pearl Harbor,
  www.cnic.navy.mil/pearlharbor/index.htm
Franklin D. Roosevelt's Pearl Harbor Speech, Dec. 8, 1941,
  ww2homefront.com/fdrspeech12-8-41.html
National Park Service—USS *Arizona* National Memorial Museum,
  www.nps.gov/usar
Centre for Research on Globalisation—Pearl Harbour: History
  Whitewashed?, www.globalresearch.ca/articles/WOO203A.html
NationalGeographic.com—Remembering Pearl Harbor,
  plasma.nationalgeographic.com/pearlharbor

Chapter 12: The Trilateral Commission

The Trilateral Commission, www.trilateral.org
North Atlantic Treaty Organization (NATO), www.nato.int
WorldNetDaily—Treasonous Agenda of the Trilateral Commission,
  www.worldnetdaily.com/news/article.asp?ARTICLE_ID=44965
The Straight Dope—Is the Trilateral Commission the Secret
  Organization that Runs the World?, www.straightdope.com/
  classics/a2_295.html

Thirst for Justice—The Council on Foreign Relations and the
   Trilateral Commission, www.prolognet.qc.ca/clyde/cfr.html
SourceWatch—Trilateral Commission,
   www.sourcewatch.org/index.php?title=Trilateral_Commission
American Institute for Economic Research—The Trilateralists,
   Road to Power, www.cooperativeindividualism.org/aier_on_
   conspiracy_06.html
Council on Foreign Relations (CFR), www.cfr.org
Conspiracy Archive—The Council on Foreign Relations (CFR) and
   The New World Order, www.conspiracyarchive.com/NWO/
   Council_Foreign_Relations.htm

Chapter 13: The Hindenburg

The Museum of UnNatural Mystery—The Mystery of the
   Hindenburg Disaster, www.unmuseum.org/hindenburg.htm
The Great Zeppelins—*Hindenburg*,
   www.ciderpresspottery.com/ZLA/greatzeps/german/
   Hindenburg.html
Wikipedia—LZ 129 *Hindenburg*,
   en.wikipedia.org/wiki/Hindenburg_disaster
Navy Lakehurst Historical Society, www.nlhs.com
RoadsideAmerica.com—*Hindenburg* Crash Site, www.roadside
   america.com/attract/NJLAKhinden.html
Federal Bureau of Investigation (FBI)—The *Hindenburg* Disaster,
   foia.fbi.gov/foiaindex/hindburg.htm
Newsfilm Online, newsfilm.bufvc.ac.uk
Hindenburg Disaster—Herb Morrison Reporting, www.otr.com/
   hindenburg.html
German Culture, www.germanculture.com.ua

Chapter 14: The Philadelphia Experiment

The Varo Edition of *The Case for the UFO*,
   www.cassiopaea.org/cass/Varo-Jessup.pdf

"Alias Carlos Allende: The Mystery Man Behind the Philadelphia Experiment," by Robert A. Goerman, web.archive.org/web/20020601165207/http://www.parascope. com/en/articles/allende.htm

Naval Historical Center—The "Philadelphia Experiment," www. history.navy.mil/faqs/faq21-1.htm

The Skeptic's Dictionary—Philadelphia Experiment, skepdic.com/philadel.html

"Anatomy Of A Hoax: The Philadelphia Experiment 50 Years Later," by Jacques Vallee, www.rense.com/ufo/philahoax.htm

The Philadelphia Experiment & Montauk Survivor Accounts, www.bielek.com

Bielek-Debunked.com, www.bielek-debunked.com

Philadelphia Experiment from A-Z, www.softwareartist.com/philexp.html

Chapter 15: Freemasonry

Wikipedia—Freemasonry, en.wikipedia.org/wiki/freemasonry

Wikipedia—Anti-Masonry, en.wikipedia.org/wiki/anti-masonry

Wikipedia—Masonic Conspiracy Theories, en.wikipedia.org/wiki/masonic_conspiracy_theories

How Freemasons Work, people.howstuffworks.com/freemason.htm

Freedom Domain—Freemasons, www.freedomdomain.com/ freemasons/freemason.html

Anti-Masonry: Points of View, www.masonicinfo.com

Freemasonry Watch: Monitoring the Invisible Empire, the World's Largest Secret Society, www.freemasonrywatch.org

Grand Lodge of British Columbia and Yukon, freemasonry.bcy.ca/grandlodge.html

The Masonic Seal of America Web page, www.geocities.com/ endtimedeception/seal.htm

Chapter 16: The JFK Assassination

Kennedy Assassination Home Page, mcadams.posc.mu.edu

The Kennedy Assassination for the Novice,
   pages.prodigy.net/whiskey99
Soundboard—JFK Assassination Conspiracy,
   www.soundboard.com/sb/JFK_assassination_conspir.aspx
The Fifties Web: Your Retro 50s, 60s and 70s Source—Kennedy
   Assassination, www.fiftiesweb.com/kennedy/kennedy-
   assassination.htm
truTV's Crime Library—The Assassination of John F. Kennedy,
   www.crimelibrary.com/terrorists_spies/assassins/jfk/1.html
What Really Happened?—The Death of John Kennedy, www.
   whatreallyhappened.com/RANCHO/POLITICS/JFK/jfk.html
Notes on a Strange World—Facts and Fiction in the Kennedy
   Assassination, www.csicop.org/si/2005-01/strange-world.html

Chapter 17: September 11, 2001

Wikipedia—September 11, 2001 Attacks, en.wikipedia.org/
   wiki/9-11
Wikipedia—9/11 Conspiracy Theories,
   en.wikipedia.org/wiki/9/11_conspiracy_theories
Loose Change, www.loosechange911.com
Screw Loose Change, www.lolloosechange.co.nr
9-11 Loose Change Second Edition Viewer Guide: And Debunking
   of Various 9/11 Conspiracy Theories,
   www.loosechangeguide.com/LooseChangeGuide.html
Sifting Through *Loose Change*,
   911research.wtc7.net/reviews/loose_change
9-11 Research, 911research.wtc7.net
9/11 Truth Movement, www.911truth.org
Popular Mechanics—Debunking the 9/11 Myths: Special Report,
   www.popularmechanics.com/technology/military_law/
   1227842.html
National Commission on Terrorist Attacks Upon the United
   States–9/11 Commission Report, www.9-11commission.
   gov/report/index.htm

National Institute of Standards and Technology—Answers to
Frequently Asked Questions, wtc.nist.gov/pubs/factsheets/
faqs_8_2006.htm

U.S. Department of State—The Top September 11 Conspiracy
Theories, usinfo.state.gov/xarchives/display.html?p=pubs-
english&y=2006&m=August&x=20060828133846esnamfuaK0.
2676355

The September 11 Digital Archive, 911digitalarchive.org

Chapter 18: Bodies of Evidence: The Lindbergh, Lincoln, Hoffa, and Morrison Mysteries in Brief

The Lindbergh Baby Kidnapping

The Lindbergh Kidnapping Hoax,
www.lindberghkidnappinghoax.com

Richard Hauptmann Trial, www.law.umkc.edu/faculty/projects/
ftrials/Hauptmann/Hauptmann.htm

PBS: *American Experience*—Lindbergh,
www.pbs.org/wgbh/amex/lindbergh/sfeature/crime.html

Time—Lindbergh Kidnapping, www.time.com/time/archive/
collections/0,21428,c_lindbergh_kidnapping,00.shtml

The Lincoln Assassination

Abraham Lincoln's Assassination,
home.att.net/~rjnorton/Lincoln74.html

Abraham Lincoln Online, showcase.netins.net/web/creative/
lincoln/education/assassin.htm

National Archives and Records Administration—Lincoln
Assassination, www.archives.gov/exhibits/american_originals/
lincoln.html

The Disappearance of Jimmy Hoffa

CoverUps.com—Jimmy Hoffa, www.coverups.com/hoffa.htm

Detroit News—"The Day Jimmy Hoffa Didn't Come Home," by Pat
Zacharias, info.detnews.com/history/story/index.cfm?id=42&
category=people

Dead Men Do Tell Tales—The Missing Teamster,
www.prairieghosts.com/hoffa.html

The Death of Jim Morrison
Time—"How Jim Morrison Died," by Vivienne Walt,
www.time.com/time/world/article/0,8599,1643884,00.html
Rolling Stone—Jim Morrison's Death May Be Reinvestigated,
www.rollingstone.com/rockdaily/index.php/2007/07/10/jim-
morrisons-death-may-be-reinvestigated
Seize the Night—Jim Morrison,
www.carpenoctem.tv/cons/lizard.html
Jim Morrison: A Living Legend,
www.rodeoswest.com/RM_JM_DOORS.html
RockandRollBadBoy.com—The Ghost of Jim Morrison,
www.rockandrollbadboy.com/hollywood_diaries/ghost_
of_jim_morrison

About the Authors

Jim Broderick, a former reporter and copy editor, currently teaches journalism at New Jersey City University in Jersey City, NJ. He is the author of two previous books. Broderick lives in Glen Ridge, NJ, with his wife Miri and his daughters Olivia and Maddy.

Darren Miller has worked as a reporter and editor for newspapers in New Jersey and North Carolina and is the recipient of several journalism awards. A resident of Asheville, North Carolina, Miller lives with his wife Heather.

Broderick and Miller previously co-authored *Consider the Source: A Critical Guide to 100 Prominent News and Information Sites on the Web* (Information Today, Inc., 2007). They can be reached through their Web site, www.TheReportersWell.com, and by email to News@TheReportersWell.com.

Index

13, appearance on dollar bill, 91
48 Hours Mystery (TV show) on
    Marilyn Monroe, 115
9/11 Commission, 219, 229
9-11 Loose Change Second Edition
    Viewer Guide: And Debunking
    of Various 9/11 Conspiracy
    Theories Web site, 227
9-11 Research Web site, 227
9/11 terrorist attacks. *See* September
    11, 2001 terrorist attacks
9/11 Truth Movement, 223, 227–228

A

Abiff, Hiram, 190
abovetopsecret.com on Jesus contro-
    versy, 91
Abraham Lincoln Online site, 236
Abraham Lincoln's Assassination site,
    236
Acquired Immune Deficiency
    Syndrome. *See* AIDS
Africa, AIDS in, 39–40, 47
African-Americans, AIDS in, 39, 49
AIDS (Acquired Immune Deficiency
    Syndrome)
    biology, 40
    compared to other conspiracy theo-
      ries, 41–42, 50–51
    conspirators, alleged, 39–40, 45,
      46–47, 48
    in specific populations, 39–40, 47,
      49
    spread, 39
    theories on, 42–44

    Web sites, 44–50
"AIDS Biowarfare" (Cantwell), 46
AIDS: USA Home-Make Evil (Segal &
    Segal), 42–43
airplane crash. *See* TWA Flight 800
    disaster
Al-Fayed, Dodi, 15, 16
Al-Fayed, Mohammed, 17, 23
"Alias Carlos Allende: The Mystery
    Man Behind the Philadelphia
    Experiment" (Goerman), 178
aliens, outerspace, 9, 40, 48. *See also*
    Roswell, New Mexico
Allen, Carl, 176, 178–179, 181–182,
    183
Allende, Carlos Miguel, 176, 178–179,
    181–182, 183
al-Qaeda, 217
American Experience (PBS episode) on
    Lindbergh kidnapping, 234
American Institute for Economic
    Research, 159–160
American Patriot Friends Network Web
    site, 101–102
*America's Secret Establishment: An
    Introduction to the Order of
    Skull & Bones* (Sutton), 72
"Anatomy Of A Hoax: The
    Philadelphia Experiment 50
    Years Later" (Vallee), 184
Anderson, Mark, 64
Andrew Furuseth, 178, 183–184
Anti-Defamation League (ADL) Web
    site, 131
anti-Masonry movement, 193

The Antiquities of Warwickshire
(Dugdale), 55
anti-Semitism. *See Protocols of the
Elders of Zion*
Apollo 11 mission, 95, 98. *See also*
Moon landing
archive.org Web site, 183
Area 51 site
activities, suspected, 1, 3–4, 7
Moon landing conspiracy, 97
secrecy, 6–7, 10
Web sites, 9–11
Arizona, 145
Armstrong, Neil, 95, 106
Ashcroft, John, 222
The Asphalt Jungle (movie), 110
Associated Retired Aviation
Professionals Web site, 36–37
AVERT, 49–50

B

Bacon, Sir Francis, 53, 60–61
Bad Astronomy Web site, 104–105
Baker, Lord, 23
Barnes, Marshall, 184–185
Bartleby Web site, 66
Bavarian Illuminati, 72–73, 192
Bay of Pigs invasion and JFK assassi-
nation, 207
Berlitz, Charles, 5, 179
Bernett, Sam, 240
Between Two Ages (Brzezinski), 151,
154
biblebelievers.com, 129–130
Bielek, Al, 185
bielek-debunked.com, 185
Bigfoot, 185
Bilderberg Web site, 77
bin Laden, Osama, 217, 218
Bloodline of the Holy Grail Web site,
87–89
Bolender, Albert and Ira, 108
Bomb Plot message, 140
The Boodle Boys. *See* Order of Skull
and Bones
Booth, John Wilkes, 234, 235
Brainy Quote Web site, 116–117
Brazel, William, 3
Brenda James Web site, 61
British Newsfilm Online Web site, 173
Brown, Dan, 82, 85
Brown, Senator Hank, 154

Bruno, Scott, 90
Brzezinski, Zbigniew, 151, 152, 154,
158
Budiansky, Stephen, 142, 143
Bullock, Steven C., 189
Burger, Neil R., 179
Bush, President George H. W., 70, 74,
75, 76, 152
Bush, President George W.
Order of Skull and Bones member-
ship, 67, 69, 74, 78
September 11, 2001 terrorist attacks,
217, 219–221

C

Cameron, Duncan, 185
Cantwell, Alan, 46–47
Capricorn One (movie), 97
Card, Andrew, 219
carpenoctem Web site, 240
Carter, President Jimmy, 151, 158
The Case for the UFO (Jessup), 176,
178, 179–180, 181–182
Cashill, Jack, 33
Cashill Web site, 33–34
Castro, Fidel, 113, 208
Catholic Church, 83, 85, 236
Central Intelligence Agency (CIA), 43,
75, 76, 207
Centre for Research on Globalisation
Web site, 145–146
Christianity, 85. *See also* Catholic
Church; Jesus controversy;
New Testament
CIA (Central Intelligence Agency), 43,
75, 76, 207
Clement XII, Pope, 192
Clemmons, Sgt. Jack, 112
Clinton, President Bill, 152
CNN.com, 103
The Codebreakers (Kahn), 143
Committee for Skeptical Inquiry Web
site, 214
Conover, David, 109
Conspiracy Archive Web site, 160–161,
194–195
ConspiracyPlanet.com, 20, 45
conspiracy theories, situations allowing,
231–232
Conspiracy Theory Research List, 74
Council on Foreign Relations, 143–144,
152, 153, 156–157, 160–161

Courson, Pamela, 239
CoverUps.com, 9, 20, 238
the Craft. *See* Freemasonry
Crystal, Ellie, 9
Crystalinks Web site, 9–10
Cuban Missile Crisis and JFK assassination, 208

D

danbrown.com, 83
da Vinci, Leonardo, 83, 86, 90–91
The Da Vinci Code (Brown), 82–83, 85, 86, 89, 91
Day of Deceit (Budiansky), 142, 143
Day of Deceit: The Truth About FDR and Pearl Harbor (Stinnett), 138
ddickerson Web site, 133
Dead Men Do Tell Tales Web site, 238
Dealey Plaza, 206, 210, 211
Dearborn Independent newspaper, 126
degaussing, 175
Densmore, John, 240
destroyer escorts, 175
Detroit News archive on Hoffa disappearance, 238
de Vere, Edward (17th Earl of Oxford), 53–54, 61–65
Diana, Princess of Wales
  biographical information, 13–15, 24
  car crash, 13, 15–19
  controversy, reasons for, 24
  death, government investigation of, 22–23
  following, 13
  murder, motivations for, 16–17, 21
  Web sites, 20–23, 24
Diana, Princess of Wales Web page, 20
Dickerson, David, 133
DiMaggio, Joe, 111, 115
DiMaggio, June, 115
dirigible flight, 163, 168–169, 170, 172. *See also Hindenburg*
Discovery Channel Web site on Jesus controversy, 91–92
dollar bill, symbolism on, 90, 91, 192, 200
Donadio, Rachel, 54–55
Donaldson, Commander William, 28
Don't Bother to Knock (movie), 110–111
Dorsch, E. C., Jr., 210–212

Dougherty, James, 109, 110
Douglass, William Campbell, 45
Dudgeon, Edward, 184
Dugdale, William, 55
Dujmovic, Nicholas, 75–76
Duke, Phillip S., 47

E

Eager, Thomas W., 230
Eckner, Dr. Hugo, 170, 171
Einstein, Albert, 176, 181
Eldridge, 176–177, 179–184, 186
Elizabeth I, Queen, 53
Ellen's Place Web site, 118–119
Emerson, Ralph Waldo on Shakespeare authorship controversy, 60, 64
Emma E. Booker Elementary School, Presidential visit, 219–221
Encyclopedia of American Conspiracy Theories (Kuzmick), 126
experimentation, medical/psychological, 43, 44

F

Fahrenheit 9/11 (movie), 220
Faked Apollo Landings Web site, 102–103
FATE magazine article on Carlos Miguel Allende, 178, 183
Federal Debt Relief System (FDRS) Web site, 143–144
the feminine sacred, 85
The Fifties Web site, 213
File and Claw, 71, 72
Finding Marilyn (Conover), 109
Fleshing Out Skull & Bones: Investigations Into America's Most Powerful Secret Society (Millegan), 74
Fletcher, Richard E., 189–190
Flight 800 disaster. *See* TWA Flight 800 disaster
Flight 800 Independent Researchers Organization (FIROS), 36
Flying Saucer Review Web site, 47
Ford, President Gerald, 214
48 Hours Mystery (TV show) on Marilyn Monroe, 115
Franklin, Benjamin, 189, 192
Freedom Domain Web site, 77, 196–197, 198

Freemasonry
  beliefs, 189
  controversy, 191–195, 200–201
  goals, suspected, 190
  history, 190–191, 192–194
  Lincoln assassination, 236
  membership process, 189
  persecution, 192–194
  practices, 189–190
  structures, 195
  symbolism, 191, 192, 200
  Web sites, 192, 194–195, 196–200
"Freemasonry, Conspiracy Within,
    Initiation and the Brotherhood"
    (Melanson), 194–195
Freemasonry Watch Web site, 199
Freud, Sigmund, 64
Frontline program on Shakespeare
    authorship controversy, 62

G

Gardner, Laurence, 88–89
General Agreement on Tariffs and
    Trade (GATT), 153–154
Geneva Bible, 62, 64
germanculture Web site, 174
"The Gnostic Gospels", Mary
    Magdalene in, 82
Goddard, Ian, 29, 103–104
Goddard's Journal, 103–104
Goddard Web site, 34, 36
Goerman, Robert, 178–179, 183, 186
The Good Shepherd (movie and Web
    site), 75
Graf Zeppelin, 170
Grand Lodge of British Columbia and
    Yukon Web site, 199–200
Graves, Dr. Boyd, 46
Graves Web site, 46
Great Zeppelins Web page, 170
Greenblatt, Stephen, 54, 55
Greenson, Dr. Ralph, 114
Groom Lake. *See* Area 51 site
Grossman, Lev, 219

H

Hall, Jim, 37
Hamas (Islamic Resistance Movement),
    127, 133, 194
Hancock, John, 192
Hathaway, Anne, 56

Hauptmann, Richard Bruno, 232, 234
Henry Neville Web site, 61
Herzl, Theodore, 130
Hindenburg
  characteristics, 163, 164
  destruction, described, 164–165,
    166, 171, 173
  destruction, investigation into,
    166–167, 168, 172
  destruction, possible causes,
    166–168
  destruction, press coverage, 164,
    165, 167, 173–174
  sabotage theory, 167–168
  Web sites, 169–174
The Hindenburg (Mooney), 167
Hitler, Adolf
  Freemasonry, 193–194
  Hindenburg, 167–168, 171, 174
  Protocols of the Elders of Zion,
    124–126, 131
  World War II, 137
HIV (human immunodeficiency virus),
    40, 41, 42–44, 49. *See also*
    AIDS
Hochheimer, Andrew, 186
Hoffa, Jimmy, 112, 236–238
Holocaust, 121, 126, 131, 132–133
Holocaust Encyclopedia, 132–133
Holocaust History Project Web site, 131
Holy Blood, Holy Grail (Brown),
    83–84, 87
Holy Grail, 83, 84, 85, 86
Holy Trinity Church representation of
    Shakespeare, 55
homosexuals, AIDS in, 39, 47
House, Edward Mandell, 157–158
"How Freemasons Work" (Watson),
    192, 196
HowStuffWorks.com, 192, 196–197
human immunodeficiency virus (HIV),
    40, 41, 42–44, 49. *See also*
    AIDS
Hussein, Saddam, 194

I

IAMAW (International Association of
    Machinists and Aerospace
    Workers), 28
Illuminati, 72–73, 192
The Impossible Zoom Climb Web site,
    34, 35

Independent Institute Web site, 142
intelligence community, 75. *See also*
    CIA
International Association of Machinists
    and Aerospace Workers
    (IAMAW), 28
*The International Jew. See Protocols of
    the Elders of Zion*
Internet Public Library's Shakespeare
    Bookshelf Web site, 66
Iraq, oppression of Freemasons, 194
Islamic Resistance Movement (Hamas),
    127, 133, 194
*Is Shakespeare Dead? From My
    Autobiography* (Twain), 55–56

J

James, Brenda, 61
James, John S., 48–49
Japanese attack on U.S. *See* Pearl
    Harbor attack
Jessup, Morris, 176, 178, 180, 181–182
The Jesus Conspiracy page, 87
Jesus controversy
    Catholic Church concerns, 83, 85
    crucifixion and resurrection, 81–82,
        89
    marriage and descendants, 81–83,
        84, 89, 91–92
    response to, 92–93
    Web sites, 86–92
Jew Watch site, 129
JFK (movie), 75, 210
Jim Morrison: A Living Legend Web
    site, 240–241
Johnson, President Lyndon and role in
    JFK assassination, 208–209
Johnson, Vice President Andrew, 235
Journot, Phillipe, 18

K

Kahn, David, 143
Kathman, David, 65
Kennedy, President John F.
    biographical information, 213
    Marilyn Monroe, 111, 112, 114,
        115–116, 117
    Moon landing pledge, 97
Kennedy, President John F.
    assassination
    conspiracy theories, 203–204,
        205–206

effects, 214–215
    investigation, 206, 207, 213, 215
    location, 206, 210, 211
    motivations, suspected, 207–209
    suspects, 74, 197, 203
    Web sites, 209–214
Kennedy, Robert F.
    involvement with Marilyn Monroe,
        111, 112, 113, 114, 116–117
    role in JFK assassination, 208
Kennedy Assassination for the Novice
    Web site, 210–212
Kennedy Assassination Web site,
    209–210
Kerry, John, 67, 68–69, 78
KGB and AIDS, 45
Khrushchev, Nikita and JFK assassina-
    tion, 208
Kidd, Devvy, 156–157
Kissinger, Henry, 152
Knights Templar, 84, 86, 190–191
Konoe, Fumimaro, 139
Ku Klux Klan, 127, 131, 132
Kuzmick, Marlon, 126

L

Lahr, Ray, 30, 34, 35, 37
The Last Supper (da Vinci painting), 86,
    91
letter C rock, 102–103
Lincoln, Mary Todd, 235
Lincoln assassination, 234–236
Lindbergh baby kidnapping, 232–234
Loeb, Bernard, 26–27
Logan Act, 159
lone gunman theory. *See* Kennedy,
    President John F. assassination
Looney, J. Thomas, 63
Loose Change Web site, 225–227
Louis XV (King of France), 192
Lovett, Robert A., 75
Luce, Henry, 70

M

Mafia, 113, 208, 238
magic bullet theory, 206
Manzarek, Ray, 240
Marcel, Major Jesse, 3, 5
marilynmonroe.com, 116
marilynmonroepages.com, 119
"The Marliad" (Marlowe Lives!
    Association), 61

Marlowe, Christopher, 53, 61, 62
Marlowe Lives! Association Web site, 61
Marrs, Jim, 144
Mary Magdalene, 81, 82, 83, 88, 92
masonicinfo.com, 197–199
Masonic Seal of America Web page, 200
Masonry. *See* Freemasonry
Mbeki, Thabo, 42
McAdams, John, 209–210
McCollum Memo, 138, 144–145
McCrarey, Lacy, 181
McKee, Grace, 108–109
Meet the Press interviews of Kerry and Bush, 68–69
Mein Kampf (Hitler), 125–126, 194
Meisner, Brett, 241–242
Melanson, Terry, 194–195
Menken, H. L., 234
Merovingian dynasty, 82
Meyer, Major Fred, 29–30
Military-Industrial Complex and JFK assassination, 207, 209
Millegan, Kris, 74
Miller, Arthur, 111
MK Ultra, 43
Monroe, Gladys Pearl, 108
Monroe, Marilyn
  biographical information, 107, 108–111
  death, conspiracy theories, 108, 111–113
  death, effects, 119
  Web sites, 113–119
Moon, fascination with, 105–106
Mooney, Michael, 167
Moon landing
  conspiracy claims, 95–96
  conspiracy theory, response to, 100–101
  evidence for/against, 96–100
  falsification, location, 7
  falsification, motivations for, 97–98, 102
  influence of, 95
  Web sites, 101–105
"Moon Landing: Myth or Fact?" (message board), 103
moonmovie.com, 105
Moore, Michael, 220
Moore, William L., 5, 179
Morgan, William, 192–193
Morrison, Herb, 165, 169, 173–174
Morrison, Jim, 239–242

Mortenson, Norma Jeane. *See* Monroe, Marilyn
Mr. William Shakespeare and the Internet Web site, 65–66
The Murder of Princess Diana Web site, 20–21
Murray, Eunice, 112, 113
Museum of Science-Boston Web site, 90–91
Museum of UnNatural Mystery Web site, 169–170
The Mysterious William Shakespeare: The Myth and the Reality (Ogburn), 62

N

NAFTA (North American Free Trade Agreement), 153
NASA (National Aeronautics and Space Administration), 100, 105
"NASA Debunks Moon Landing Hoax Conspiracy" (CNN), 103
National Archives and Records Administration Web site, 236
National Geographic Channel on TWA Flight 800, 33
National Geographic's Remembering Pearl Harbor Web page, 146–147
National Institute of Standards and Technology and September 11, 2001 terrorist attacks, 229
National Transportation Safety Board (NTSB) Web site, 32–33
NATO (North Atlantic Treaty Organization), 154, 155
Naval Historical Center Web site, 145, 183
Naval Station Pearl Harbor Web site, 145
Navy Lakehurst Historical Society (NLHS) Web site, 172
Nazis. *See also* Hitler, Adolf
  Freemasonry, 193–194
  Hindenburg, 167–168, 171, 174
  Jewish persecution, 127
  Protocols of the Elders of Zion, 126, 132
  zeppelins, 170
Nehlsen, Charles, 174
Neville, Sir Henry, 53–54, 61
New Testament, 81, 85, 86

Nilus, Sergei, 124, 125
9/11 Commission, 219, 229
9-11 Loose Change Second Edition
      Viewer Guide: And Debunking
      of Various 9/11 Conspiracy
      Theories Web site, 227
9-11 Research Web site, 227
9/11 terrorist attacks. *See* September
      11, 2001 terrorist attacks
9/11 Truth Movement, 223, 227–228
NLHS (Navy Lakehurst Historical
      Society) Web site, 172
North American Free Trade Agreement
      (NAFTA), 153
North Atlantic Treaty Organization
      (NATO), 154, 155
Notes on a Strange World Web site, 214
NTSB (National Transportation Safety
      Board) Web site, 32–33

O

Office of Strategic Services (OSS), 75
Ogburn, Charlton, 62
Olberman, Keith, 77
Operation Northwoods, 229–230
"The Operation Paget inquiry report
      into the allegation of conspir-
      acy to murder" (British report),
      22–23
Order of File and Claw, 71, 72
Order of Free and Accepted Masons.
      See Freemasonry
Order of Skull and Bones
2004 presidential election, 67–69,
      76–77, 78
      history, 68, 69, 72–73
      influence, 73–75, 78–79
      interest in, 76–77
      prominent members, 69–71
      rituals and practices, 67, 71–72, 73
      symbolism, 68
      Web sites, 74–77
organized crime, 113, 208, 238
"The Origins of HIV" (AVERT), 49
OSS (Office of Strategic Services), 75
Oswald, Lee Harvey, 205, 206–207
otr.com Web site, 173–174
Oxford, Edward de Vere, Earl of,
      53–54, 61–65
Oxfordians (supporters of de Vere as
      Shakespeare author), 61–65

P

Pajamas Media Web site, 133–134
Paul, Henri, 15–16, 18
PBS Web site on Shakespeare author-
      ship, 62
Pearl Harbor, aerial view, 144
Pearl Harbor attack
      controversy, motivations for,
            135–136
      described, 136–137
      effects, 137–138, 147
      precursors, 138, 139
      Roosevelt's role, 135–136, 137, 141,
            145
      September 11, 2001 connections,
            145–146
      Web sites, 140–147
"Pearl Harbor: History Whitewashed?"
      (Woods), 145–146
Pearl Harbor: Mother of All
      Conspiracies Web site,
            140–142
Pence, Colonel Lawrence, 34
Pentagon terrorist attacks, 217, 223
The People's Almanac (Wallechinsky &
      Wallace), 112
Philadelphia Experiment
      conspiracy, motivations for, 187
      effects, 175, 176–178
      investigation, 178–181
      Web sites, 182–186
The Philadelphia Experiment (movie),
      179, 185
Philadelphia Experiment & Montauk
      Survivor Accounts Web site,
            185
Philadelphia Experiment from A-Z Web
      site, 186
*The Philadelphia Experiment: Project
      Invisibility* (Moore), 179
Philip IV (King of France), 190
Pitts, Gerald, 240–241
Plait, Phil, 104
Plantard, Pierre, 90
Playboy magazine, Marilyn Monroe in,
      110, 111
Popular Mechanics Web site on
      September 11, 2001 terrorist
      attacks, 228–229
Priory De Scion & Secret Societies
      Web site, 90
Priory of Sion, 82–83, 84, 86, 90, 91

Project for a New American Century, 222

Project Rainbow. *See* Philadelphia Experiment

Proofs of a Conspiracy against All Religions and Governments of Europe (Robison), 192

Propaganda Matrix Web site, 77

Protocols of the Elders of Zion
content, 123–124
effects, 121, 124–125, 126–128, 134
Freemasonry, 193–194
history, 122–123, 124, 126
symbolism, 122
Web sites, 128–134

Pruss, Max, 167

PubMed Web site on AIDS, 49

Q

Quarantine Act, 46

R

Rachovsky, Pytor, 124
Rather, Dan, 214
Reagan, President Ronald, 161
Rebuilding America's Defenses: Strategy, Forces and Resources for a New Century (Project for a New American Century), 222
Rees-Jones, Trevor, 15, 16
rense.com Web site, 184
Revere, Paul, 192
Revolutionary Brotherhood: Freemasonry and the Transformation of the American Social Order (Bullock), 189
Richard Hauptmann Trial site, 234
RoadsideAmerica.com, 172
Robbins, Alexandra, 72, 73, 74, 77, 78–79
Robison, John, 192
Rockefeller, David, 151, 159
Rolling Stone, on Jim Morrison death, 240
Roosevelt, President Franklin D., 135–136, 141, 145, 192
Rosenbaum, Ron, 73–74, 77, 79
Ross, Terry, 65
Roswell, New Mexico
community response, 6, 8, 11, 12

conspiracy theories, 1–2, 3–6
events, 3–4
Web sites, 8–12

The Roswell Incident (Berlitz), 5
The Roswell Incident page, 8
Ruby, Jack, 205, 212
Rumsfeld, Donald, 222
Russell, William H., 69, 72
Russell Trust Association, 71. *See also* Order of Skull and Bones
Russert, Tim and interviews of Kerry and Bush, 68–69
Rylance, Mark, 64

S

Safer, Morley, 77
Santayana, George, 146
Sarah, daughter of Jesus, 82
Save the Males Web site, 130
scottbruno.com, 90
Screw Loose Change Web site, 227
"Seconds From Disaster" (National Geographic Channel), 33
secret societies, 71, 90. *See also* Freemasonry; Order of Skull and Bones
Secrets of the Tomb: Skull and Bones, the Ivy League, and the Hidden Paths of Power (Robbins), 73
Segal, Jakob and Lilli, 42–43
Seize the Night Web site, 87, 240
September 11, 2001 terrorist attacks
conspiracy theories, 219, 221–225, 229–230
described, 218, 219, 223
effects, 217–218, 230
investigation, 219, 229
Pearl Harbor connections, 145–146
political response, 217, 219–221
warning events, 221–222
Web sites, 225–229
September 11 Digital Archive, 229
Shakespeare, William
biographical information, 53, 54, 56
signatures, 56, 57
Web sites on, 66
will, 56
Shakespeare authorship controversy
alleged authors, 53–54, 60–65
defense of Shakespeare as author, 57–60
described, 53–57
history, 53–54

importance, 66
Web sites, 60–65
Shakespeare authorship Web site, 65
"Shakespeare" By Another Name: The Life of Edward de Vere, Earl of Oxford, the Man Who Was Shakespeare (Anderson), 64–65
Shakespeare Fellowship Web site, 63–64
"Shakespeare" Identified (Looney), 63
"The Shakespeare Mystery" (*Frontline*), 62
Shakespeare: Who Was He? (Whalen), 59–60
Shakspere, William. *See* Shakespeare, William
Shaw, 146
Sheldon, Michael, 230
Shenandoah, 169, 170
Sibrel, Bart, 105
Sickler, Melvin, 153, 157–158
Sifting Through Loose Change Web site, 227
Silenced (Cashill), 33
Simpson, George, 179
Sir Francis Bacon's New Advancement of Learning Web site, 60–61
Skeptic's Dictionary, 8–9, 184
Skull and Bones. *See* Order of Skull and Bones
The Skulls (movie), 76
Sonic.net on JFK assassination, 46
Soundboard Web site on JFK assassination, 212–213
SourceWatch Web site, 45, 158–159
Spah, Joseph, 170
Spehl, Eric, 170
spook (term), 76
Spoto, Donald, 113
Square and Compass, 191
SS *Andrew Furuseth*, 178, 183–184
Stanley, Harold, 70
Stanton, Edwin and Lincoln's assassination, 236
Stevens, John Paul, 64
Stevens, Lord, 23
Stinnett, Robert, 138, 142–143
The Straight Dope Web site, 157
Stratfordians (supporters of Shakespeare as author), 54, 57, 58, 63, 65
submarines, 175
Subversive Element Web site on Roswell, 8
Summers, Anthony, 116

Surratt, Mary, 234
Sutton, Anthony, 72, 77

T

Taft, Alphonso, 69
Taft, William Howard, 70–71
TheTruthAboutDaVinci.com, 89–90
Thin Air (Simpson & Burger), 179
Thirst for Justice Web site, 157–158
13, appearance on dollar bill, 91
Thomas Paine's Origin of Free-Masonry (Paine), 199
"Three Debates/Mock Trials" (Boston Bar Association), 62
ThreeWorldWars.com, 131
Time magazine Web site, 23, 219, 234, 239
Toland, John, 146
the Tomb, 71–72
Totse.com, 48–49
Trilateral Commission
    activities, 149, 153, 155
    agenda, alleged, 149–152, 153–156, 161–162
    agenda, public, 149
    history, 152, 156
    influence, 161–162
    Web sites, 149, 150, 153, 156–161
Trimble, South, Jr., 167
The Truth About Pearl Harbor: A Debate Web page, 142
The Truth Will Out: Unmasking the Real Shakespeare (James), 61
truTV's Crime Library Web site, 113–115, 213
Tuskegee Study of Untreated Syphilis, 43, 44
TWA Flight 800 disaster
    alternate theories, 32–38
    described, 25–26
    investigation, 26–28, 30
    sightings, 28–31, 38
    Web sites, 32–37
Twain, Mark and Shakespeare authorship controversy, 55–56, 64

U

U-boats, 175
UFO Evidence Web site, 7–8
UFOs (unidentified flying objects), 6, 7–8, 11–12, 176. *See also* Roswell, New Mexico

Unified Field Theory, Naval experimentation with, 176, 181
U.S. Army medical/psychological experimentation, 43
U.S. Department of State and September 11, 2001 terrorist attacks, 229
U.S. Public Health Service medical experimentation, 43, 44
USS *Arizona*, 145
USS *Arizona* National Memorial Museum Web site, 145
USS *Eldridge*, 176–177, 179–184, 186
USS *Shaw*, 146
USS *West Virginia*, 137

V

Valentine, Dr. Mason, 180
Vallee, Jacques, 184–185
Varo Edition, 178, 179–180, 181–182
Vietnam war and JFK assassination, 207, 209
Voice of Reason Web site on Jesus controversy, 91
Von Hindenburg, Paul, 163

W

Wallace, Irving, 112
Wallechinsky, David, 112
Warren Commission, 206, 207, 213, 215
Washington, D.C. Masonic symbolism, 198
Washington, President George, 192, 193
Was the Apollo Moon Landing Fake? Web site, 101–102
Watson, Stephanie, 192
Weishaupt, Adam, 192
Wells, Orson, 64
Westminster Theological Seminary Web site, 89–90
West Virginia, 137
WeThePeople Web site on Diana, Princess of Wales, 21–22
Whalen, Richard, 59–60, 62
What Really Happened? Web site on JFK assassination, 213–214
Whitman, Walt, 64

WHO (World Health Organization), 45, 47
Wikipedia
    Freemasonry, 196
    Hindenburg, 170–171
    Marilyn Monroe, 119
    Pearl Harbor controversy, 145
    Roswell, New Mexico, 10–11
    September 11, 2001 terrorist attacks, 220, 225
    UFOs, 10–11
Wilcox, George, 3
Willer, Dean, 70
Will in the World: How Shakespeare Became Shakespeare (Greenblatt), 54
Wilmot, James, 53
Woods, Ian, 145–146
The Work Continues Web site, 23
World Conquest Through World Jewish Government Web page, 129–130
World Health Organization (WHO), 45, 47
WorldNetDaily Web site, 115, 156–157
"World Shadow Government". *See* Trilateral Commission
World Trade Center terrorist attacks. *See* September 11, 2001 terrorist attacks
World Trade Organization (WTO), 153
World War II, Pearl Harbor role, 137–138

X

X, Malcolm, 64

Y

Yale secret societies, 71

Z

Zakheim, Dov, 222
Zapruder, Abraham, 212
Zapruder film, 204, 206, 214
zeppelins, 163, 168–169, 170, 172. *See also Hindenburg*